SEASONAL GUIDE TO THE NATURAL YEAR

SEASONAL GUIDE TO THE NATURAL YEAR

A Month by Month Guide to Natural Events

Minnesota, Michigan and Wisconsin

John Bates

Fulcrum Publishing
Golden, Colorado

*For my daughters, Eowyn and Callie,
and my wife, Mary.*

We gratefully acknowledge the following contributors for the use of their materials:

Excerpt on page 36 from John Eastman's *The Ghost Forest* is used with permission from *Natural History* (January, 1986). Copyright the American Museum of Natural History (1986).

Excerpt on page 44 from Diana Kappel-Smith's *Wintering* is reprinted by permission of McIntosh and Otis, Inc. Copyright © 1979, 1980, 1982, 1983, 1984 Diana Kappel-Smith.

Excerpt on page 55 from Justin Isherwood's "Sugarin.'" *Wisconsin Natural Resources* (1978): March/April.

Maps included in this book are for general reference only. For more detailed maps and additional infor-mation, contact the agencies or specific sites listed in the text or in the appendix.

Library of Congress Cataloging-in-Publication Data

Bates, John.
    Seasonal guide to the natural year : a month by month guide to
natural events. Minnesota, Michigan, and Wisconsin / John Bates.
        p.   cm. — (The Seasonal guide to the natural year series)
    Includes bibliographical references (p.) and index.
    ISBN 1-55591-273-7 (pbk.)
    1. Natural history—Minnesota—Guidebooks. 2. Natural history—
Michigan—Guidebooks. 3. Natural history—Wisconsin—Guidebooks.
4. Seasons—Minnesota—Guidebooks. 5. Seasons—Michigan—
Guidebooks. 6. Seasons—Wisconsin—Guidebooks. 7. Minnesota—
Guidebooks. 8. Michigan—Guidebooks. 9. Wisconsin—Guidebooks.
I. Title. II. Series.
QH104.5.M47B37 1997
508.2'0977—dc21   96-48511
                                            CIP

Printed in the United States of America

0 9 8 7 6 5 4 3 2 1

Fulcrum Publishing
350 Indiana Street, Suite 350
Golden, Colorado 80401-5093
(800) 992-2908 • (303) 277-1623

The Seasonal Guide to the Natural Year Series

Pennsylvania, New Jersey, Maryland, Delaware, Virginia, West Virginia and Washington, D.C., Scott Weidensaul

New England and New York, Scott Weidensaul

Illinois, Missouri and Arkansas, Barbara Perry Lawton

Colorado, New Mexico, Arizona and Utah, Ben Guterson

Northern California, Bill McMillon

Oregon, Washington and British Columbia, James L. Davis

Texas, Steve Price

North Carolina, South Carolina and Tennessee, John Rucker

Florida with Georgia and Alabama Coasts, M. Timothy O'Keefe

Southern California and Baja, Judy Wade

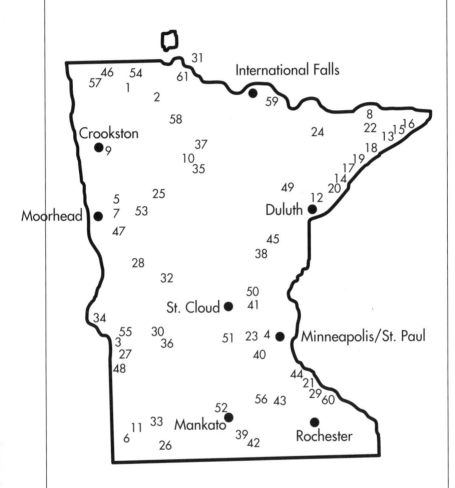

MINNESOTA HOTSPOTS

31
46 54   61   International Falls
57   1
2   59
58   8
24   22   16
Crookston   37   13 15
●9   10 35   18
5   25   17 19
Moorhead   7   53   49   14
●   47   12   20
Duluth ●
45
38
28
32
50
St. Cloud ●   41
34
55   30   51   23 4 ●
3   36   40   Minneapolis/St. Paul
27
48
44
21
56 43   29 60
52
11 33 Mankato
6   26   39 42   Rochester

Seasonal Guide to
the Natural Year

N

SITE LOCATOR MAP

LIST OF SITES
Minnesota

1. Agassiz National Wildlife Refuge
2. Beltrami Island State Forest
3. Big Stone National Wildlife Refuge
4. Minneapolis/St. Paul sites (Black Dog Lake, Lake Calhoun, etc.)
5. Borup area sites (Blazing Star Prairie, Zimmerman Prairie, etc.)
6. Blue Mounds State Park
7. Bluestem Prairie
8. Boundary Waters Canoe Area Wilderness
9. Crookston area sites (Burnham Creek Wildlife Management Area, Chicog Wildlife Management Area, Dugdale Wildlife Management Area, Pankratz Prairie, Tympanuchus Wildlife Management Area, etc.)
10. Chippewa National Forest
11. Coteau des Prairies
12. Duluth sites (Hawk Ridge, Minnesota Point, Lakewood Pumping Station, Jay Cooke State Park, etc.)
13. Cascade River State Park
14. Gooseberry Falls State Park
15. Grand Marais
16. Judge C.R. Magney State Park
17. Split Rock Lighthouse State Park
18. Temperance River State Park
19. Tettegouche State Park
20. Two Harbors
21. Frontenac State Park
22. Superior National Forest
23. Hennepin County Park Reserve District
24. International Wolf Center
25. Itaska State Park
26. Kilen Woods State Park
27. Lac Qui Parle Wildlife Management Area
28. Lake Christina
29. Wabasha
30. Lake Johanna
31. Lake of the Woods
32. Lake Osakis
33. Lake Shetek State Park
34. Lake Traverse
35. Lake Winnibigoshish
36. Long Lake
37. Lost Forty
38. Mille Lacs Lake
39. Minnesota Lake
40. Minnesota Valley National Wildlife Refuge
41. Monticello
42. Myre–Big Island State Park
43. Nerstrand Big Woods State Park
44. Red Wing
45. Rice Lake National Wildlife Refuge
46. Roseau River Wildlife Management Area
47. Rothsay Wildlife Management Area
48. Salt Lake
49. Sax-Zim Bog
50. Sherburne National Wildlife Refuge
51. Silver Lake
52. Swan Lake
53. Tamarac National Wildlife Refuge
54. Thief Lake Wildlife Management Area
55. Thiekle Lake
56. Townsend Woods State Natural Area
57. Twin Lakes Wildlife Management Area
58. Upper Red Lake
59. Voyageurs National Park
60. Weavers Bottoms
61. Zippel Bay State Park

MICHIGAN HOTSPOTS

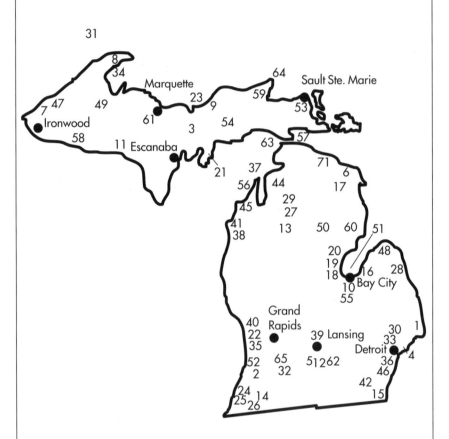

31

8
34
Marquette
64
Sault Ste. Marie
23
59
9
47
49
53
7
Ironwood
61
3
54
58
11 Escanaba
63
57
21
71
6
37
44
17
56
29
45
27
41
13
50
60
51
38
20
48
19
16
28
18
10 Bay City
55
Grand
Rapids
40
30
1
22
39 Lansing
33
35
Detroit
52
65
51262
36
4
2
32
46
42
24
14
15
25
26

Seasonal Guide to
the Natural Year

N

SITE LOCATOR MAP

LIST OF SITES
Michigan

1. Algonac State Park
2. Allegan State Game Area
3. Baldy Lake Sharptail Area
4. Detroit sites (Belle Isle, Harsen's Island, Metrobeach Metropark, St. Clair Flats Wildlife Area, etc.)
5. Bernard Baker Sanctuary
6. Besser Natural Area
7. Black River Harbor Recreation Area
8. Copper Harbor sites (Brockway Mountain Drive, Estivant Pines Sanctuary, etc.)
9. Pictured Rocks National Lakeshore
10. Crow Island State Game Area
11. Crystal Falls
12. Phyllis Haehnle Memorial Sanctuary
13. Dead Stream Flooding
14. Dowagiac Woods
15. Erie Marsh Preserve
16. Fish Point State Game Area
17. Fletcher Floodwaters
18. Tobico Marsh State Game Area
19. Nyanquing Point
20. Wigwam Bay State Wildlife Area
21. Garden Peninsula
22. P.J. Hoffmaster State Park
23. Grand Island National Recreation Area
24. Grand Mere State Park
25. Warren Dunes State Park
26. Warren Woods National Area
27. Grayling
28. Harbor Beach Harbor
29. Hartwick Pines State Park
30. Indian Springs Metropark
31. Isle Royale National Park
32. Kellogg Bird Sanctuary
33. Kensington Metropark
34. Keweenaw Peninsula
35. Kitchel–Lindquist Dunes Preserve
36. Lake Erie Metropark
37. Leelanau State Park
38. Ludington State Park
39. Maple River State Game Area
40. Muskegon State Park
41. Nordhouse Dunes
42. Petersburg State Game Area
43. P.H. Hoeft State Park
44. Pigeon River Country State Forest
45. Point Betsie
46. Pointe Mouillee State Game Area
47. Porcupine Mountains Wilderness State Park
48. Port Crescent State Park
49. Silver Mountain
50. Rifle River Recreation Area
51. Saginaw Bay
52. Saugatuck Dunes State Park
53. Sault Ste. Marie
54. Seney National Wildlife Refuge
55. Shiawassee National Wildlife Refuge
56. Sleeping Bear Dunes National Lakeshore
57. Straits of Mackinac
58. Sylvania WIlderness and Recreation Area
59. Tahquamenon Falls State Park
60. Tawas Point State Park
61. Van Riper State Park
62. Waterloo Recreation Area
63. Wilderness State Park
64. Whitefish Point Bird Observatory
65. Yankee Springs Recreation Area

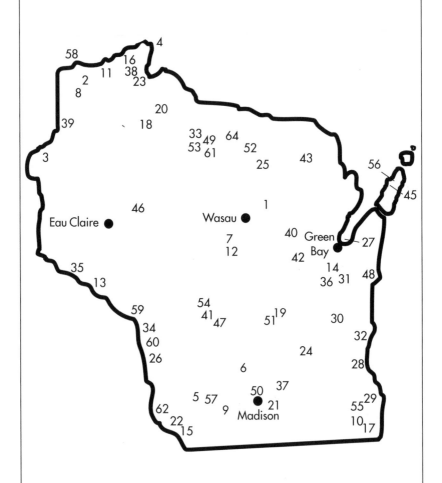

58
16
11 38
2   23
8

4

20
18

39

3

33 49 64
53 61 52
25 43

56

45

46

Eau Claire ●

1

Wasau ●

40 Green
7   Bay 27
12

42

14
36 31 48

35
13

54
41 47 51 19 30

59
34
60
26

32

24 28

6

50 37
5 57   21
62 9 Madison
22
15

55 29
10 17

Seasonal Guide to
the Natural Year

N

SITE LOCATOR MAP

LIST OF SITES
Wisconsin

1. Ackley Wildlife Area
2. Amnicon Falls State Park
3. Crex Meadows area sites (Amsterdam Sloughs Wildlife Area, Fish Lake Wildlife Area, etc.)
4. Apostle Islands National Lakeshore
5. Avoca Prairie State Natural Area
6. Baraboo Hills sites (Baxter's Hollow, Hemlock Draw, International Crane Foundation, Devils Lake State Park, etc.)
7. Mead Wildlife Area
8. Pattison State Park
9. Black Earth Rettenmund Prairie
10. Bong State Recreation Area
11. Brule River State Forest
12. Buena Vista Marsh
13. Reick's Lake
14. High Cliff State Park
15. Cassville
16. Chequamegon National Forest
17. Chiwaukee Prairie
18. Clam Lake
19. White River Marsh Wildlife Area
20. Copper Falls State Park
21. Madison sites (University of Wisconsin Arboretum, Goose Pond Sanctuary, Schoeneberg Marsh, etc.)
22. Nelson Dewey State Park
23. Ashland sites (Fish Creek Marsh, Sigurd Olson Institute, Kakagon Sloughs, etc.)
24. Horicon Marsh
25. Thunder Lake Wildlife Area
26. Goose Island
27. Green Bay
28. Harrington Beach State Park
29. Milwaukee sites (Juneau Park Lagoon, Milwaukee Harbor, etc.)
30. Kettle Moraine State Forest
31. Killsnake Wildlife Area
32. Kohler–Andrae State Park
33. Turtle–Flambeau Flowage
34. Lake Onalaska
35. Lake Pepin
36. Lake Winnebago
37. Rocky Run Oak Opening State Natural Area
38. Moquah Barrens
39. Namekagon Barrens
40. Navarino Wildlife Area
41. Necedah National Wildlife Refuge
42. New London
43. Nicolet National Forest
44. Northern Highlands/American Legion State Forest
45. Peninsula State Park
46. Pershing Wildlife Area
47. Petenwell Dam
48. Point Beach State Forest
49. Powell Marsh Wildlife Area
50. Prairie du Sac
51. Quincy Bluff and Wetlands Preserve
52. Rainbow Flowage
53. Riley Lake Wildlife Area
54. Sandhill Wildlife Area
55. Scuppernong Prairie
56. Ridges Sanctuary
57. Spring Green Preserve
58. Wisconsin Point
59. Trempealeau National Wildlife Refuge
60. Upper Mississippi River National Wildlife Refuge
61. Willow Flowage
62. Wyalusing State Park

Contents

CONTENTS

Acknowledgments

Many people contributed their knowledge, guiding hands, and ideas to this project. Some of the people who helped me considerably along the way include Ross Hier, assistant wildlife manager with the Crookston Department of Natural Resources; Kim Risen, a truly expert birder from Minnesota who shared many of his birding hotspots with me; Jeff Roth, fish manager in the Mercer Department of Natural Resources; Linda Parker, ecologist with the Chequamegon National Forest, and John Krause, natural areas specialist; Bob Pleznac, an expert on the prairies of Michigan; Jim Hammill, Michigan wolf biologist; Gary Tischer, assistant manager at Agassiz National Wildlife Refuge; John Williams, assistant manager at Thief Lake Wildlife Management Area; Pete Reaman, former director at Whitefish Point Bird Observatory; Adam Byrne, ace Whitefish Point Bird Observatory counter; Ann Swengel, Wisconsin butterfly expert; Jim Rooks, Cooper Harbor resident naturalist; Gordon Dietzman, with the International Crane Foundation; many other natural resources personnel and rabid outdoor enthusiasts who love the Upper Midwest.

Several professional photographers contributed greatly to this book: Carol Christensen, whose photography graces many of these pages; Jeff Richter, of R Images Photography; Bruce Bacon, Wisconsin Department of Natural Resources wildlife manager and photographer; Woody Hagge, Hazelhurst photographer; and the Wisconsin Department of Natural Resources (thanks to Bob Queen).

Additional thanks must go to Carmel Huestis, Sara Hanson, and the Fulcrum staff for their commitment to this series and to publishing outdoor books of high quality.

The greatest thanks, as always, goes to my wife, Mary, who is always ready and willing to go exploring at the drop of a hat and whose editing wisdom kept me on track. We've got lots more exploring to do, MB.

Introduction

Every year in late April as the snow slowly dissipates from the woods around our northern Wisconsin home, my wife and I go to one spot we know will have trailing arbutus in flower. We await that flower with the same high expectations with which we await the sap rising in the sugar maples, the loons wailing on the lakes, the blackberries coming ripe, and the leaves of the silver and red maples turning scarlet. Over time we have learned some of the whens and wheres of how the natural world operates, and these have provided us with infinite pleasure in our explorations. Finding that same stand of arbutus along that same south-facing lakeshore gives us a true sense of place, and a sense of belonging. We gain greater faith when the natural world keeps presenting its gifts with such timeliness and timelessness.

This book will help you know when to go and where to go to experience some of nature's splendors. Each section focuses on one month and is divided into six chapters. The first four chapters direct you to a natural event of unusual interest. The fifth chapter offers brief hints on other events and sites you could explore, and the sixth, "closer look" chapter offers you an in-depth look at the natural history of a plant or animal or a view of a natural process that influences the lives of wild things. Each section provides directions to specific sites, or "hotspots," with viewing tips, background on the event, and maps when possible.

The Upper Midwest includes Minnesota, Wisconsin, and Michigan, an amazingly rich and variable region that is so large that generalizations about the area are very difficult to make. Take Michigan, for instance. The distance from the northwestern corner of the state to the southeastern corner is nearly 500 miles. The same summer day could have temperatures ranging from 70°F in Copper Harbor along Lake Superior in a boreal tamarack bog to 100°F in dry farm country along Lake Erie and the Ohio border. To give you a sense of how different the climates and habitats can be, consider that Copper Harbor in Keweenaw County in the northernmost tip of the state is closer to James Bay in Canada than it is to Monroe, in far southeastern Michigan. For that matter, Monroe is closer to Tennessee than it is to Copper Harbor.

All three states are rich in water resources. Minnesota is known as the land of 10,000 lakes (it really has thousands more—no other state has as much surface water area), but Michigan also has 11,000 inland lakes, and

Wisconsin boasts nearly 15,000 lakes, from 1-acre ponds to the 137,708-acre Lake Winnebago.

The three states cover a lot of territory, too. Minnesota's 84,000 square miles make it the twelfth largest state and, except for Texas, the largest state east of the Rocky Mountains. St. Louis County in northeastern Minnesota alone sprawls over 6,700 square miles, an area larger than Connecticut. Fortunately, the states' populations remain relatively moderate, ranging from 4 to 9 million people, most of whom are concentrated in southern and central metropolitan areas. So there's still plenty of open and wild spaces to explore, and room for native flora and fauna to thrive. One can hike virgin tracts of tall-grass prairie, canoe the river bottomlands of the Mississippi River, or howl with nearly 2,000 timber wolves in the greatest lake country wilderness in the United States, in northeastern Minnesota.

People in the Upper Midwest take to their public lands in great numbers, and participation in nonconsumptive outdoor activities continues to be on the rise. A 1991 national survey of fishing, hunting, and wildlife-associated recreation estimates 40 percent of the entire U.S. population over 16 years of age participates in nonconsumptive wildlife-associated recreation, which translates into more than 76 million people who feed, observe, or photograph wildlife. In Michigan, nearly 3.3 million residents over age 16 participate in nonconsumptive wildlife recreation, and the economic impact of their activities is estimated at $893 million in annual trip-related expenses and equipment purchases. Michiganders spend $123 million each year on birdseed alone.

Michigan contains 3 national parks, 3 national forests, 33 state forests, and 80 state parks and recreation areas. Wisconsin has 3 national parks, 2 national forests, and 50 state parks. Minnesota's public lands include 2 national parks, 2 national forests, 57 state forests, 66 state parks and recreation areas, and 812 wildlife management areas.

I hope this book stimulates your interest in investigating these beautifully diverse states—there's a lifetime and more of exploration available here. Use this book as a starting point, because no one book can do justice to the natural wealth these states contain.

General Advice and Counsel

Detailed maps are an absolute must if you wish to spend more time enjoying a site than looking for it. State highway maps provide the big picture, but to navigate you will need maps that guide you along backcountry roads. If you can carry only one set of maps, get the DeLorme atlas for each of the three states. The scale of 1:150,000 and usual remarkable accuracy down to the dirt roads make exploring an area much easier. These maps also show topographic contours, forest cover, and even some foot trails.

At a site, the 1:24,000 scale U.S. Geological Survey topographic maps (7.5-minute quadrangles that cover an area about 6.5 miles by 7.5 miles) are the best friends you can take with you (except for the local naturalist or longtime resident who knows the area). Check the date on the bottom right-hand corner of the topo map, though. Many topos were printed 20 or more years ago, and a lot of features have changed with recent developments. Trust your maps overall, but exercise some critical assessment now and again, too.

Nearly all of the sites listed in this book are on public lands or on private property owned by conservation groups, like The Nature Conservancy, that allow public access. But a few sites take you on roads through private land, or the public land identified abuts private land that may or may not be marked with signs. Treat all land, but in particular private land, with excessive respect—the landowners' generosity in permitting access cannot be abused in any form or we all risk losing the opportunity to enjoy the site. More important, the wildlife or flora that we seek is often shy or at risk. Explore whenever possible with binoculars from a respectful distance, and remain on designated trails when this is requested.

Remember also that though the seasonal march of biological events is surprisingly predictable, seldom is any event so regular that it can be seen on the same day every year (the swallows don't really all come back on the same day to Capistrano, you know). A range of probable days works best, because even though the day length (or *photoperiod*) cocks the trigger for much seasonal activity, the variables of weather play a major role in whether and when the trigger is pulled.

And need it be said that wildlife have minds of their own, which is what makes the viewing of them so much more richly enjoyable? Wildlife viewing is fraught with uncertainties because the animals are not on tethers. They live by biological clocks quite different from ours. Many animals have large home ranges and move around constantly in search of critical needs like cover and food. The very rarity of sighting certain fauna is what heightens the joy of the experience. You may need to go back to a site many times to see something, or get out of the car and spend a day on foot exploring. Even then, circumstances beyond anyone's control may limit your seeing what you came to see. I humbly suggest that the philosophy necessary to take with you wherever you go is to be flexible and thankful for whatever gifts you are given, even the rain that keeps the migrating hawks on the ground (a phenomenon I've experienced a number of times). It's sometimes hard to do, but take what the moment offers.

Know the hunting seasons and laws for the area you are exploring. For instance, waterfowl viewing in October near refuge land can seem like a shooting gallery, and viewing opportunities will obviously be rather slim.

Wear blaze orange when in doubt. Hunting is permitted on nearly all national and state forests, wildlife management areas, and portions of some state parks and national wildlife refuges.

Many of the phone numbers for the sites' headquarters are listed in the text or in the Appendix. When in doubt, call ahead for more information.

Good trail maps, a compass, rain gear, a first-aid kit, extra food and water, waterproof matches, binoculars, and a flashlight with good batteries are essentials to carry along in a daypack. You never know what may occur in the backcountry, so err on the overprepared side.

Your Help Is Needed

The directions and information in this book were researched carefully, but in the time between writing and publication, and in the years thereafter, some things may change. If you note in your explorations that signs are removed, roads are altered, sites are closed, and other changes have taken place, please write the author, c/o Fulcrum Publishing, 350 Indiana Street, Suite 350, Golden CO 80401-5093. Your corrections for future editions will be invaluable.

The seasonal events listed in this guide represent only some of what can be seen in any given month in the Upper Midwest. Your explorations will undoubtedly turn up other spectacles of note. If you have suggestions for future additions to this book, please send them to the address above with as much information as you can muster (particularly directions) so the event can be adequately researched. These events should occur on public land or private land that is open to the public, should be generally consistent from year to year, and should be of significant and unusual interest to the average outdoor person. Thank you for your help.

Abbreviations Used Frequently in the Text

NWR: National Wildlife Refuge
WMA: Wildlife Management Area
SNA: State Natural Area

January

Notes

1

Ice Caves along the Great Lakes

Probably the last place most people would want to be in a North Woods winter is out on the ice of Lake Superior, where windchill factors can exceed most imaginations, and where the ice can change in a matter of hours. Yet there may be no more beautiful place to be than the Squaw Bay ice caves in the Apostle Islands National Lakeshore. Here, thin layered sandstone has been carved into architectural wonders by the moving ice in the winter and by the winds and waves that crash relentlessly onshore in the spring, summer, and fall. Sea kayakers explore the caves during summer's open water and exult over their beauty, but the ice formations that coat the caves in the winter raise them to yet another aesthetic level. Seeps of melting snow, spring water from the rocky cliffs, and icy mists off the open lake congeal in formations that often seem to defy the laws of nature while creating masterpieces of color and shape that astonish most viewers. Colors may vary from turquoise to blue to green to rust to orange. And shapes often diverge wildly depending on the conditions when the ice was formed, which can range from winter gales to a calm minus 30°F in the sun.

The trip to the ice caves isn't an easy jaunt. Ice along the shores of the largest lake in the world seldom freezes into a picturesque smooth sheen. It's 1,700 miles around the lake and a very rare winter when the waters freeze all the way across. The ice breaks, reforms, is pushed back upon itself by winds and waves, and thus is often traversed only by stumbling across broken shards, plates, and humps of ice in an unrelenting wind. But the rigors of the trip, as always, make the moment of arrival all the sweeter.

Before you consider the adventure, a call to the National Park Service in Bayfield for their advice on ice conditions is an absolute necessity. During the intensely cold winter of 1993–1994, Lake Superior froze over completely, and the ice was excellent. The mild winter of 1994–1995 was just the opposite, and the ice was never passable. Within the same day, conditions can and do change rapidly, so exercise extreme caution in proceeding. National Park Service employees often carry pocket-size ice picks to help yank themselves out of the ice if they fall through. To be on the safe side, if conditions are questionable, either cancel your trip or join an organized National Park Service trip.

Even in the coldest of winters, pools of open water often form at the backs of the caves, so observations are best made from the shoreline or only as far as the cave entrances.

Don't let these essential precautions deter you from taking this journey. Those who have been here use superlatives like "magical," "cathedral-like," and "a wonderland" to describe the caves. They are a true natural wonder.

The shorelines along the Great Lakes anywhere in the Midwest can offer dazzling ice formations that may reform and change again and again in any given year. Ice formations are one of the performance arts of the natural world, along with the wind sweep of sand dunes, the saturated tapestry of autumn leaves, and the ephemeral flowers of spring in a maple woods.

Ice may be explored in other forms, too. A 2-mile ice bridge across Lake Superior marked by old Christmas trees may be crossed to reach Madeline Island in the Apostle Islands. Ice boat races on mirror ice in Pewaukee, Wisconsin, take place every winter. And the groans and booms of ice cracking and forming on a frigid night may be one of the greatest natural audio concerts to be experienced anywhere.

Hot Spots

To get to **Squaw Bay ice caves,** take Hwy. 13 west from Bayfield for 17 miles to Meyers Road. Or from the junction of County Hwy. C in Cornucopia, head east on Hwy. 13 for 4.5 miles. Meyers Road has no signs and may not be plowed. Either drive or walk the 0.5 mile to the National Park Service's shore overlook and take the wooden steps down to the beach. The caves begin about 0.75 mile to the east and stretch for another mile to Sand Point—there should be tracks of others to lead the way.

You may also call the Bayfield Chamber of Commerce at (715) 779-3335 for ice-condition information, as well as for accommodations on this very beautiful peninsula.

In Michigan, the **Grand Island National Recreation Area** on **Munising Bay** in Lake Superior has beautiful ice caves, although large numbers of snowmobilers traverse the edges to look, altering the quiet of the place and, for some, the beauty. Munising Bay ice is safe only in cold years, so check with the recreation area office in Munising before doing any exploration: (906) 387-2512.

At the **Pictured Rocks National Lakeshore** near Munising, park personnel warn that the pack ice is usually pretty shaky—ice travel is not recommended except in extremely cold years.

In Minnesota, the **state parks along the North Shore of Lake Superior** offer beautiful ice formations. Three prominent points gather ice floating by and catch the brunt of the waves. Northeastern storms coat the rocks and vegetation along these points, glazing most of the area with a coating of translucent ice. In cold winters the ice can climb 25 feet in thick pieces. And the ice is all the more remarkable for its transparency—you will be amazed how far you are able to see into it.

The points at **Gooseberry Falls, Split Rock Lighthouse,** and **Tettegouche** (both Palisade Head and Shovel Point) **State Parks** are most easily accessed. Trails lead to all the points and are usually well packed from previous ice-watchers, so you can often walk right to the points. Try also **Artist's Point** in **Grand Marais Harbor** and the **Two Harbors** rock ledge out by the lighthouse, where the sloping rocks can pile ice up to extreme heights.

2

Wintering Eagles

Adult bald eagles move only as far south in the winter as good fishing requires them to, and no better sites for winter fishing exist than below dams on the Wisconsin and Mississippi Rivers. Here on any given day several to a hundred or more eagles may congregate, actively fishing in the early morning and roosting in trees in the afternoon. A good perching tree may have five to ten eagles lined up on its branches apparently just passing the time in communal reverie. In the evening the eagles retire to roosting sites most often in undisturbed bottomlands where heavy forest cover and cliff banks protect them from winter winds.

Early mornings, while the eagles are actively fishing, offer the most exciting viewing opportunities. The fishing can be particularly good below the dams, where fish are often sucked through the turbines and thus are stunned or killed, making for some easy catches. Because eagles, unlike ospreys, don't dive into the water to catch fish but instead skim over the surface and grab fish with their talons, the floating fish below the dams must seem like a dinner at a five-star restaurant on the company payroll.

Sometimes the eagles are seen catching rather small fish that barely look like enough for a snack, and indeed those little fish may simply be french fries for an eagle, but an hour of swallowing those can easily fill a stomach. Eagles can hoist big fish, too, like a 6- to 7-pound fish, if one swims close to the surface. That's impressive work, for an eagle only weighs 8 to 14 pounds (females average 10 to 14 pounds, males 8 to 11 pounds).

But fish are only part of an eagle's winter diet. Eagles are opportunistic feeders, taking whatever the moment offers. So some of the best winter viewing of bald eagles can be done inland, on a roadkill deer carcass. Eagles readily eat carrion (one eagle-bander I know goes so far as to heretically refer to eagles as "glorified vultures"). In early March, my wife and I often put out beaver carcasses, supplied by a local trapper, in the wetlands below our house. As many as eight eagles come down onto the marsh ice to feed while we watch with our spotting scope from the comfort of our house.

Bald eagles return in late February and early March to their nesting areas, but the ice doesn't usually go off northern lakes until mid-April at the earliest. During that time, feeding on carrion may be the most important means of survival for bald eagles.

Eagles may be seen from mid-November to early March on any of the sites listed here until they turn northward to reestablish their mating territories.

Eagle etiquette requires observing eagles from designated sites or from the inside of your car in order not to disturb the birds, which have limited amounts of energy to spend on flying away from curious humans. A car-window mount for a spotting scope is ideal for watching the eagles. You can stay out of the wind and cold, and the eagles don't seem to mind the presence of cars, which serve as blinds.

The Wisconsin Bureau of Endangered Resources' work with eagles is funded by tax-form checkoffs and by the Adopt an Eagle Nest Program. For $100, individuals or organizations can "adopt" a nest and help pay for its protection

A bald eagle sits in winter snow. Photo by Jeff Richter.

and management. Donors receive information on the breeding success of "their" nests, a photograph of young eagles in the nest, and a copy of *Birds of Prey in Wisconsin*. Contact the Wisconsin Bureau of Endangered Resources at (608) 266-7012.

Hot Spots

In Wisconsin, the Wisconsin Department of Natural Resources (DNR) hosts Bald Eagle Watching Days in the month of January in **Sauk City** and **Prairie du Sac** (sister cities located on the Wisconsin River and called together "Sauk Prairie"), and at **Cassville** on the Mississippi River. Each Saturday in January, with the assistance of DNR Bureau of Endangered Species biologists, you can watch scores of bald eagles. Contact the Wisconsin DNR or the local chambers of commerce for exact times and dates. Additional programs throughout the day, such as slide shows, talks, environmental music, and displays, make an Eagle Watching Day into a full-day event if you wish to learn about eagles and have a lot of fun at the same time.

At Sauk City and Prairie du Sac, the Ferry Bluff Eagle Council maintains an overlook with a spotting scope in a parking lot next to CJ's Restaurant on Hwy. 78 (Water Street) in the middle of Prairie du Sac. An island in the middle of the Wisconsin River below the parking lot usually has a number of eagles perched in its trees. The best eagle site, though, is at the dam north of Prairie du Sac. Take Hwy. 78 north out of town for about 1 mile, and turn right on Dam Road. Go 0.5 mile, and take the right fork in the road to the dam.

The *Eagle Watcher's Guide* for Sauk Prairie is readily available at the parking lot or in town and lists the six best sites in the area for observing eagles. An average of about 80 eagles may be seen in the general vicinity. Free guided bus tours leave every half hour in the mornings: call (608) 643-4168, or 1 (800) 68EAGLE for the local chamber of commerce. The Wollersheim Winery even produces "Eagle Wine," which can be tasted at the winery.

Cassville is one of the nation's best winter eagle-viewing sites, often concentrating 100 or more eagles at a time below Lock and Dam 10 and the power generating station on the Mississippi. Start by checking the **Wisconsin Power and Light Company power plant** off Hwy. 133. To find the plant, take County Road VV, which is just northwest of Cassville, about 0.5 mile, and turn left on the road marked Boat Landing.

Also check the **Dairyland Power Plant** on the south side of Cassville—as you come into Cassville from the south on Hwy. 133, take the first left and drive about 0.2 mile to the river. A third area to check may be found as you are heading south out of town on Hwy. 133. Take the first right off Hwy. 133 just before you cross the railroad tracks. This 1.5-mile road loops back to Hwy. 133 and may have eagles perched anywhere along its entire stretch. The Wisconsin DNR usually has a full weekend of activities planned in late January for eagle-watching in the Cassville area. Call the Wisconsin DNR or the Cassville Department of Tourism at (608) 725-5855 for more information.

Wyalusing State Park offers excellent viewing as well, as may any other site along the Mississippi River where a dam keeps the water open, where there's fish to catch, and where large shoreline trees are available for perching and roosting. **Blackhawk Park,** south of Victory in Vernon County on Hwy. 35 along the Mississippi River, commonly has 20 bald eagles fishing in the area. **Goose Island,** located 2 miles south of the junction of Hwys. 14 and 35, just south of La Crosse, has good eagle-viewing too. From Hwy. 35 south, look for the marked entrance to Goose Island on the right (west), and drive the main road into the park. Search snags and trees rooted in the river bottoms for eagles.

Eagles also winter over along the mile-long stretch of open water below the **Petenwell Dam.** The dam was built in 1950 and created a 14-mile-long flowage, second only to Lake Winnebago as the largest body of water lying entirely within Wisconsin. The flowage above the dam ices over in the winter, but below the dam are stands of old trees attractive

Bald Eagle Viewing Areas near Wabasha, Minnesota, and the Surrounding Riverfront

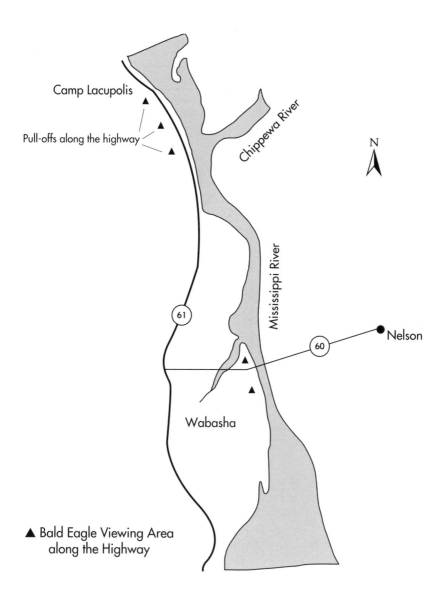

Camp Lacupolis

Pull-offs along the highway

Chippewa River

N

Mississippi River

61

60

Nelson

Wabasha

▲ Bald Eagle Viewing Area along the Highway

Sauk City/Prairie du Sac Bald Eagle Viewing Areas

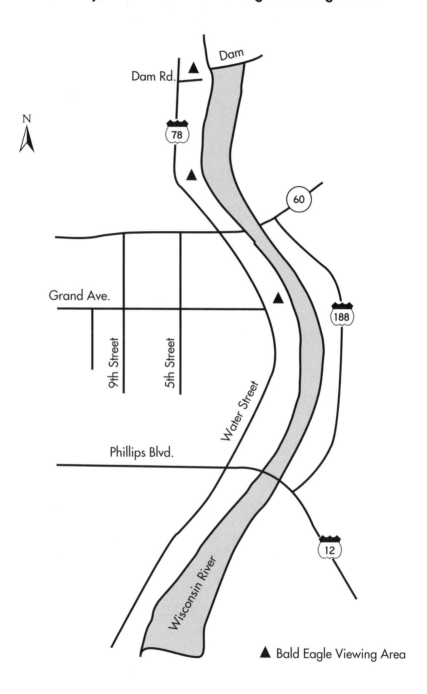

▲ Bald Eagle Viewing Area

to perching birds like wintering bald eagles, who fish the open water most actively in the early morning.

Take Hwy. 21 3 miles east from Necedah to the Petenwell bridge, where Hwy. 21 crosses the Wisconsin River. There is a parking lot at the east end of the bridge, and a hiking trail goes south along the east riverbank. The western end of the bridge may be better for viewing, however—look for eagles perched in tall trees on a large island north of the bridge. Dozens are commonly seen.

The **Wisconsin River Power Company** maintains an excellent observation tower at the dam for public use. After crossing the bridge heading west, turn right onto 18th Avenue, drive north 1 mile, and park just below the dam in a large lot with an interpretive signpost.

Necedah National Wildlife Refuge (NWR) has an observation blind available for photography and general observation, and it's free to the public. This is an opportunity to see both bald and golden eagles. In the winter of 1994–1995, 10 bald and 3 golden eagles fed near this blind, which is located on a barrens habitat between two large pools in the interior of the refuge. Refuge personnel put roadkill deer carcasses near the blind to draw in the eagles. The best times for viewing are when fresh carcasses are put out and when it hasn't snowed for a while, so the carcasses aren't covered up. Contact the refuge for information at (608) 565-2551.

In Minnesota, at Wabasha, an eagle watch takes place every Sunday in the winter from 1:00 to 3:00 P.M. at **Wabasha's City Deck** on the riverfront. From November through March you can join volunteers trained by the Raptor Center of St. Paul in watching bald eagles fish the Mississippi River (the observation deck is not staffed if it's raining or if temperatures drop below 10°F). Approximately 50 to 75 eagles congregate in the Wabasha area because the current from the inflowing Chippewa River keeps the Mississippi open here. Contact the Wabasha Area Chamber of Commerce, P.O. Box 105, Wabasha, MN 55981; (612) 565-4158. Just north of Wabasha and between Camp Lacupolis and Read's Landing on Hwy. 61 are good highway turnouts from which to scan for eagles over the river and the south end of Lake Pepin.

Along the waterfront in **Red Wing** and in **Colville Park** wintering eagles also concentrate along the Mississippi. Follow Hwy. 61 south to Red Wing (55 miles south of the Twin Cities) and watch for signs to the parks on the waterfront. If you miss the signs, follow Hwy. 61 through the downtown district, and as the highway turns to the right, look for a small road that turns to the right and then doubles back, paralleling Hwy. 61 for about 2 blocks and passing under it. This road will lead you into Colville Park.

3

Winter Seabirds and Rare Gulls

Come late January in the Upper Midwest, the winter often seems as if it will stretch on forever. The first migrant birds won't be back until March (late March for the North Woods), and those weary of seeing snow and limited bird activity need a wildlife fix. One of the best ways to get the wildlife-watching adrenaline surging again is to find open water. And because the lake ice in the North Woods doesn't go out until mid- to late April, one usually needs to head south along the Great Lakes to find open water with waterfowl and gulls.

Waterfowl are widely appreciated by humans, but gulls are often seen in the opposite light, regarded more as nuisances than as birds worth watching. Credit the herring gull armies that swarm landfill sites for the bad press gulls often get. But really, gulls are beautiful birds, well worth studying for their aesthetic appeal and their interesting behaviors.

In North America, 25 species of gull, including two called *kittiwakes,* are known to nest. Of those 25, 21 species have been seen in Minnesota, though many are accidentals blown there on a storm. Still, the array of gull species and their often extremely distant origins make gull-watching always interesting. For instance, glaucous gulls nest in the Arctic and usually winter out on the pack ice, but some come as far south as the Upper Midwest or the Northeast Coast. A sighting of a rarity like the Iceland gull, which only breeds in Greenland and winters usually well to our east, or of the pelagic Sabine's gull, which breeds in the high Arctic and winters in the Pacific down to Peru, can make careful scanning of flocks of gulls highly rewarding. Gulls imitate the hungry teenagers of the world, eating most anything they spot. As scavengers, they help clean up dead fish and other sea animals that wash up on shore, and so provide a useful disposal service. Flocks of gulls often follow a farmer's plow to eat unearthed insects. The California gull has had a monument erected in its honor in Salt Lake City. Its appetite for insects saved the Mormons in the 1840s from losing their crops to a locust invasion.

Gulls take live food from the lakes and seas, too, often hovering in the air and then diving to the surface to pick up a fish, or simply lighting on the water and feeding by dipping their heads and necks underneath for organisms near the surface. Their aerial skills seem effortless, and the beauty of a white gull in a blue sky can be as striking as that of any bird.

Gulls are social animals and always gregarious, whether during breeding, while incubating in nesting colonies, or during feeding and roosting.

Twenty-one species of gulls have been seen in Minnesota. Photo by Carol Christensen.

They steal one another's eggs and often fight aerial duels for fish. Some gulls, such as the herring gull, show little fear of humans and can even be fed by hand from a boat. Other gulls, such as the laughing gull, are quite sensitive to human disturbance and have declined in numbers as humans continue to encroach on their nesting habitat.

Don't think of gulls as just big white birds. They come in all sizes and are often strikingly patterned. The great black-backed gull of the north Atlantic Coast is 30 inches long with a wingspread of $5^1/_2$ feet, while the little gull is only 11 inches long, about the size of a pigeon. For color variation, Franklin's gull has a black hood, a reddish bill, and a rosy bloom on its breast, and the ivory gull is white with black legs.

The sexes usually look very much alike, and the identification of immature gulls challenges the best of birders. Usually immatures are darkest in their first year and become progressively lighter until they attain maturity, in their third or fourth year. Given that several plumages can occur in these intermediate stages of development, if you're an amateur birder, do yourself a favor by not trying to identify every last gull—the frustration isn't worth it.

Have you ever wondered how an oceangoing gull gets fresh water? A pair of "salt glands" located on the top of the skull enables pelagic gulls to drink saltwater, separate the salt into a clear liquid concentrate, and then eliminate it through the nostrils.

Hot Spots

In Wisconsin, **Milwaukee's Harbor** is the most likely site for a variety of waterfowl and gulls. The Milwaukee, Kinnickinnic, and Menominee Rivers come together to flow out into the natural harbor that in times past teemed with wintering birds. Milwaukee often serves up rarities and has earned its reputation as one of the best midwestern winter birding locales. Diving ducks like scaup and mergansers are common, but the occasional rarity, such as Barrow's goldeneye, seems to show up every year. Gulls such as the little, Thayer's, and glaucous often highlight the winter offering.

Don't bother getting up early to bird this area—unless it's overcast, the sun will blind you until late in the morning. And like nearly every site mentioned in this section, although the birding might be hot, the air almost certainly won't be, with screamer winds off the Great Lakes accentuating the cold. As a rule, the birding is best when the weather is at its worst, because birds often seek the safe haven of the calmer harbors during storms. Strong northeastern winds often drive the most seaworthy of birds inside the Milwaukee breakwaters, and if you can stand up to the wind, the opportunities for rare-bird sightings are often good. An average winter around Milwaukee might bring in and hold 20,000 loafing waterfowl and another 10,000 herring gulls who enjoy the pickings at the landfills.

The Milwaukee Harbor isn't a single site. It actually includes a number of areas behind the man-made breakwaters as well as other areas north and south of the breakwaters that often turn up excellent sightings. **Juneau Park Lagoon**, along Lincoln Memorial Drive, traditionally has drawn thousands of waterfowl and gulls (the first state record sighting of a mew gull occurred here in 1986) into its open water, but the lagoon's aerator was turned off in the 1994–1995 winter because too many birds were concentrating here, so call ahead to see what the city has in mind in the year of your visit.

You can make a day of driving and stopping along the Milwaukee shoreline. Get a copy of *Wisconsin's Favorite Bird Haunts,* published by the Wisconsin Society for Ornithology, for explicit directions to a host of sites in and around the harbor.

Much farther south along Lake Michigan, the protected **Kenosha Harbor** often has numerous oldsquaws and various other diving ducks, and **Wind Point** in Racine is good for rarities all year round and in winter may turn up harlequin ducks, scoters, and oldsquaws, as well as rare gulls. To get to Wind Point, from the intersection of Hwys. 31 and 20, take Hwy. 31 north to 4 Mile Road. Turn east and follow the road until it turns right and becomes Lighthouse Drive and brings you to a lighthouse and Shoop Park. Park at either the lighthouse or the golf course and scan the open water off the lake.

North of Milwaukee you can jump from harbor to harbor all the way to the tip of Door County if you so choose, but the best stops along the way are **Virmond Park,** where Pacific and red-throated loons have been seen; **Port Washington Harbor,** where a mew gull was spotted in February 1995; then north to **Harrington Beach State Park,** which is well-known for its fall hawk migrations, but which also turns up scoters, harlequin ducks, and loons. Still driving north, **Sheboygan Harbor** had four harlequin ducks reported in February of 1995, and **Two Rivers Harbor** was home briefly to an Iceland gull during that same month. **Manitowoc Harbor** offers an impoundment that attracts a large variety of rare gulls, including several sightings of royal terns among a host of Caspian terns, and an Arctic tern among flocks of Forster's and common terns.

Kewaunee, Algoma, and **Northport Harbors,** farther north along the coast, also offer open-water opportunities to see wintering gulls and waterfowl.

The Wisconsin Birders Hotline can steer you to the right harbor at the right time, because wintering birds tend to be fickle critters. Call first to save yourself a trip or to discover a site you might not have considered before: (414) 352-3857.

In Michigan, **Harbor Beach Harbor** on Lake Huron in Huron County is a large man-made harbor protected by a breakwall and is kept open during the winter by a warmwater discharge near the Coast Guard station. Look for wintering waterfowl and gulls such as the glaucous, Iceland, and great black-backed. The Coast Guard station parking lot may be found by taking Michigan 25 north for 4 blocks from the traffic signal in Harbor Beach. Turn east onto Pack Street and drive to its end and park.

Between Lake Huron and Lake Erie, the St. Clair and Detroit Rivers don't freeze over entirely and often harbor an unusual variety of rare ducks and gulls in any given year. The **St. Clair River** is usually open from Port Huron to Marine City in almost every winter, and opportunities to view oldsquaws and glaucous and Iceland gulls are good, and king or common eiders and Thayer's gulls are rare but possible.

Harsen's Island in the **St. Clair Flats Wildlife Area,** an area of several islands in the northwestern part of Lake St. Clair where the St. Clair River enters, is reachable by car—look for small open-water areas where waterfowl may concentrate. Flotillas of canvasbacks and redheads are common. Check the **North, Middle,** and **South Channels,** the St. Clair River, and **Anchor Bay** along Michigan 29 to the northwest of Harsen's Island.

Farther south, **Belle Isle** is a city park on an island in the **Detroit River.** The best winter viewing opportunities are off the southwestern corner of the island and off the swimming beach on the west side. If the water stays open, large concentrations of canvasbacks may be seen in rafts off the swimming beach, as well as a host of diving ducks such as oldsquaws and hooded mergansers. In the fall, all three species of scoters, red-throated loons, and red-necked grebes are likely. From U.S. 10 or I-75, go south to East Jefferson and drive east for 2 miles to East Grand Boulevard. Cross the bridge here to Belle Isle.

Lake Erie Metropark, where the Detroit River empties into Lake Erie, is an ideal location for wintering birds because of its more than 2 miles of Lake Erie shoreline. The waterfront remains open throughout the winter due to a hot-water discharge from the Trenton power plant. Good viewings of ducks, geese, and swans are very likely. This area is superb for fall hawk migrations, too (see chapter 51). From Detroit, take I-75 south to the Gibraltar Road exit. Turn left (east) onto Gibraltar and drive about 1.8 miles to Jefferson Road. Turn right (south) and continue another 1.8 miles to the park entrance.

For hotspots along **Lake Michigan,** head far northwest to the **Lake Bluff Audubon Center,** which often has good concentrations of oldsquaws, mergansers, and harlequin ducks through March. From Manistee, go north on U.S. 31 and turn north (left) onto Michigan 110. After 1 mile, Michigan 110 turns into Lakeshore Road, and the Lake Bluff center is located on the left (east) side of the road at 2890 Lakeshore Road. Call the Michigan Audubon Society at (616) 889-4761 for more information.

In Ottawa County, well south of Lake Bluff, **Port Sheldon** and **Pigeon Lake** remain open all winter. The Pigeon River widens into Pigeon Lake and then flows into Lake Michigan. The warmwater discharge from the Consumers Power plant keeps the lake open throughout the winter, attracting rare birds such as harlequin ducks, red-necked grebes, and scoters. Port Sheldon is located on Lake Shore Avenue between Holland and Grand Haven, approximately 5 miles south of Michigan 45, which ends at Hwy. 31.

As for the last and biggest of the Great Lakes, the **Lake Superior** shoreline usually freezes in the winter, but **Sault Ste. Marie,** located on the **Saint Marys River** in northern Michigan, often holds many northern birds usually seen only in southern areas in winter. Parts of Saint Marys River and **Lake Nicolet** stay open all winter and, as usual, the best spots are warmwater discharge sites from power companies, in this case the Sault Edison Power plant. Expect good close-up views of diving ducks like oldsquaws, and occasional harlequin ducks or Barrow's goldeneyes. Bald eagles hang out on the ice floes, and this may be the best place in Michigan for gyrfalcons. Keep an eye out for glaucous and Iceland gulls, too. The electric plant is only a few blocks east of the locks. Travel north or south on roads adjacent to the river to find other open water.

In Minnesota, **Lake Calhoun** and **Lake Harriet,** just west of downtown Minneapolis, are excellent bets for winter birds, though they do usually freeze over by late November and early December. Still, they often get roosting flocks of gulls on the ice well into December and, if the winter is mild, January. Glaucous and Thayer's gulls are uncommon but possible, and record sightings of strays such as California, Iceland, and lesser black-backed gulls have occurred here. Red-throated and Pacific loons; grebes; ducks, including harlequin and oldsquaw; scoters; and Barrow's goldeneyes may also be seen. Lake Calhoun can be viewed from the Lake Calhoun Parkway, which goes around its perimeter, and Lake Harriet can be scanned from the Lake Harriet Parkway, which also encircles the lake.

Black Dog Lake is the single best site in Minnesota for winter birding and probably the most popular year-round birding spot in the Twin Cities. Rare gulls are frequently seen here, and the Minnesota record for the most gulls seen in one day was taken here. Thayer's and glaucous gulls are seen every winter, and there have been record sightings of California, Iceland, great black-backed, and lesser black-backed gulls, and black-legged kittiwakes.

Take the 113th Street exit off I-35W and follow Black Dog Road, which runs between the lake and the Minnesota River. Part of the lake usually remains open throughout the winter due to the warmwater discharge from a power plant. Scan from the road just west of the power plant. Black Dog Road crosses Hwy. 77 at the northeastern end of the lake.

To bird the south side of Black Dog Lake, take the 122nd Street (Cliff Road) exit off I-35W and follow River Ridge Boulevard east across the railroad tracks. Turn east on Cliff Road just over the tracks, and a half-mile later stop at the Park and Ride lot. From here the main trail leads to Black Dog Park, which provides good vistas of both halves of the lake.

On **Lake Superior, Grand Marais** has a fish-cleaning operation that has been active in recent years in the harbor, and it attracts gulls, although the harbor is a natural for attracting waterfowl and gulls without the added food source. Record sightings of rare gulls are the best here of anywhere in Minnesota. Look for ivory gulls from November through January, as well as lesser black-backed, great black-backed, and Iceland gulls. Waterfowl specialties include harlequin duck, oldsquaw, scoters, and rarities like brant, king eider, and Barrow's goldeneye.

4

Wolves Howling

One of the most exciting, and sometimes chilling, moments in anyone's outdoor experience is hearing wolves howl for the first time. If we had any fur left to raise on our backs, we probably would (though that's why we still get goose bumps—it's an attempt to raise our long-gone fur). No other sound may signify wildness more, or strike a deeper primordial chord within us. Wolf howling includes barklike yips, yaps, yowls, and deep bass notes, a cacophony of sounds unanticipated by human listeners new to the communication repertoire of a wolf pack.

Only seven states in the lower forty-eight have viable wolf packs, and Michigan, Wisconsin, and Minnesota are three of them (Washington, Montana, Idaho, and Wyoming are the other four). The northern gray timber wolf is listed as endangered everywhere except in Minnesota, where it is considered threatened. Minnesota's population of nearly 1,700 wolves is far greater than all the other states put together.

In 1996, Wisconsin's timber wolf population jumped to around 100 wolves, up from 83 wolves in 18 small packs in 1995. This unexpected increase meant that for the first time, the statewide goal of 80 overwintering individuals had been reached, though the population must remain at this number for at least three years before the goal is considered fully met. At that point, Wisconsin will be in the business of managing wolves, not in the wolf recovery phase.

Michigan's wolf population in the winter of 1996 was 116 wolves in at least 16 packs across the Upper Peninsula (UP), up from the 1995 count of around 80 individuals in 12 territorial areas across the UP. Michigan has a three-tiered management goal: Level 1 is to reach 100 wolves; level 2 is for a minimum viable population of 200 wolves in 10 packs; and level 3 is to reach 500 wolves, a number based on what humans can be expected to tolerate. The UP, given its excellent wolf habitat and limited habitat fragmentation, may be able to support up to 1,000 wolves if the public is willing to accept them.

Minnesota's wolf numbers are still growing and are currently in the range of 1,700. The 1992 Eastern Timber Wolf Recovery Plan called for a population goal of 1,250 to 1,400 by the year 2000. Here is one wildlife recovery plan that has exceeded its goals. The highest number of wolves Minnesota will likely be able to sustain is about 2,000.

The likelihood of seeing a timber wolf pack is very slim, but the chances of hearing one, or of seeing its tracks, grow considerably if you know where

*The highest population of timber wolves in the Lower 48 lives in northeastern Minnesota.
Photo by Woody Hagge.*

wolf territories are located. Still, an average wolf's territory stretches over 50 square miles, and may be as large as 120 square miles if the food base is minimal. So although many territories are discussed in this chapter, the wolves may be anywhere within them, and are adept at remaining invisible.

Eastern timber wolves mate from late January into early March. The dominant pair within the pack are usually the only ones to breed, and after a 63-day gestation period, a litter averaging 5 to 6 pups may be born in late April or May, usually in a cavity dug in the ground.

Some folks like to go out and howl for wolves in hopes of receiving a response. I'd like to encourage you instead to go on an organized hike with a trained wolf biologist. It's not a good idea to go out howling on your own, particularly at this time of year. Let me explain why.

Wolf packs usually occupy territories ranging from 25 to 100 square miles. In prime wolf habitat like northeastern Minnesota, various packs claim nearly every square mile of forest and often overlap into adjacent wolf territories, sharing a mile-or-so-wide territorial strip with other packs. These "demilitarized" areas are usually avoided by neighboring packs to prevent often-fatal territorial encounters. Lone unattached wolves make frequent use of these zones because of the safety they offer.

A Canadian researcher, Fred Harrington, studied timber wolves in Superior National Forest in northeastern Minnesota in an attempt to determine

Wolf Activity in the Upper Peninsula of Michigan

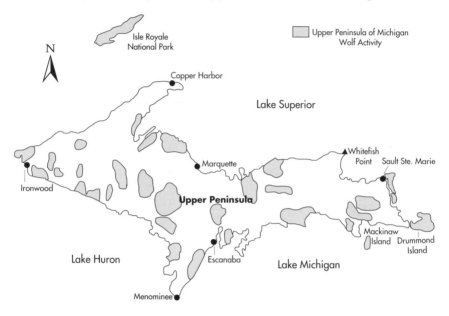

what role howling plays in establishing and maintaining territories. By tracking radio-collar signals and locating the packs, Harrington forced encounters with the packs by entering their territories and howling. He found that if a pack howled back, it nearly always stood its ground, but if the pack kept quiet, it retreated one-third of the time and stayed put the other two-thirds. Retreat probably occurred to avoid a direct encounter with the intruding "pack," because such clashes often result in serious injury or death to at least one member of the pack. Harrington concluded that howling serves as a long-distance defense system, allowing packs to announce their locations to prevent accidental meetings. Howling can be heard up to 5 miles away, giving a traveling pack sufficient warning to avoid invading an established territory.

Still, researchers have witnessed packs purposely leave their territories and invade neighboring territories either to steal a kill or to attack, such battles motivated by reasons still unknown to us. So a wolf pack, upon hearing howling nearby, has a dilemma. Howling back will invite the intruding wolves to leave, if they are willing to do so. However, if the intruders intend to attack, the howling pack has given away its location. Harrington received responses to his howling on only half of his attempted contacts, the internal conflict of "to howl or not to howl" perhaps accounting for the inconsistent responses.

Wolf Territories in Wisconsin

Probable Wolf Range

Territories with Wolves Present

Harrington found a number of patterns that apparently explain how a pack decides to risk howling back, keep quiet, or retreat. If the pack had just made an important kill, their response rate was very high. If pups were still at the den site, or at a rendezvous site where they spend three to four months maturing, the response rate was very high—one pack responded at a rendezvous site to Harrington on each of the 24 nights in July and August he howled to it.

Once the pups were grown—from November to January—howl responses seldom were made unless the pack had just made a kill.

In late January, with the onset of the breeding season, reply rates went way up but declined to virtually none by April, after mating activity ceased.

The size of the pack influenced the reply rate, too: The larger packs appeared to feel more confident in their ability to defend themselves, and so howled more frequently.

And did the phase of the moon affect reply rates? Not at all. Wolves howl to protect their families and food from intruders, needs the moon has no bearing upon.

Thus, it's best for the wolves if people do not go into their territories and howl, for howling serves as an important means of wolf communication. The adverse affects of too many "howlers" in a territory could affect a pack significantly.

If you would like to snowshoe or backcountry ski into wolf territory to look for sign, refer to the maps for the locations of known territories as of 1995. Territories may change over time, however. Radio-collared yearling wolves have traveled from their natal territories as far as 550 miles in less than a year to find a new home. And given the small size of many wolf packs—the average pack in Wisconsin ranges from three to five members— the loss of one or two wolves may force the remaining individuals to reform elsewhere.

The tracks of wolves dwarf those of coyotes. The average pad size in wolves is 4.5 inches long and 3.5 inches wide; a coyote's pad measures 2.75 inches long and a little less than 1.5 inches wide. Wolves stand $2^1/_2$ feet at the shoulder and weigh 50 to 100 pounds; coyotes stand $1^1/_2$ feet and average only 25 to 40 pounds. Differentiating wolf tracks from dog tracks is another matter, because five breeds of very large dogs have tracks similar to those of wolves. A variety of measures taken on a series of tracks is required to be certain of a wolf's identity.

Look for scent markings (urine) too. Breeding wolves will urinate differently than will nonbreeding animals. The male will urinate off to one side of his track and normally on a raised object, whereas nonbreeders usually urinate right in their tracks. Blood in the urine usually indicates a female in estrus (heat).

Hot Spots

In Minnesota, the **Superior National Forest** and the **Boundary Waters Canoe Area** in the northeastern corner of the state provide the best territory for wolves anywhere in the continental United States. But packs are found in northwestern Minnesota as well. **Agassiz NWR** has a pack with 8 to 12 individuals and maintains a blind that the public can use, complete with a tape of wolves howling for use in enticing wild wolves to respond. Winter isn't the only time to listen and watch for wolves. August at Agassiz may be the best time—the pups are larger, the weather's still warm, and the bugs are fewer. **Tamarac NWR** also has an established pack within its boundaries.

In Michigan, wolves crossed the pack ice from Canada back in 1948 onto **Isle Royale National Park**, an island wilderness in Lake Superior. The study of the interaction of the resident moose population with its predator, the wolf, has been one of the finest long-term ecological studies in the nation. The wolves on Isle Royale make up the only fully protected wild wolf population in the world. Their numbers dropped from an average in the mid-twenties to less than ten in the early 1990s, raising great concern among researchers, but fourteen were counted in late winter 1995, and the population seems to have stabilized for the moment.

No access to the island is possible during the winter, but ferries travel from the mainland in Michigan or Minnesota from late April to October, and once on the island, an attentive visitor can often see the tracks of moose and wolves overlapping.

In Michigan's **Upper Peninsula,** the western half currently has more wolves than the eastern half. Consult the map for areas you might explore in hopes of seeing sign or hearing some howling.

In Wisconsin, contact the Timber Wolf Alliance, (715) 682-1223, at the **Sigurd Olson Institute** in Ashland for a raft of educational materials and current programs. You might consider joining the Adopt a Wolfpack Program to aid in the further restoration of wolves in the Upper Midwest. Consult the map of Wisconsin's wolf territories for areas you might search for sign.

The best opportunities to hear wolves probably come out of organized trips led by wolf biologists or educators. In Minnesota, the **International Wolf Center,** a nonprofit educational center in Ely, offers a variety of "wolf weekend" courses, often traveling by dogsled through wolf country. Call them at (800) ELY-WOLF. Or visit their 6,000-square-foot "Wolves and Humans" exhibit at the center in Ely.

In Wisconsin, **Treehaven,** a beautiful 1,400-acre natural resource and education center in Tomahawk, operated by the University of Wisconsin at Stevens Point, runs several winter weekend classes on wolves, usually including a walk in a known wolf territory. Call (715) 453-4106, or write 2540 Pickerel Creek Road, Tomahawk, WI 54487, for more information.

The **Sigurd Olson Institute** in Ashland runs "wolf weekends" twice a year and also houses the Timber Wolf Alliance, an educational organization devoted entirely to wolves. Call the institute at (715) 682-1223.

The **Timber Wolf Information Network** (TWIN) runs workshops every year as well. Give them a call at (414) 731-5278.

In Michigan, the Sigurd Olson Institute maintains an office in Watersmeet and coordinates educational wolf activities in many UP cities and is trying to establish active centers in the larger cities like Houghton and Marquette. Call (906) 358-4350 for more information.

5

January Shorttakes

Short-Eared Owls

Just before sunset around open country like marshes, meadows, and prairies, short-eared owls become very active hunters, often perching on signs, muskrat houses, and various low objects. Their buoyant flight and barrel-shaped bodies distinguish them easily. "Squeaking" may work to draw a short-eared closer to you. Short-eareds often hunt and roost in good-sized numbers—10 or 20 may be seen at a good winter hunting ground. In January 1995, 10 short-eared owls were seen from a parking lot in the **White River Marsh Wildlife Area** in south-central Wisconsin (see chapter 19 for directions).

That same January, 19 owls were seen in the **Killsnake Wildlife Area** in Calumet County, Wisconsin. Take Hwy. 151 east from Chilton for 4 miles, then turn north on Lemke Road and follow it to the marsh.

In Michigan, try the **Maple River State Game Area.** From U.S. 27 9 miles north of St. John's, turn right (east) on Ranger Road (first road north of the Maple River), and go 2 miles to Crapo Road and park.

The open country around **Sault Ste. Marie** is usually excellent short-eared owl country (see directions in chapter 7).

Deer Yards

White-tailed deer "yard up" in winter in areas that provide good cover from snow and wind and ample browse. The **Jonvick Deer Yard** in northeastern Minnesota is 22 miles long and 2 miles wide, along Hwy. 61 from Temperance State Park to just past Cascade River State Park. Its south-exposed slope has a much thinner snow cover—deer are forced here to get out of deeper snows inland. Deer can be seen from area ski trails as well as along Hwy. 61. The campground area in Cascade usually has quite a few. If the snow is deep enough, moose may move into the area, as well as predators like coyotes, wolves, and cats. The greatest concentration is from Hall Road to County Road 7. The Minnesota Department of Natural Resources does "deer enhancement," creating shear cuts and openings from which to feed the deer.

Jay Cooke State Park, just southwest of Duluth, is another excellent winter deer site. Deer are almost always seen in the campground parking lot area. The combination of good cover and south slopes makes this a desirable yarding area. Take Hwy. 210 west from the south end of Duluth along the St. Louis River to reach the park.

Ravens Staging

Each day, before roosting for the night, ravens perform aerial displays and make calls as part of a staging ritual. Hundreds may be seen in the **Brule River State Forest.** The roost site changes every year, but it can be found by following the aggregation of ravens in the late afternoon, or ask at the forestry station in Brule, Wisconsin. The Brule State Forest is located north and south of the town of Brule on U.S. 2 about 30 miles east of Superior.

6

A Closer Look:
Survival in the Cold

Somewhere in the North Woods, the temperature falls to minus 40°F at least once every other year. Survival in this type of deep freeze separates the very hardy from the just plain hardy. Arctic-dwelling conifers like jack pine, tamarack, white and black spruce, and balsam fir, and hardwoods like white birch, trembling aspen, balsam poplar, and willow and alder shrub are "very hardy," able to tolerate temperatures down to minus 80°F! How can anything survive that level of cold? Their solution is rather ingenious—they perform extracellular freezing. By drawing most of the liquid out from their cell walls and allowing it to freeze in the spaces between the cells, the living tissue escapes the killing cold.

Many Upper Midwest plants escape frost injury by supercooling, which protects them down to about minus 40°F. The liquids in the cells remain liquid because there are no rough particles inside the cell walls to act as nuclei for the ice crystals to form around. But if the temperature falls below minus 40°, the cell liquids freeze anyway. A range map for most North Woods trees, such as sugar and red maples, basswood, red oak, eastern hemlock, and white and red pine, shows a cutoff line in southern Canada that generally corresponds to where minus 40° occurs with some regularity.

That makes sense for plants, but what about animals? Some perform extracellular freezing too—in fact, they freeze hard. If you were to open up frozen wood frogs, painted turtles, and garter snakes, you would see chunks of ice dotted among their organs. In a painted turtle, about 53 percent of its total body water freezes. The wood frog pumps a glycogen solution into its body that protects the cells from ice damage. The high sugar levels would trigger diabetic coma and death in us, but the solution saturates the frog's cells in such a concentrated form that the cellular fluids can't freeze, even though the rest of the frog freezes. When thawed in spring, these frogs hop away as if nothing has happened.

Painted turtles lay their eggs in underground nests from mid-June on. The eggs hatch 10 or 11 weeks later, but some babies don't leave the nest until next spring, spending the winter instead in the shallow cavity. The little turtles are safe from predators, but the temperature drops below freezing in the nests frequently, even with insulating depths of snow above. When the nest temperature reaches 26°F the hatchlings freeze and can survive in this state for at least 11 days. When they freeze, ice first coats their skin, then travels inward, cutting off all circulation to the periphery until only the blood corridor between the heart and brain is left open. Incredibly, even this corridor eventually closes, and no muscle movement, no breathing, no heartbeat, and no blood flow occur, though minimal brain activity somehow continues.

After their first winter, painted turtles lose this ability, and they spend the rest of their winters hibernating underwater on bottom sediments or buried in the mud. Because turtles use their lungs to breathe, this isn't any less magical than being able to survive freezing as hatchlings. How do they survive without breathing? Their blood oxygen content falls to near zero, which would be certain fatality to humans within minutes, but a condition a hibernating turtle can tolerate for more than 150 days. And that's in totally deoxygenated water! Painted turtles win the vertebrate animal award for being able to endure the longest period of oxygen deprivation. They go into a state of metabolic arrest and are able to live off their stored body-fuel reserves until the ice goes off in the spring. Then up they come, ready to bask in the sun and gulp a breath of fresh air.

Frogs that hibernate underwater don't go to quite the extreme that painted turtles do, but their ability to maintain nearly normal levels of oxygen in their tissues by gas exchange through the skin is "magic" too.

How about our closer relatives, the mammals? Black bears go into a winter torpor where the breathing slows, body temperature decreases to about 86°F, and they lightly "sleep" away the winter. But as any bear researcher who has gone into a winter den knows, the female can be awakened instantly. Remarkably, the bears never defecate or urinate while in torpor but instead reprocess urea back into the building of muscle tissue. If they were to lose body fluids they would die of thirst, because they don't take in any fluids to replace those lost when hibernating.

The study of these processes, from freezing to torpor, rightfully excites scientists, who look to these animals for answers to how humans can live in a form of suspended animation while in space travel or how doctors could prevent death in situations where a patient is not getting any oxygen.

More easily understood is the wintering strategy of the beaver, who constructs a superinsulated lodge that any human home builder would be impressed by. The foot-thick walls and the body heat generated by the beavers huddling keep the inside temperatures at 45°F to 50°F, a very livable environment. Beavers put up a large supply of sticks (their food cache) about 30 feet from the lodge, and then swim underwater to grab something from the cupboard whenever their hunger rises.

The fox grows an exceptional winter coat, and with a tail one-third as long as its body, it simply curls up with its tail draped across its nose and feet for maximum warmth. An Arctic fox can rest comfortably at minus 40°F without changing its behavior or physiology one bit—a red fox can do the same down to 8°F. Colder temperatures force red foxes to increase their metabolism, seek shelter, or even shiver to produce heat.

Birds have a very hard time in cold weather, and that's why, of the nearly 180 species that nest in the North Woods, only about 20 remain in the winter. Birds must eat every day if they want to survive—they have enough fat to usually get them through one winter night, but that's it. The black-capped chickadee has evolved another way to reduce its heat loss at night. It goes into a regulated hypothermic state where its body temperature drops about 20°F, so less fuel is needed to keep warm.

Many birds shiver to keep warm. Even large birds like ravens and crows will shiver continuously on a cold night until morning to stay warm. The avian method for staying warm is when a bird fluffs out its feathers until it looks like it has swallowed a softball. This reduces heat loss by 30 to 50 percent through the increased insulative qualities of the air spaces between the feathers. But even then, a redpoll still needs to eat 40 percent of its body weight every day to keep its internal furnace stoked. So keep your feeders stocked, particularly on days below 15°F, when the birds may need you to help them survive a cold night.

February

Notes

7

Arctic Owls

Winter sends most of the Upper Midwest's nesting birds scurrying south; but winter, like all things, is relative. To the great gray owl, boreal owl, northern hawk owl, and snowy owl, who usually spend their winters in more arctic conditions, our snow and cold must seem positively balmy. Every year a few of these Arctic owls drop down to sample the rodent fare, and if you'd like to see one, Sault Ste. Marie, Michigan (commonly referred to as "the Soo"), may be the Arctic owl capital of the United States. In the most recent major invasion winter of 1991–1992, 55 great gray owls were counted near the Soo. Twenty-eight of those were seen on Sugar Island alone, and up to 14 of these birds were observable at one time from one location on the island. Fifteen hawk owls were also seen in the farmlands south of the Soo, as were 3 boreal owls (2 of which were located in evergreens in private yards), and at least 21 snowy owls.

These numbers are, of course, the exception. Invasion years occur on an average of every four years, and the *big* invasion years occur every 10 years or so, as in the 1991–1992 season, when the owls almost became commonplace. In a normal year around the Soo, though, snowies average about six to eight individuals and great grays three to four, still very respectable numbers that draw birding enthusiasts from all over the country.

Hot Spots The easiest way to get the best looks at the Soo's wintering owls is to sign up for a birding weekend with the **Whitefish Point Bird Observatory.** Expert volunteers lead trips nearly every weekend in January and February to the areas around the Soo that have over the years consistently drawn and held owls (plus other birds, like gyrfalcon, sharp-tailed grouse, and various winter finches). The cost in 1995 was $75 per person ($65 if you're a member of the observatory), all of which goes to the research efforts of the observatory. Write or call Whitefish Point Bird Observatory, HC 48, Box 115, Paradise, MI 49768, (906) 492-3596, for more information on the trips.

If you wish to go on your own, there's lots of ground to cover. **The Soo** is an excellent winter birding area because, in the midst of so much dense boreal forest in the Upper Peninsula of Michigan, the Soo provides a surprising mix of open fields and scattered woodlots ideal for rodent hunting. Plus, there is always open water in the Soo due to the power plants along the Saint Marys River. The ornamental plantings and house feeders in the city and country draw birds, too.

For the best opportunities to see Arctic owls, take a day and drive slowly all the roads east of I-75 and south of the city in the thumb of land between the freeway and Saint Marys River. If the ferries are running to **Neebish Island** and **Sugar Island,** be sure to take them and explore the few roads on each island. The ferries run frequently every day, but only if the water is open (the river usually freezes in early January), so either call ahead or simply stop and see if they're in operation. The crossings take only five minutes. Call the Eastern Upper Peninsula Transportation Authority for current information: (906) 495-5656. Despite Sugar Island's extraordinary great gray owl numbers in 1991–1992, Neebish Island often is the best bet for finding great grays—in fact, great grays are thought to breed on the island.

Michigan 129 and **9 Mile Road** are good roads to watch for snowies perched on the top of telephone poles, and they also offer viewing opportunities for sharp-tailed grouse and rough-legged hawks. But just about every road in the area has good potential. Late one morning in early February 1995, during a Whitefish Point Bird Observatory tour, we saw a pepper-and-salt snowy owl sitting atop a telephone pole across from a farmhouse on Maple Road; saw another pepper-and-salt snowy on another pole in midafternoon on Michigan 129; and saw a third snowie, this time a pure white one, again on Maple Road, sitting on top of a shed roof. Maple Road, west of I-75, usually offers excellent viewing at dusk for short-eared owls, too (see chapter 5).

Be sure to call the **Michigan Bird Alert Hotline** before you visit the Soo for information about what has been seen and where to go: (616) 471-4919. In addition, call the specific bird alert for Sault Ste. Marie: (705) 256-2790. Keep in mind that the extreme northern latitude of the Soo, its location on Lake Superior, and its open farmlands make for bitterly cold and windy days. Be prepared for blowing and drifting snow across the country roads, and to stay warm, wear enough layers of clothing to make it nearly impossible to get in and out of your car.

Do not plan on birding the Soo on the first weekend in February. Snowmobile races at that time make birds and accommodations rather difficult to find.

In Minnesota and Wisconsin, the **Duluth/Superior area,** at the traditional birding hotspots of **Duluth Harbor/Minnesota Point/Wisconsin Point,** is the most reliable place to see snowy owls. More snowy owls winter in Duluth/Superior than anywhere south of Canada.

Wisconsin Point is only 2 miles long and very narrow, but its wide variety of habitats and position at the very southwestern edge of Lake

Spectacular snowy owls invade the Upper Midwest usually every four years. Photo by Woody Hagge.

Superior make it an exceptional area for migrant birds. Minnesota Point (also called Park Point) is a 6-mile-long peninsula that nearly reaches to the tip of Wisconsin Point and offers the same migrant observation opportunities as Wisconsin Point. In fact, Park Point, which is usually considered the recreation area between the bus turnaround at 43rd Street and the airport, may be the best site in all Minnesota for observing migrant birds of all kinds.

The **Duluth Harbor Port Terminal** area usually harbors a gyrfalcon as well as snowies. Along Garfield Avenue, especially around the grain elevators and the railroad tracks, spilled grain feeds a community of mice, rats, and pigeons that in turn provide an excellent diet for snowy owls and others. This is considered the most reliable spot in Minnesota for observing snowies.

Across the bridge from Duluth, **Superior, Wisconsin,** industrial areas also offer structures for the owls to hunt from, and usually a very good supply of prey to hunt. Remember that snowy owls will perch most anywhere, from TV antennas to fence posts to ice humps, so look at any possible perching site.

In Superior, while traveling on Hwy. 2, go 1 block northwest of the Belknap Street intersection to Main Street and turn right. The next left puts you on Connor's Point, and a grain elevator to your right is prime raptor habitat—look for gyrfalcons and peregrine falcons here as well. Or try the open fields off Stinson Avenue and Hill Avenue near the oil refinery.

The two best spots in Minnesota for great gray and hawk owls are the **Sax-Zim Bog** area northwest of Duluth, and **Aitkin County.** In the Sax-Zim Bog great gray owls are found year-round, and the Minnesota record for hawk owl sightings occurred here—nine in a Christmas Bird Count one year. Miles of bog habitat mixed in with alder thickets, black ash swamp forest, and upland fields and sedge meadows offer an exceptional variety of hunting opportunities for wintering owls. Slowly drive the parallel County Roads 213 and 788, and County Road 7 between County Road 52 and Zim for good viewing opportunities of great gray and hawk owls.

In Aiken County you can expect snowy, hawk, and great gray owls every year, and also goshawks and rough-legged hawks. One year this area had six snowies, six grays, and six hawk owls in it. The 3-mile-long **Pietz's Road** is considered the best single location in Minnesota to find a great gray owl. No sign identifies where to turn off County Road 18 onto this road, but go 4 miles east of Hwy. 169 on County Road 18 and turn left (north). The best sighting opportunities usually occur at dawn and dusk, and at the edges of clearings. Be sure to scan perches at the midtree level and down.

One other general area to find great grays is Hwy. 3 from just west of Roseau to the Canadian border in the **Roseau River Wildlife Area,** and the bogs of the **Lost River State Forest** along Hwy. 310 from Roseau to the border. From the Canadian border, scan carefully in the first 2 miles south on Hwy. 310—this is one of the most reliable sites in Minnesota for great grays.

The "big" bog country of the **Beltrami State Forest** and **Lake of the Woods** area also harbors consistent wintering and breeding owls, but much of the area is inaccessible wilderness.

8

Big Pines in Deep Snows

White pines are the gatekeepers of the North Woods, occupying the same symbolic niche for the flora of the north that common loons occupy for the fauna. You know you're "Up North" when you see stands of big white pines. As the tallest and longest-lived tree of the northern forest, mature white pines most often live in the supercanopy of a forest, usually numbering no more than 12 to 15 an acre, but making up for their lack of numbers with extraordinary size. The big ones harvested in the heyday of lumbering dated to the early 1400s, and were 4–7 feet in diameter and up to 200 feet tall. Today our largest pines are 3–4 feet in diameter and 150 feet tall, but they still inspire awe.

In the Manitowish River Wilderness Area adjoining my home in northern Wisconsin, old white pines stick well above the canopy like giant green feathers in the wind. Whatever the season, my family and I hike, mountain bike, pick berries, ski, and snowshoe in among those pines, following old logging trails that now sprout hazelbrush and blackberry canes determined to swallow up the openings. The majority of the pines here were cut down, and their stumps endure among the aspen that has pioneered the cutover area. But a number of upland pine stands remain intact, as do islands of pine scattered in wetlands too historically problematic or unprofitable for the loggers to cross.

The stump fields, and the aspen, white birch, and jack pine that pioneered the open ground throughout the Upper Midwest, are the remains of a ghost forest. The historical destruction of the northern pinery was rapid and thorough, beginning in the mid-1800s, peaking at a cut of 3.4 billion board feet in Wisconsin alone in 1899, and ending for all intents and purposes by 1930. In Wisconsin an estimated 103 billion board feet of pine was cut. Because an average house uses about 10,000 board feet of lumber, the math comes out at 10.3 million homes, give or take a few, which could have been built from Wisconsin's pinery alone. St. Louis, Chicago, and other prairie cities were originally built with the pine of the Upper Midwest.

The magnitude of the clearing is hard to imagine. Filibert Roth wrote in 1898 about northern Wisconsin: "During forty years of lumbering nearly the entire territory has been logged over .... Nearly half has been burned over at least once, about three million acres are without any forest cover whatever, and several million more are but partly covered by the dead and dying remnants of the former forest." This destruction was seldom questioned and in fact was most often appreciated. Alexis de Tocqueville wrote in *Democracy in America* of pioneer life in Michigan: "The pioneer living in the wilds ... only prizes the works of man. He will gladly send you off to see a road, a bridge, or a fine village. But that one should appreciate great trees and the beauties of solitude, that possibility completely passes him by."

The few remaining stands of pine today were either missed by some twist of fate, protected by the land barons for their personal use, or saved by the first conservationists of our time. In Minnesota only 15,000 acres remain, less than 1 percent of the original old-growth pine forest. Most of the old-growth pine is found in Itasca State Park and the Boundary Waters Canoe Area. Itasca contains over 25 percent of the state's last old-growth red and white pine forests, as well as Minnesota's record white pine and red pine.

The good news is that much of the aspen/birch forest that came up in the place of the cutover pinery has aged. If not clear-cut again, it will die, allowing white pine and other trees that live in the shade of pioneer species to take off. This is happening now, and much of the original pine forest lands are coming back into white pine, red maple, red oak, and balsam fir. In Wisconsin from 1968 to 1983, white pine increased nearly 50 percent in area, and in Michigan from 1966 to 1980, white pine timberlands increased nearly 66 percent. In a hundred years, if these stands aren't disturbed by humankind or natural forces, we'll have good-sized, abundant white pine to appreciate.

Why take the effort to snowshoe or ski into a stand of old pines? John Eastman offers the best of reasons: "Pine is the larynx of the wind. No other trees unravel, comb, and disperse moving air so thoroughly. Yet they also seem to concentrate the winds, wringing mosaics of sound from gale weather—voice echos, cries, sobs, conversations, maniacal calls. With the help of only slight imagination, they are receiving stations to which all winds check in, filtering out their loads of B-flats, and F minors, processing auditory debris swept from all corners of the sound-bearing world."

Hot Spots

In Michigan, the 58,000 acres of the **Porcupine Mountains Wilderness State Park** is one of the few remaining large wilderness areas left in the Midwest. Much of the forest is old-growth hemlock, yellow birch, and sugar maple, with supercanopy white pines rising above them. Traveling into the "Porkies" turns back the clock, giving you an understanding of the presettlement landscape. The rugged, steep slopes offer skiing and snowshoeing challenges not found anywhere else in the Midwest (though the Sawtooth Mountains along Lake Superior's north shore compare favorably).

The South Boundary Road isn't open in the winter, so the park must be approached from the south on Michigan 64 into Silver City, and then west on Michigan 107. Lake-effect snows provide up to 20 feet of powder in a season, usually more than enough to cover the 42-kilometer network of groomed double-track ski trails from November through March. The Porkies have a vertical drop of 600 feet—stunning panoramas over Lake Superior and inland lakes are the rule. No-frills ski-in cabins are available for winter use and should be booked in advance.

The **Estivant Pines Sanctuary,** owned by the Michigan Nature Association, is a 200-acre tract with many of the largest white pines left in Michigan. The "Leaning Giant," once 23 feet in circumference, has fallen, but other supercanopy pines remain.

The road to the stand is not open in winter—you must ski in. Contact Bear Track Tours in Copper Harbor for a naturalist-led excursion, which is recommended, given that the trails are poorly marked, and one can easily get turned around. Take a compass to be sure of your location. From U.S. 41 at the stoplight in Copper Harbor near the tip of the Keweenaw Peninsula, go east 0.2 mile and turn right. If by some miracle the road is open (the Keweenaw gets more snow than any other area in the eastern United States), drive for 2.3 miles and turn right onto Burma Road, which can be followed for 0.6 mile to the sanctuary entrance.

Hartwick Pines State Park protected 49 acres of virgin white pine back in 1910. One giant known as "The Monarch" is 300 years old, 45 inches in diameter, and 155 feet tall. From the interpretive center, ski or snowshoe the paved Virgin Pines Foot Trail through the big pines. From Grayling, take I-75 north to Exit 259 (the Hartwick Pines exit). Go northeast on Michigan 93 for 2 miles to the park entrance.

The **Besser Natural Area,** a 137-acre preserve with nearly 1 mile of undeveloped Lake Huron shoreline, has a 1-mile self-guiding trail through one of the last remaining virgin stands of white pine. From U.S. 23 just north of Lakewood in Presque Isle County, take Grand Lake Road (County Road 405) north 3.5 miles. Turn right (east) when County Road 405 jogs east, and drive about 1 mile to the entrance. For more information, contact the Alpena Chamber of Commerce, P.O. Box 65, Alpena, MI 49707.

The **Black River Harbor Recreation Area** in the **Ottawa National Forest** offers old-growth hemlock and hardwoods with supercanopy white pine. Snowshoe on the North Country National Scenic Trail through this area. From U.S. 2 in Bessemer, take Michigan 513 for 14.5 miles to the harbor at Lake Superior. Several waterfall sites are identified with signs before you reach the harbor (see chapter 68), all of which can be used to access the North Country Trail. Or go all the way to the harbor, park on the side of the road, and cross the footbridge over the Black River. A trail leads up the hill to Rainbow Falls and through some beautiful old-growth stands.

The **Sylvania Wilderness and Recreation Area** in the Ottawa National Forest offers 21,000 acres of pristine lakes and old-growth forests protected originally as a getaway for U.S. Steel executives. Twenty-six miles of trails wind through the old growth.

An 8-mile hiking trail skirts **Clark Lake**, going through gorgeous stands of virgin hemlock, hardwoods, and white pine. Contact the Ottawa National Forest Service at (906) 358-4724. From Watersmeet, go west about 4 miles on U.S. 2 to County Road 535 and turn left (south). Continue for another 4 miles, to the entrance sign to Sylvania, on the left.

Tahquamenon Falls State Park has old-growth stands of beech and sugar maple and groves of virgin hemlock. The Giant Pines ski trail goes through a stand of old-growth white pines on the north side of Michigan 123 near the Upper Falls (see directions in chapter 68).

Wilderness State Park preserved stands of virgin hemlock and has stands of tall second-growth red pine in the eastern portion of the park. Call the Michigan DNR at (616) 436-5381 for more information. From Mackinaw City, go west on Central Avenue, which becomes Wilderness Park Drive. The park office is 11 miles west of Mackinaw City.

In Wisconsin, the **Franklin Lake Interpretive Trail** in the **Nicolet National Forest** goes through huge 400-year-old pines. The trail is located between Franklin and Butternut Lakes, east of Eagle River. From Hwy. 70 east, turn right on Forest Road 2178 (the old Military Road), then left on Forest Road 2181 (Butternut Lake Road) to the Franklin Lake Campground area and trailhead, where brochures are available. The 1-mile loop connects with the 4-mile Hidden Lakes Trail and is near the 6-mile-long Anvil Lake Trail, if you wish to do more skiing or snowshoeing.

The **Giant Pine Trail** in the Nicolet National Forest has a loop where you can ski through old-growth hemlocks and supercanopy pines. Travel south on Hwy. 32 from Three Lakes for about 5 miles to Forest Road 2183. Turn left and go to Forest Road 2414. Turn left again and go north for about 1.6 miles to the trail parking lot.

Also in the Nicolet National Forest, the **Cathedral Pines** in Oconto County is a 10-acre stand of mature white and red pines, with hemlock 100 feet or more high. The pines are dying and falling and succeeding into the climax beech/hemlock forest, which reaches its westernmost edge just 15 miles west. A newly developed two-loop trail leads up the hill to the stand.

Sylvania Wilderness and Recreation Area

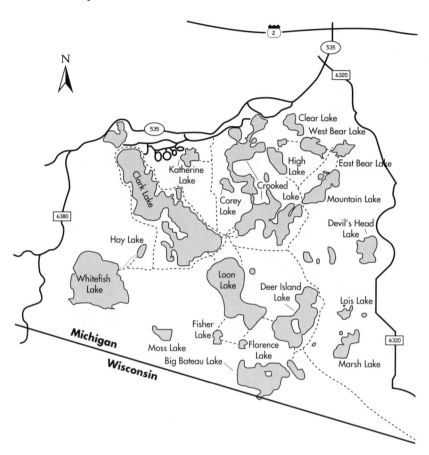

In April, a heron rookery is located in the large white pines, a rather remarkable occurrence. Eighty nests make up the rookery, and the trail leads very close to the site. Take Hwy. 32 west from Lakewood for 0.9 mile, and turn southwest on Forest Road 221 (Archibald Lake Road). Proceed to Cathedral Drive, a dirt road, and turn to drive northwest for 0.4 mile to the stand. A Watchable Wildlife binocular sign will guide you off of Hwy. 32 to the site.

The **Raven Ski Trail** in the **Northern Highlands State Forest** takes you through mature hemlock and white and red pines along the marked interpretive trail. Take Hwy. 47 south from Woodruff for about 2 miles and turn left onto Woodruff Road (a sign for the Clear Lake Campground is at the intersection). Go about 0.5 mile to the signed trail and parking lot on your right.

In Minnesota, the **Lost Forty** in the **Chippewa National Forest** was preserved due to a mapping error by the original government land survey in 1882. The site was described as part of Coddington Lake, allowing the virgin pine of the area to be saved from logging at the turn of the century. A quarter-mile loop trail winds its way through the mature red and white pines found on the east end of the Lost Forty. The pines here are as old as 350 years and have diameters between 22 and 48 inches. The Lost Forty is actually 144 acres. From Blackduck, take County Roads 30/13 for 13 miles to Alvwood. Turn north on Minnesota 46 for 0.5 mile to County 29. Take 29 east for 11 miles to Dora Lake and County Road 26. Follow 26 north for 2 miles to Forest Road 2240 and turn west. About 1.5 miles later you will see a sign for the Lost Forty.

Itasca State Park has over 3,000 acres of mature red pines. The trees at Preacher's Grove on Hwy. 1 originated from fires in the 1700s and are now over 200 years old. The **Big Pine Trail** off Wilderness Drive is the location of Minnesota's largest red pine, and the **Bohall Wilderness Trail**, also off Wilderness Drive, passes through large fire-origin white and red pines. A network of cross-country ski trails runs throughout the park, and snowshoeing opportunities abound in the 2,000-acre **Itasca Wilderness Sanctuary Scientific and Natural Area**. Take Hwy. 71 north from Park Rapids about 22 miles to the south entrance to the park.

9

Life under the Ice

Sealed off by layers of snow and ice, lakes and rivers take on an even greater mystery in winter than during the warm seasons. The first time I tagged along with an ice-fishing friend I was skeptical—how did he have any idea where the fish were? I helped him drill about a half-dozen holes, the green water rushing up and out the hole once the auger bit down to liquid. We set the holes one by one, and by the time we were setting the sixth, the first flag had gone up. We raced over, pulled up the line, and, miracle of miracles, out came a big walleye. It was beautiful and lay there quietly, apparently in greater shock at its sudden exposure to sun and wind than the shock I felt that it had come out of those green depths we had walked over so casually.

The surface waters of 48 percent of the Northern Hemisphere freeze every winter—19 million square miles of ice. That anything survives five months under a cover of ice is a matter science explains with relative ease. Still, like northern lights and bird migration, all the scientific explanations seem wanting when compared to the event itself—words just seem too little sometimes.

Ice is a wonder in itself. Consider the "miracle" of floating ice. If it weren't for a quirk of physics, lakes would freeze from the bottom up instead of the top down, and the life we know in our lakes and rivers would be absent. The magic occurs at 39°F, when water, which had become heavier and denser as it became colder, suddenly does an about-face and becomes less dense and lighter as it continues dropping in temperature, until it freezes at 32°F.

We all have swum in lakes in the summer where, as we venture into deeper water, the bottom layers become very cold. The denser, colder water sinks to the bottom and stays there because it's heavier than the warmer water. Many lakes stratify in the summer into layers that don't mix due to the differences in water density. But as the autumn progresses and the upper water temperatures drop, the water eventually reaches a temperature equilibrium throughout the water column, and then the top layers sink and the bottom layers rise. This is called autumn turnover, and the mixing brings the nutrient-rich waters up from the bottom while sending the oxygen-rich top waters to the bottom. The lake literally takes a breath and shares a meal throughout its area.

Then as the fall progresses and the water temperatures continue to drop throughout the water column, eventually reaching 39°F, the essential ecological miracle occurs—warmer water begins to sink and colder water remains at the surface. So if you were to cut a hole in the winter ice and dive to the bottom of a lake, you would find the temperature a "warm" 39°F at the bottom and a "cold" 32°F at the iced surface.

Once the ice skin forms over a lake, what do the fish and other aquatic creatures do? As cold-blooded animals, they must function within the same narrow temperature range as the water. Frogs and turtles don't even try, but just bury themselves in the mud and wait it out (see chapter 6). Most fish slow down the pace of eating, growth, movement, and reproduction. Catfish slow *way* down, appearing almost like they're in a state of suspended animation. Divers can actually pick them up and play with them when they're in this state.

As a general rule, for every change in temperature of 10° Celsius, the metabolic rate of a cold-blooded animal increases or decreases by a factor of two. So fish in water changing from 25°C (75°F) in summer to 5°C (42°F) in winter should slow their body functions by one-fourth of their normal rate. But as with most rules, there are many exceptions. Numerous fish seem to acclimate themselves to the colder temperatures by shifting to a higher metabolic rate.

Life under the ice can get difficult as the winter progresses and the oxygen cupboard becomes more and more bare. The only way oxygen can be added to the water column is through photosynthesis by aquatic plants, because the lake is capped like a canning jar against any atmospheric oxygen sneaking in. Elodea, a common submerged plant in many northern lakes, will grow under the ice even under very low light conditions. During daylight hours elodea produces oxygen through photosynthesis, but because all plants also respire, elodea only produces about half as much oxygen during the day as it uses in a 24-hour period for respiration. It's engaged in deficit spending, in the red like every other creature in the lake.

Bacteria are also consuming oxygen in the sediments as they perform their essential task of decomposition, so as the winter progresses the oxygen level in the water declines. In large, well-oxygenated lakes, as the oxygen depletes closest to the bottom where the bacteria are at work, the fish simply move up the water column, and winter survival poses few problems (except for those ice fishermen lurking above). In shallow and smaller lakes, a winterkill of organisms can occur if the ice stays on too long and the oxygen reaches intolerably low levels.

So it's a game of endurance in the end. The ice rarely goes off the lakes in the North Woods until the last days of April, nearly six months after its formation in mid-November. In February, we can only walk the snowy surfaces and wonder what is happening below.

Hot Spots

Some lakes take on the appearance of shantytowns in the winter. Ice-fishing villages of more than 5,000 huts are erected on lakes in Minnesota, such as Mille Lacs, Gull, Leech, and Minnetonka Lakes. The Minnesota DNR issued 117,583 ice-house licenses during the 1995–1996 winter!

Ice fishermen run the comfort gamut from sitting in the open on a 5-gallon plastic pail to resting within an insulated, heated, window-adorned structure that may include a sound system and TV so the big games aren't missed. If you are a novice angler, these temporary ice cities will tell you all you need to know about where to try your luck at ice fishing. And every ice fisher, if he or she is willing to share hard-won information, will have a different story on where the fish are and how to catch them. That's the beauty of fishing. Who needs casinos?

Some folks swear **University Bay** on **Lake Mendota** in Madison, Wisconsin, is the best place in the state for ice fishing. For two weeks every February you can try to spear lake sturgeon through the ice on **Lake Winnebago** near Oshkosh, Wisconsin, along with 7,000 other people, though your odds are one in ten of having one swim by your hole.

In the **Chippewa National Forest** in Minnesota, **Leech Lake** is known for its walleye and musky, and **Lake Winnibigoshish** is good for everything, particularly perch.

Of all the months of the year, February is probably the worst for fishing. Months closer to ice-on and ice-off tend to produce more active fish.

The traditional Native American method for spearing fish involved cutting a 2-foot by 3-foot hole in the ice and tenting a blanket over the hole, allowing the spearfisher to see into the water. Lying prone, the spearfisher would move a carved wooden decoy in the water with one hand with the spear at the ready in case a fish should rise to try to take the decoy.

10

Great Horned Owls

Diana Kappel-Smith describes great horned owls in her book, *Wintering:* "I heard them begin their courtship one night at the end of January. It was dark and the hills were locked in black and silver forest; and then: 'Hoo-hoo-HOO-hooo-hooo-hooo …' The owls' booming ventriloqual song filled the whole air. And again: 'Hooo-hoo-HOO-hooo! …' There were holes in the singing, pauses, oases filled with a vertiginous sky full of stars; and then another burst of 'hooo!'s came—from where? It was as if mountain trolls were tooting granitic bassoons."

The nesting of great horneds fires the first signal flare that winter has reached its peak and may be on the decline. But even before this awaited transitional moment their courting has begun, impossibly early it seems, starting in September, and then quickening in October and November. By December the adults have set up their territories, and no one is welcome for a visit, not even their own young from last year. In January, as egg-laying time approaches, the male and female call back and forth to each other consistently, night after night, their deep and slow vocalizations giving birth to the name "hoot owl."

The eggs are laid in late January in southern counties to mid-February in the north, and once the adults initiate the month-long incubation, they quiet down, apparently not wishing to draw attention to the nest. Snow still blankets the ground (as well as the adult incubating the eggs), but neither cold nor snow prevents the owlets from hatching in late February to March. Late in the winter like this, most other bird species haven't even begun to return from their wintering grounds—nearly all are still two months away from nesting—but not the great horneds.

By mid- to late April the young owlets have grown to nearly the size of the adults, though their flight feathers have yet to grow in. And by May the owlets are "branching," hopping from branch to branch around the nest, but they're still unable to fly. In 63 to 70 days from their hatching, the owlets fledge, though they remain dependent on the adults for food for several months yet, and you may hear their raspy begging calls near sunset.

In some winters, when the prey base declines in the north, great horneds migrate southward, as evidenced by band recoveries, though most great horneds winter in their breeding territories and do not migrate. They rarely build their own nests, usually "borrowing" (what animal would dare argue?)

nests of red-tailed hawks, crows, squirrels, and even great blue herons. Some nest in tree cavities, some in stick nests, some on rock faces. Because great horneds nest many months before leaves appear on the trees, their nests are often very visible.

Great horneds seem adaptable to virtually any habitat. They're found in all the counties of all three states. They are so adaptable that they are the most widespread and abundant North American owl species, found in every state in the United States north into the Arctic and south throughout Central America all the way to Tierra del Fuego.

Great horneds rule the avian roost. Their huge talons

Great horned owls may be readily found in the Upper Midwest. Photo by Carol Christensen.

rank them as one of North America's most powerful birds of prey, capable of taking anything from beetles to crayfish to young fox, with snakes, frogs, fish, muskrats, skunks, and smaller hawks and owls in between. They're even known to fish in water up to their stomachs trying to take turtles, frogs, and other aquatic animals. Stories abound about their predaceous abilities. One author writes of a friend who had just bagged a raccoon on an evening hunt and was heading home with it slung across his shoulder, when a great horned owl suddenly hit the raccoon hard in an attempt to make off with it. They struggled momentarily, the owl eventually loosening its grip and flying off. Another story describes a well-known hawk-watcher, who witnessed a great horned owl catch and kill a red-tailed hawk.

Great horned owls may be found virtually everywhere but, knowing that, the question remains, How does one go about spotting an owl? Great horneds usually come out at dusk to the edges of their feeding habitats along fields, lakes, marshes, or clearings. Scan these edges just before full dark to catch them on the perch or in flight to the perch. Although their crepuscular habits (moving about at twilight) may make for difficult viewing, finding an owl in this unique light is often magical.

Because great horneds are ordinarily so vocal, you needn't use a tape recording to try to induce them to call—use of a tape may instead succeed in disrupting territorial birds. Try "squeaking" to imitate an injured mouse by loudly sucking or kissing the side of your hand or index finger—the louder the better. Vary the squeaks and an owl may be lured in; they usually respond quickly. Stay hidden while squeaking and intersperse the squeaking with silent stretches for listening and watching.

Learn to look for signs during the day, like the whitewash of owl excrement in the branches of a favorite roost tree, or a pile of regurgitated food pellets at the base of the tree. Pellets are expelled about $6^1/_2$ hours after a meal, and usually twice a day—once at the daytime roost and once at the nighttime feeding site.

If you discover an owl at a distance and you wish to approach it, remember that owls have exceptional hearing and eyesight (even during the day). Stay low, and move very slowly and quietly toward it.

Spotting an owl requires patience, practice, and perseverance more than anything—their camouflage is ingenious, and you could be literally standing next to the perch tree of most owls and never see them. Learn to check every likely tree from many angles. And if you see crows mobbing something or songbirds in a tizzy, drop everything and see what's going on—owls are universally hated, and most birds will try to harass them out of their habitat.

Owls fly silently, and one can flush without our even knowing it. The serrated leading edges of the wing feathers are soft and velvety and muffle sound very effectively.

Take along a good flashlight, like one of the larger "mag" lights or a six-volt handheld lantern. Don't use a 12-volt, 300,000+ candlepower light on an owl—you can thus impair its night vision for a long time. A good pair of binoculars is also a necessity. Make sure you buy a pair with good twilight capabilities. Look for binoculars with the second number above 40, such as a 7 X 42 or 7 X 50. Lower-power binoculars let in more light, so you may want to sacrifice magnification for better light (the first number tells you how many times the lens will magnify the image).

Hot Spots There are many areas where great horneds are commonly seen. In Michigan, great horned owls and barred owls are common the year around at the **Grass River Natural Area**. Take U.S. 131 to Mancelona and turn west on Michigan 88. Go 2.5 miles and take County Road 618 (Michigan 88 turns to the right at this intersection). Drive 6 miles to the site entrance on the right side of the road, 0.5 mile past Comfort Road.

Nesting great horned owls may be seen from an observation deck behind the visitor center of the **Blandford Nature Center** in Grand Rapids. Take U.S. 131 north and take the Leonard Street exit. Head west for

3.5 miles to Hillburn Avenue and turn right (north). The 143-acre nature center is at the end of the street and is administered by the Public Museum of Grand Rapids, (616) 453-6192.

Metrobeach Metropark has nesting great horned owls in the nature area. From Detroit, take I-94 east to Exit 236. Turn right onto Metro Parkway (16 Mile Road) and follow it about 3 miles to the park entrance.

To see an owl-banding station, and often a variety of species of owls, visit the **Whitefish Point Bird Observatory** in the northeastern Upper Peninsula in spring and fall (see directions in chapter 46).

In Wisconsin, the **Bubolz Nature Center** just north of Appleton has nesting great horned owls. From the junction of County Roads A and OO, take A north for 1.5 miles to the preserve.

11

February Shorttakes

Gyrfalcons

Gyrfalcons have resided in the winter along the Saint Marys River in Sault Ste. Marie for at least 20 years. Usually only one is present, though three spent the winter of 1990–1991 here. The **Sault Edison power plant,** which straddles the Edison Sault Power Canal, almost always has a gyrfalcon perched on its cupola or on one of its many windowsills. Park in the lot in the **James Alford Waterfront Park** at the east end of the power plant and scan the riverside of this enormous and beautiful building. Gyrfalcons do range widely in their pursuit of waterfowl and pigeons, so try early in the morning before the gyrfalcon has much of a chance to wander elsewhere.

The **Duluth and Superior Harbor** areas often have a gyrfalcon over-wintering. Check around the grain elevators as described in chapter 7.

Spruce Grouse

The place to look for spruce grouse, the rarely seen "fool hen," is during the winter on **County Road 2 in Lake County,** northeastern Minnesota. They come to the roadsides to pick up salt and grit, and dawn is the time to see them, for traffic will scare them off as the morning progresses. The most consistent spot, says Kim Eckert in his exceptionally thorough book, *A Birder's Guide to Minnesota,* is just beyond Sand River, some 41.5 miles north of Two Harbors. Look along the roadsides for the following 2 miles.

Snow Fleas

Snow fleas hardly inspire the oohs and aahs of glamour species like falcons and owls, but in February, millions (if not billions, but who wants to count?) dot the snow on warmer sunny days. When you're out skiing or snowshoeing, look around the bases of trees, where they tend to congregate because the dark tree bark absorbs heat and radiates it out again. The snow will look like someone has shaken pepper all over it.

Snow fleas aren't fleas at all, but *springtails.* Watch them leap several inches through the air—they're the kangaroos of the insect world.

12

A Closer Look: Great Gray Owls

Great gray owls while hovering above the snow in readiness to drop on their prey have been likened to gigantic moths. The largest of all North American owls, with broad wings that span 5 feet, a standing height of $2^1/_2$ feet, and yellow eyes that gleam from concentric gray circles on its facial disc, the great gray usually sends birders into paroxysms of excitement as the birding hotlines light up with sighting news. In an invasion year, the beauty and rarity of this boreal forest denizen draws birders from all over the country.

Though the dimensions of a great gray seem immense, they are more feathers than true bulk. Snowy owls and great horned owls outweigh them, and great horneds, probably the fiercest predator in the wild, regularly prey upon their larger cousins—one study turned up 13 radio-marked great grays that died at the talons of great horned owls.

The great gray's impressive size, rounded head without ear tufts, and white "bow tie" under the chin make its identification unmistakable. The prominent circles on the facial disc bestow a solemnity upon the bird that is particularly characteristic, as is its deep booming call, *whoo-hooo-hooo,* which thrums low and slow.

Great grays nest uncommonly in the far northern reaches of the Upper Midwest and are rarely seen except in the winters of invasion years, when their prey base crashes in Ontario and Manitoba. Then they usually filter south until they discover a good stock of rodents, and there they'll stay as long as the prey numbers hold up. Sometimes they head north, too—one radio-tagged great gray nested in southeastern Manitoba, and her signal was heard three months later near Hudson Bay, 500 miles northeast.

Usually great grays inhabit deep boreal forests and bogs, but winter often brings them out to roadsides and field edges, where the grassy habitat supports large populations of voles and mice. This behavior makes for good viewing for humans but can concentrate the owls in such a manner that many die from collisions with cars. Along one 35-mile stretch of the Trans-Canada Highway in the winter of 1980–1981, researchers found the remains of 50 great grays, most of which were thought to have been killed by cars.

Although they are considered elusive and retiring, great grays can also exhibit remarkably tame behaviors. One researcher was trying to locate a brood of recently fledged great grays, and he imitated the call of the female parent. All three young came immediately to him, and one landed on top of his head, where it remained for eight minutes, every so often peering over the brim of his cap, probably to see when the food was going to appear.

Courtship usually begins in mid-February. The male may display to the female by imitating typical behaviors like searching for food, nest-building, and feeding young. He exaggerates these behaviors, performing them over and over again. Robert Nero, a longtime researcher of great grays and the author of a book on the owls, writes about watching a male plunge into the snow as if to catch a vole a dozen times, then flying to the watching female in hopes of breeding.

Because great grays don't build their own nests, once breeding is successful they frequently take over old hawk nests or use man-made structures, both of which are usually placed in large deformed trees. Thus, great gray nesting success appears tied to the success of goshawks, ravens, red-tailed hawks, and broad-winged hawks, or to the efforts of researchers who build artificial nests. Maintenance of older-growth forest is equally necessary, for all these hawks usually build nests in these habitats.

Two to five eggs may be laid, and after a month of incubation by the female, who is fed by the male, the eggs hatch over a period of several days, resulting in owlets that develop at varying rates. Remarkably, observations have been made of nonbreeding males bringing food to nesting females, and of hungry fledglings being fed by unrelated males, too. Apparently, great grays may socialize to some extent within a community of nesting owls, a unique behavior among North American owls.

To see great grays in winter, it's easiest simply to call the birding hotlines in each state to hear about the most recent sightings and where they are. Then be ready to drop what you're doing and head north. The last Arctic owl invasion year was 1991–1992 (previous years were in 1981–1982 and 1986–1987). Dusk and dawn are the best times to find them hunting, usually until 10:00 A.M. and after 4:00 P.M., though if they're particularly hungry they may perch in the open all day.

Though you may have to wait five years for an invasion, drive a long way, and endure cold weather, the first time you see a great gray in the wild is worth all the effort.

March

Notes

13

Maple Syruping

I have been accused for many years by my so-called friends of secretly drinking pure maple syrup directly from the bottle. It's just not true. I merely sample the syrup now and again to make sure it has retained its purity, a service I perform for the safety of my family and friends, a fatherly duty among many others.

We have few extravagant habits in our household, but real maple syrup is an absolute must, and we gladly pay the $25 a gallon to support our habit. Part of the reason may be that both Mary and I have helped make syrup in the past, a long and rather magical process that distills a tasteless sap (though Mary claims she can taste the sweetness in it) into an amber elixir that has no equal. Staying up all night tending a wood fire under an evaporator tends to heighten the taste of the pancakes drowned in syrup in the morning, too.

John Burroughs said it best back in 1886: "A sap-run is the sweet good-by of winter. It is the fruit of the equal marriage of the sun and frost." The sap run begins before bird migrations and spring flowerings. It carries the flag of spring, though you would never know that this herald has arrived unless you know when to tap into a maple in order to hear the sap *ping, ping, ping* into a metal pail.

No one can foretell the exact date when the sap will start to flow. Dripping eaves may be as good a signal as any. Daytime temperatures of above freezing with nights below freezing trigger the sap to rise. The official moment could be as early as mid-February in southern counties or as late as the end of March up north. Once it rises, the run can be a sprint ending in a week or two after a quick warm-up, or a long-distance jog lasting for three weeks or more as spring gradually comes on. When the sap is truly running, a 3-gallon bucket will usually fill within 24 hours. Because it takes 40 gallons or so of sap to make 1 gallon of syrup, there's more work to collecting and hauling the sap than one might think.

Native Americans were the first to "sugar." The Ojibwa would go to their sugar camps in March and stay the month until they had boiled the syrup all the way into pure maple sugar, which they would pack in small birchbark cones. They sugar-flavored everything, from lake water (the first pop?) to soups to meats, and they used the maple sugar as a valued trade item. Along with wild rice, maple sugar was the most important plant-derived food of the Native tribes of our region.

I've often wondered how the Native people figured out that this nearly tasteless liquid could produce such a wondrous sugar. I think the red squirrel gave it away. Red squirrels are often seen in spring piercing maples with their sharp teeth and licking the sap. Surely the Natives saw this, but more likely the sap ran down the trees and gradually evaporated, leaving behind the sugary residue, ample evidence that if the water could be removed, generations of children could be raised with sweet tooths.

The sugar maple (or "hard" maple) contains the most sucrose—from 3 percent up to 8 percent in a "sweet tree." Red maple, silver maple, even box elder, which is in the maple family too, can be tapped (for that matter so can trees in the birch family), but none yield the volume and concentrated sweetness of the sugar maple.

Have I convinced you to try your hand at making syrup and not just buying it? Take your children and give them the opportunity to see trees in a whole new light. Wisconsin essayist Justin Isherwood writes of one night in the sugar house: "Kids come to watch once more before going to bed, eyes brightened by the fire, surprised that such sweetness can come from trees. Children will never be the same again, having once tasted hot syrup submerged in steam and surrounded by a darkness kept barely at bay by the firelight."

Hot Spots

In all three states, a wide array of environmental centers offer maple syruping programs to the public. In Wisconsin: the Department of Natural Resources **MacKenzie Environmental Education Center** in Poynette; the **Riveredge Nature Center** in Newburg, (414) 675-6888; the **Ledge View Nature Study Area** in Chilton, (414) 849-7094; the **Bubolz Nature Preserve** in Appleton, (414) 731-6041; the **Wehr Nature Center** in Franklin, (414) 425-8558; the **1000 Island Environmental Center** near Kaukanna, (414) 766-4733; the **River Bend Nature Center** in Racine, (414) 639-0930.

In Michigan, the Maple Sugar Festival is held in the **Eddy Geology Center at the Waterloo Recreation Area** in Chelsea, (313) 475-8307; the Maple Syrup Fest is held in the **Kalamazoo Nature Center** in Kalamazoo, (616) 381-1574; **Blandford Nature Center** in Grand Rapids educates 13,000 visitors every year in the art of maple syruping, (616) 453-6192; and Maple Syrup Day takes place at the **Chippewa Nature Center** in Midland, (517) 631-0830.

In Minnesota, **Myre–Big Island State Park** conducts hands-on syruping near Albert Lea, (507) 373-4492.

14

Waterfowl Migration

March skies may appear gray and drab to the inexperienced bird-watcher but, along the southern Great Lakes coastal areas, waterfowl abound during this month. No March morning should be dreary to the early riser who has an eye open and an ear attuned to the first avian harbingers of spring.

If there's open water, the ducks, geese, and swans seem to know it. No sooner does a river or lake open than within a day or two, or sometimes within only hours, a few ducks are there diving or dabbling for food, as if they had never left. It's difficult for North Woods residents to believe the waterfowl are returning this early in the southern counties, but they are indeed on the wing, and often in substantial numbers. A word to the wise: I visited Erie Marsh in southeastern Michigan on April 10 one year, and by then I had already missed the bulk of the waterfowl migration!

The tundra swans often lead the vanguard. Our only native swan to pass through in large numbers (trumpeter swans now nest in all three states but are tiny in total number—see chapter 15), the tundras herald the advent of spring. Pure white, with a nearly 7-foot wingspan, they appear to take winter with them as they disappear northward. They nest in the far northern tundra, from the top of Hudson Bay to the Bering Sea. And though summer won't come until June there, they arrive well before the ice and snows are off, bargaining that incubating eggs with protective snow all around is worth the risk of their fat reserves dwindling.

Nearly 30 waterfowl species join or follow the tundras in their northern flight. Sea ducks like scoters, harlequin ducks, and oldsquaws usually remain well off the coast, but March storms can drive them to calmer bays and shorelines. Storms are prime birding weather, believe it or not, and one seldom wonders if suffering the weather's abuse was worth it when rare migrants ride the storm-tossed waves within binocular range.

Many of the divers (ducks that dive to feed), such as goldeneye, ringnecked, scaup, canvasback, redhead, and bufflehead, arrive early. Some, like the common goldeneye, may even precede the tundras. I've seen goldeneye on open water in Sault Ste. Marie in early January in minus 20°F weather with windchills down to minus 70°F. Hardy may be too limited an adjective to describe their winter adaptability. For identification purposes, the large white spot between the eye and the bill gives the male away immediately.

The dabblers (they tip up their tail high in the air to feed), such as mallard, black, ruddy, pintail, wigeon, shoveler, teal, and gadwall, tend to arrive a bit later, except for mallards and the blacks who often last out the winter on open water, particularly if someone is willing to feed them.

The loss of wetland habitat is by now a well-known story. Lake Erie was famed for its marshes, as was the southern end of Green Bay on Lake Michigan. Both now offer vestiges at best of their once exuberant wealth, yet there's still much to see. Today what few coastal marshes remain are usually protected by state and federal agencies. This lack of stopover habitat often concentrates waterfowl into refuges, certainly a gain for the bird-watcher who wishes to see the most variety and the greatest abundance of birds.

Waterfowl arrive in their breeding plumages, the males often so brilliantly colored and marked that one may only wonder in admiration of nature's exceptional artistry.

Remember that March is, shall we say, "playful." Others might use the words "devious," "unfaithful," or "fickle." The promise and the reality differ enormously.

March gestures charmingly, and leads us on, playing up to our wishful thinking and then hammering us with snow and wind and sleet. The wild weather swings are the only consistent occurrences one can bank on in March. Dress appropriately.

Aldo Leopold devoted a chapter in his unsurpassed book *A Sand County Almanac* to migrating geese in March. The geese, said Leopold, were a wild poem carried through midwestern skies to the Arctic tundra. No one who has listened intently for the first flight of geese on a tempestuous March morning would disagree.

Nothing more but Leopold's words need ever be said about the return of geese and the wild joys of March.

Hot Spots

If I had to choose two areas upon which to concentrate my waterfowl-watching efforts in March, it would be southeastern Michigan along Lake Erie and in Saginaw Bay along Lake Huron. I'd begin in **Monroe County.** Even though the area is heavily industrialized, it's the best county in Michigan for finding waterfowl, marsh birds, and shorebirds, given its extreme southeastern location. Visit first the **Michigan Nature Conservancy's Erie Marsh Preserve.** Its 2,618 acres, about half of which are a shallow portion of North Maumee Bay, constitute 11 percent of the state's wetlands on Lake Erie and Lake St. Clair. The land was donated by the Erie Gun Club to the Michigan Nature Conservancy, but club members have retained hunting rights. Many miles of dikes run through extensive marshlands and open water, and much to a birder's delight, the dikes may only be walked. The best waterfowl birding is usually the last week in March. I visited in early April, and the great egrets had just returned the night before. I saw eight within 50 yards of my car, so if your schedule doesn't permit a March waterfowl trip, try an early April heron trip. This is an important feeding area for great blue herons, black-crowned night herons, and great egrets. Don't forget to look up, too; raptors soar by throughout April.

Take I-75 south to Exit 2 (Summit Street), and go 0.8 mile across the bridge to a crossover. Make a U-turn here and go north for 0.2 mile to Bay Creek Road and turn right. Take Bay Creek for 0.8 mile to Dean Road (scan the shoreline and flooded fields along the way), then go another 0.4 mile to the parking lot. Ignore the sign reading Erie Shooting Club—Private. This is Nature Conservancy property, and although it is still private, is open to the public. Walk the dikes to either side of the cottages (owned by the shooting club); the dikes that lead out to the left, past the fronts of the cottages, offer a 6-mile loop hike (expect mud!).

From the Erie Marsh Preserve, drive north to **Pointe Mouillee State Game Area,** which offers 4 miles of Lake Erie marsh system shoreline and many miles of generally dry dikes to explore by foot or bicycle. Pointe Mouillee owes its migrant success to the construction of dikes, which allow water levels to be manipulated for maximum attractiveness to waterfowl. Here is one case where wetlands are far better off with human intervention—otherwise, the area would be mostly a vast, shallow, muddy expanse, generally undesirable to most birds. Call (313) 379-9692 for more information.

Farther north, the **Metro Beach Metropark** on Lake St. Clair between Lake Erie and Lake Huron can serve up huge numbers of waterfowl, particularly if the winter has been mild and the lake remains open (see chapter 10). From Detroit, take I-94 east to Exit 236, and turn right onto the Metro Parkway (16 Mile Road). Follow the parkway for 3 miles to the park entrance.

St. Clair Flats Wildlife Area, also on Lake St. Clair, usually has large numbers of tundra swans and thousands of geese and ducks. Take I-94 to the Algonac exit (Michigan 29, Exit 243) and follow Michigan 29 east for 17 miles to the Harsen's Island Ferry at the Port-O-Call Restaurant.

Continue heading north, now for the shallow waters of **Saginaw Bay. Fish Point State Game Area** is a 3,200-acre peninsula pushing into Saginaw Bay that has been called the "Chesapeake of the Midwest" for its exceptional variety and numbers of waterfowl. An observation tower and hiking trail provide good viewing opportunities. The tower is at the intersections of Seagull and Ridge Roads. Up to 3,000 tundra swans may be seen in March in the fields, along with thousands of ducks and geese, including snow and white-fronted geese. Rarities such as brant, cinnamon teal, and oldsquaw are possible. The wildlife area is open to hunting in the fall and thus spring is the best time for observing waterfowl. Write to the Michigan DNR for a map of this area to help you understand the multiple ownership: Wildlife Division of Michigan DNR, Box 30028, Lansing, MI 48909; or call (517) 674-2511. Fish Point itself is privately owned, for instance, and viewing opportunities there are limited. From Unionville, take Michigan 25 west for 2.5 miles. Where it bends left, head straight on Bay Park Road to Ringle Road. Turn right (north) and go another 3 miles to the Fish Point headquarters.

Nayanquing Point State Wildlife Area provides resting and nesting habitat for large numbers of ducks, geese, and tundra swans. Marsh and open water on Saginaw Bay are the dominant habitats, and there are a few dikes and roads that provide access, and an observation tower on Saginaw Bay. Rare species occur regularly, and this is one of the few areas in Michigan with a nesting yellow-headed blackbird colony. Waterfowl hunting in October and November limits good birding to spring and summer. Nine miles north of Kawkawlin (north of Bay City) on Michigan 13, take Kitchen Road (a Nayanquing sign is at the road junction) east for 1.5 miles to Tower Beach Road. Turn left (north) to the area headquarters immediately on your right. Get a map and ask where the current hot spots are. Mallard Point Road (take the next right off Kitchen Road) ends at an observation tower where one can also continue hiking out into marshland. The tundra swans are actually better here in the first week of November than in spring—about 2,500 to 3,000 on the average may be seen by the observation tower.

Tobico Marsh State Game Area in **Bay City State Park** is another excellent area, and only 5 miles south. A boardwalk, two observation towers, and a hiking trail help make for easier marsh viewing. From I-75, take the Beaver Road exit (#168), and head east for 5 miles to the entrance of Bay City State Park. Park in the day-use parking lot next to the Jennison Nature Center, which will have maps of the area, though it's closed this early in the spring. Write ahead for information.

Wigwam Bay Wildlife Area, a relatively newly purchased 1,000-acre marsh with a network of dry dikes to hike, is considered one of the top marshes left along Saginaw Bay. From Standish on Michigan 13, take Pine River Road east toward the lake for 3.5 miles. Turn left (north) onto Arenac State Road, and go 1.5 miles to Stover Road. Turn right (east), and in 3.5 miles you will reach the site entrance.

Crow Island State Game Area, 2,200 acres of marsh and floodplain habitat inland on the Saginaw River, offers particularly good viewing of spring migrants like tundra swans. Take I-75 north from Saginaw to the East Bay City Road exit (Michigan 13). The marsh is on your right side as you wind around the exit loop. The area parallels Michigan 13 immediately and for 1.5 miles to a power line tower. A dike may be seen just before the tower on the right.

15

Return of the Trumpeter Swans

The early spring wind pummels the wetlands of the Mead Wildlife Area in central Wisconsin, stirring the open water into waves. Any migrating birds that may have stopped off here are harbored in the marsh vegetation. I wander about, trying this slough and that, hoping to stumble upon loafing waterfowl waiting out the wind. But I am luckless until I see the white shapes far in the distance on a large open marsh. I move rapidly toward them along the dike, stopping and watching through my binoculars as I go, and, remarkably, the pair seems to be swimming my way. Our paths intersect five minutes later. I hide in the shoreline shrubs, and they cruise back and forth in front of me while I try to keep my excitement under control. Eventually it dawns on me that they are watching me as much as I am watching them, and so I gradually come out into the open. They remain a mere 10 yards out from me, an odd combination of wildness and curiosity.

I am in a stare-down with trumpeter swans, the largest waterfowl in the world—5 feet long in flight, with a wingspan of 7 feet and body weight up to 30 pounds. But their extraordinary size is secondary to their elegance; their grace is a subject for poets.

I stand and watch a long while, trying to fully appreciate that I am enjoying a privilege few people in Wisconsin have ever enjoyed. Until the 1980s, trumpeters had only been seen twice in Wisconsin in all of the twentieth century. One individual in 1904 in Waukesha County was observed and summarily shot, then hung in a billiard hall in Chicago. And once in 1937 four trumpeters landed briefly near Oconto as part of a larger flock of tundra swans on their way to northern nesting areas.

Existing records of trumpeter observations in nineteenth-century Wisconsin were rather rare too, suggesting an irregular historical presence of swans in widely scattered locations. The swans' return in recent years is all the more remarkable given that the closing of the twentieth century will be remembered ecologically for the loss of thousands of species worldwide. In this time of continued global destruction, the restoration and enhancement of a rare species are truly something to celebrate.

Nationally, trumpeter swans were so hard to find that Arthur Cleveland Bent, the author in 1925 of *The Life Histories of North American Wild Fowl*, had to rely on essays by John James Audubon from nearly 100 years earlier to describe significant details of the life histories of the swan. A 1932 national

Trumpeter swans have made an extraordinary comeback in all three states due to intensive restoration efforts. Photo by Carol Christensen.

census of trumpeters confirmed their rarity, yielding only 69 swans, all of which were found in an area near Yellowstone National Park. Although some swans were known to nest in Canada and Alaska, their future appeared bleak.

Swan skins had been used in ladies' powder puffs and the feathers tufted into fashionable hats. The Hudson's Bay Company records show that from 1853 to 1877 a total of 17,671 swan skins, mostly from trumpeters, were sold. Their decline was evident from 1888 to 1897, when only 57 swan skins were in the fur-sale offerings in London, and in 1897, 1900, 1902, and 1903, when none appeared.

"A swan seen at any time of the year in most parts of the United States is the signal for every man with a gun to pursue it," observed E.H. Forbush in 1912. "Only the younger are savory, and the gunners might well have spared the adult birds, but it was 'sport' to kill them and fashion called for swan's-down." Even Audubon was most fond of writing with a swan quill.

The Migratory Bird Treaty of 1918 offered the first protection for the trumpeter from hunters. The establishment of wildlife refuges, particularly the Red Rock Lakes National Wildlife Refuge in Montana in 1935, brought the next measure of protection. Wild cygnets (swans in their first year) were soon transplanted from Red Rock Lakes to national wildlife refuges in Wyoming, Oregon, Nevada, Washington, and South Dakota. Eventually Hennepin Parks in Minnesota obtained a pair of Red Rock Lakes cygnets in 1966, and with the restoration efforts of the Minnesota DNR, a breeding population of some 13 pairs and nearly 200 free-flying birds now graces Minnesota.

On the heels of Minnesota's efforts came the Michigan and Wisconsin natural resource departments' swan recovery programs. The results of these pioneering efforts are trumpeter swans breeding in all three upper midwestern states, and March is a good time to see them because they return to the area early.

Hot Spots

In Minnesota, 21 swans were released on **Tamarac NWR** in 1987, 41 in 1988, and 33 in 1989. Other swans have been released in recent years in **Nicollet County on Swan Lake** and in the **Chippewa National Forest** near Grand Rapids. A new release site on **Heron Lake** was just started in a cooperative restoration effort with the Iowa DNR. In 1994, 13 pairs statewide fledged 52 cygnets. Overall, the Minnesota DNR has turned loose 230 trumpeters. The last planned release year was 1994, so the swans, now an estimated population of nearly 350, are on their own.

The core area in which to find the swans is the great complex of wetlands in the **Detroit Lakes** region near and in **Tamarac NWR.** Most swans were released in Detroit Lakes, but they're dispersing now on their own. Some Minnesota swans are nesting in Canada now.

Tamarac NWR had been averaging two active nests per year but had a record five successful nests in 1994. Trumpeters are often seen on Blackbird Lake, so drive the Blackbird Auto Tour Route if the road is open— it may not be open until May. Take County Road 26 from just south of Callaway to the refuge headquarters, and check with the refuge manager for the best sites from which to view trumpeters this early in the year.

Hennepin Parks, 30 miles west of the Twin Cities, had 100 free-flying swans and 53 cygnets in 1995, with 15 potential breeding pairs. Note the maps indicating the best trumpeter swan viewing locations in the Hennepin Parks Reserve system.

Near **Monticello,** a nuclear power plant 45 miles northwest of Minneapolis keeps the Mississippi River open. A large number of trumpeters, as many as 50, winter here beginning in late November. Report trumpeter sightings to the Nongame Wildlife Program in St. Paul (see the Appendix for address and phone number).

In Wisconsin, state biologists have released 227 swans to the wild since 1987. In 1994, 130 free-flying swans were counted in the state, including 10 nesting pairs that produced 25 young. In 1996, a record 18 pairs nested! The swan recovery program's goal is to establish a breeding and migratory population of at least 20 nesting pairs by the year 2000.

The bulk of Wisconsin's release program has taken place in the **Crex Meadows Wildlife Area** just north of Grantsburg. I've seen swans on the

Hennepin Parks Reserves

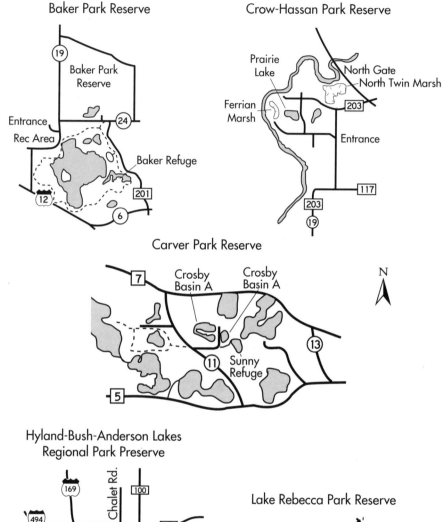

Baker Park Reserve

19
Baker Park
Reserve
24
Entrance
Rec Area
Baker Refuge
12
201
6

Crow-Hassan Park Reserve

Prairie
Lake
North Gate
North Twin Marsh
Ferrian
Marsh
203
Entrance
117
203
19

Carver Park Reserve

7
Crosby
Basin A
Crosby
Basin A
N
13
11
Sunny
Refuge
5

Hyland-Bush-Anderson Lakes
Regional Park Preserve

169
Chalet Rd.
100
494
5
Prairie
Trail
Richardson
Nature Center
18
1
34
E. Bush Lk. Rd.
1
18

Lake Rebecca Park Reserve

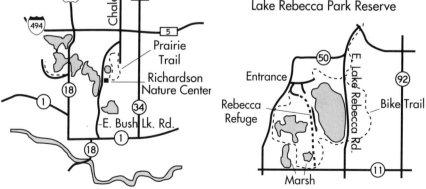

50
E. Lake Rebecca Rd.
92
Entrance
Bike Trail
Rebecca
Refuge
11
Marsh

North Fork Flowage, Phantom Flowage, and the Refuge Extension Flowage, but drive the myriad dike roads to discover where the open water is (see chapter 37 for directions).

Mead Wildlife Area encompasses nearly 30,000 acres of wetlands, forests, and upland fields and maintains a series of dikes that offer excellent vantage points for viewing swans and other waterfowl. Take Hwy. 10 west from Stevens Point to County Road S. Turn right (north), and follow S to the area headquarters. Also try the first small flowage to your right (south) on the Berkhahn Flowage dike trail.

At **Oakridge Lake** in St. Croix County, trumpeter swans from Minnesota's release program have crossed the border and taken up residence and, it is hoped, are nesting as well. Take Hwy. 65 north out of New Richmond for 3 miles and turn right (east) on 220th Avenue. Drive 2 miles to the south side of the lake.

Observations of trumpeter swans in Wisconsin should be reported. Call the Swan Hotline at (800) 815-8151.

In Michigan, the goal is for 200 trumpeters and 15 breeding pairs by the year 2000. Forty birds were released each year in 1991–1993. Attempts have been made since 1986 to cross-foster trumpeter cygnets with mute swan parents, but through 1988 only six trumpeters survived to flight. Free-flying adults number 108 in Michigan as of the 1994 census.

At the **Rifle River Recreation Area,** trumpeters were released by the Michigan DNR and may be seen on any of the lakes. Of 18 birds released here in 1993, 12 returned, 10 of which were males. From Rose City on Michigan 33, take F-28 (Rose City Road) about 5 miles to the entrance to the site.

The **Kellogg Bird Sanctuary** is a good site for wintering trumpeters from November through February, as well as for breeding pairs in March. From Battle Creek, take Michigan 89 west to 40th Street. Turn right (north) and go 1.5 miles to C Avenue, turn left, and the entrance is the first driveway on the right.

Seney NWR recently counted 34 individual trumpeter swans and five breeding pairs, but the waters at Seney are usually locked up in March—better to wait until May to view the swans. Take the self-guided auto tour, which opens on May 15. To reach Seney from the Mackinac Bridge, take U.S. 2 for 65 miles to Michigan 77. Turn right (north) on 77 and travel 13 miles to the refuge entrance.

At the **Allegan State Game Area,** trumpeter and mute swans are regularly found in the impoundment where Michigan 40/89 crosses the Kalamazoo River. To reach the headquarters, take 40/89 northwest from Allegan and turn left (west) on Monroe Road. Travel 6.5 miles to the game area office (Monroe becomes 118th Avenue after 5 miles).

As a final note, although many of the trumpeters have returned to their nesting sites in March, not all have. Trumpeters will come back and stand on the ice waiting for the lakes to open up, but they are difficult to see under these circumstances. The hardy wildlife viewer is out looking for the trumpeters in March, but better viewing opportunities will exist later in spring as more roads become passable and the lakes open. So don't forget to try April and May, too.

16

Booming Prairie Chickens

We were up at 3:30 A.M., in the van by 4:00, and out into the blind by 4:30, the dark night still close around us. Soon the eastern sky began to lighten, and about a half hour before sunrise the males suddenly flew onto the booming ground. Immediately, each began a series of calls that ranged from cackles to deep-throated "booming," and what had been a silent and barren grassland was transformed into the stage for the ritualized courtship displays of the greater prairie chicken. Sixteen males took up their territories, each strutting his stuff, engaging alternately in behaviors that included inflating a brilliant orange sac along his neck, bowing forward and flaring stunning orange eyebrows that any punk rocker would be proud of, spreading his primary feathers in a sort of cloak around him, raising a set of retractable long black feathers over his head in a tight V, and "dancing"— rapidly stamping the ground. Frequently, two males would square off and jump into the air in a clash of feathers, each protecting his invisible territorial boundaries. All this was done in hopes of enticing a female who would consent to mating into their territories.

For their part, the females entered a half hour later, 11 of them eventually, each nonchalantly picking her way through the manic displaying males, who, with the arrival of the females, stepped up their acts to a fever pitch. The males fought and called and flashed their colors, and for nearly two hours the females ignored the advances as if they were alone on a desert. Suddenly a male mounted a female, and within seconds the act was over, the female at length shaking her feathers and then walking away from the group. In several days she would lay a clutch of 10 to 14 eggs and incubate them for 24 days, all in the hope that the prairie chicken cycle might continue another year.

The other 10 females managed to continue to ignore the males and soon flew off. Instantly the booming ground was quiet, the males realizing their audience had departed and the play needn't go on. It was as if the air had been taken out of a balloon.

The booming of the males has been described as "deep as a bassoon, eerie as the oboe." The three-syllable call sounds to me like the birds are asking "Who are you?" but others characterize it as "Old Muldoon" or *oo-loo-woo.* The deep notes sound like a baritone mourning dove or the sound made by blowing across the mouth of a bottle, and in the stillness of a prairie morning, they can be heard over a mile away.

A male prairie chicken inflates the sacs along his neck and dances feverishly in his courtship display. Photo by Bruce Bacon.

Males begin their courtship displays at the end of February and proceed until May. The females don't usually deign to show up until early April, in the apparent knowledge that even though the males are ready, the weather for nesting isn't. The best times for watching the full act are in April, but males may be viewed every morning in March.

As with nearly all prairie species, today's prairie chicken numbers represent a flickering of what once was. The far horizons, wide skies, and grassland seas have been replaced by seas of corn and other crops, or by urban sprawl, and in the midst of so much development, prairie chicken populations hang on rather precariously.

Hot Spots

In Wisconsin, the prairie chicken is designated as threatened by the state. The 1994 fall count estimated the total state population at around 2,000. The good news in Wisconsin is that nearly half of these prairie chickens live on the **Buena Vista Marsh** in Portage County, a nearly 12,000-acre patchwork of grasslands managed by the Wisconsin DNR. The efforts of nearly 25 years of pioneering research by Drs. Frederick and Frances Hamerstrom brought the plight of Wisconsin's prairie chickens into the public mind and culminated in the purchase of these lands. The Buena Vista is the largest grassland tract remaining east of the Mississippi, and thus represents a biological treasure.

The booming is easily observed (if getting up at 3:00 A.M. is easy) by reserving a blind on the marsh or by signing up for programs given at

Wildlife Management Areas in Northwestern Minnesota

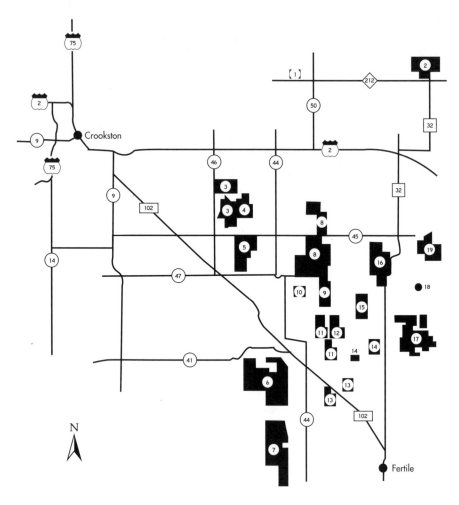

1. Stipa (Red Lake Co.)
2. Marcoux WMA (Red Lake Co.]
3. Pankratz SNA (TNC)
4. Kertsonville WMA
5. Tympanuchus WMA
6. Chicog WMA
7. Liberty WMA
8. Pembina WMA*
9. Burnham Creek WMA
10. Foxboro Creek WMA
11. Burnham WMA
12. Trail WMA
13. Onstad WMA
14. Godfrey WMA
15. Shypoke WMA
16. Dugdale WMA
17. Maple Meadows WMA
18. Oak Ridge WMA
19. Tilden WMA

*North end is Crookston Prairie Addition (SNA)/(TNC)
SNA = Science and National Area
WMA = Wildlife Management Area

the **Central Wisconsin Environmental Station,** (715) 824-2428, near Amherst Junction. These programs, cosponsored by the Natural Resources Foundation of Wisconsin, are called "Boom with a View," and begin on Friday night with a lecture and slide show on the natural history of the chickens, then overnight accommodations in the Environmental Station's dorms, a morning van ride to a blind, and finally a telemetry discussion later that morning. Contact either organization for details, preferably by January, because the programs often fill up. Contact the University of Wisconsin Stevens Point College of Natural Resources to rent a blind on your own at (715) 346-4109.

The Buena Vista Marsh is located along Hwys. F and W about 10 miles east of Wisconsin Rapids. Travel slowly any of the town roads in this area to view the grasslands, but remember that much of the area is privately farmed, so scouting is a piecemeal affair. Look too for sandhill cranes, northern harriers, bobolinks, western and eastern meadowlarks, upland sandpipers, and acres of grassland flowers in season.

Another area in Wisconsin in which to see prairie chickens is the **Mead Wildlife Area,** a 25,000-acre tract of lowland marshes, reservoirs, and upland grasslands. Prairie chicken numbers have been declining in the early 1990s here, and the Wisconsin DNR no longer (as of 1995) sets up blinds for public viewing of the booming grounds. Total numbers are down to around 200, and display sites are remote. Still, there is hope of a population upswing. Contact wildlife area office for current information: (715) 457-6771. From Hwy. 51, take County Road C west to County Road S and turn south (left). Take S for 2.5 miles to the area headquarters.

In Minnesota, prairie chicken populations are much higher than in Wisconsin, but the chickens are still on a state "special concern" list. Their numbers have been stable if not slightly increasing in the mid-1990s, particularly because of lands set aside in the federal Conservation Reserve Program (CRP). These lands are often actively planted to grasses that greatly benefit grassland bird species.

Most of Minnesota's prairie chickens live in the west-central and northwestern regions, from Wilkin County north to Marshall County. The **Rothsay Wildlife Management Area** is considered the prairie chicken capital of Minnesota (Rothsay even has a giant fiberglass prairie chicken wayside stop). Located along the shoreline of glacial Lake Agassiz, it is a favorite spot for booming prairie chickens as well as migrant prairie falcons, short-eared owls, and Smith's longspurs.

The Minnesota Nature Conservancy owns and manages six prairies in the management area, all of which may support booming grounds: **Western North, Western South, Anna Gronseth, Town Hall,**

Kettledrummer, and **Foxhome.** Contact The Nature Conservancy for information on how to access the areas and regulations.

Other areas include the grasslands around **Felton** in Clay County, and **southeast of Crookston** in Polk County, particularly the Nature Conservancy's 2,044-acre **Pembina Trail tract** and its **Pankratz Memorial Prairie tract,** as well as the DNR's **Tympanuchus Wildlife Management Area.**

Pankratz is reached by taking U.S. 2 east from Crookston to County Road 46. Turn right (south) and you will see the Nature Conservancy sign on your left in 1.75 miles designating the site.

To find Tympanuchus, continue south on County Road 46 from Pankratz Memorial Prairie, and turn left (east) onto County Road 45. Go 1 mile to reach the northwestern edge of the unit—a small WMA sign will identify the site.

To reach the Pembina tract, follow County Road 45, a dirt road, east about 7 miles until you see The Nature Conservancy (TNC) sign on the south side of the road. Another TNC sign, on the north side of the road and across the railroad tracks, can be found farther east on 45. Some 200 native plants, including 7 rare species, may also be seen here.

Minnesota offers a large number of free blinds for watching the show, but they must be reserved in advance. Call the following numbers for information on reservations and directions:

Cass County Land Department: (218) 947-3338
Park Rapids DNR Office: (218) 732-8452
Crookston DNR Office: (218) 281-8452
Detroit Lakes DNR Office: (218) 847-1578
Fergus Falls DNR Office: (218) 739-7575

In Michigan, no prairie chickens remain, though the **Prairie Chicken Management Area,** a 1,280-acre tract north from Clare, was one of the few places in Michigan where prairie chickens recently gathered to display. Their last dance took place in the mid-1980s. Reintroduction in Michigan is not contemplated in the future—there just isn't suitable habitat left. For permanent populations to thrive, an area at least the size of one-half of a township, or 18 square miles, 25 percent of which is in permanent grasslands, is theorized to be the minimum habitat requirement. Better yet to have an entire township, or 36 square miles, with 25 percent in grassland. And of that 25 percent grassland, the core areas need to be at least a square mile in size, with a minimum size of 80 acres for outlying areas, and preferably 160 acres. These large habitat requirements demonstrate the enormous management commitments that must be made if we wish to maintain one of the most remarkable birds in the Upper Midwest.

17

March Shorttakes

Steelhead Runs

Steelhead go by two names—rainbow trout and steelhead—and they offer top-notch fishing during their spring spawning runs. They also can be seen at some DNR fish hatchery areas along the Great Lakes when they "run" the tributary streams. You can see steelhead through a glass viewing window at the **Root River Egg-Taking Facility** in Racine (see chapter 56 for directions). Or try observing them in the water at **Big Rock County Park** on the Sioux River near Washburn in Bayfield County.

Eagle Territorial Battles

When the ice begins to go off many lakes and rivers in March is the best time to see eagles fighting aerial duals for territorial claims. **Indianhead Flowage,** a lake formed by the hydroelectric dam at St. Croix Falls in Wisconsin, often has 15 to 30 eagles concentrated on the ice or in the trees. The eagles are best viewed from the headquarters of the **St. Croix National Scenic Riverway** at the north end of town.

Tundra Swans

Large flocks of tundra swans may be seen in Michigan at **St. Clair Flats,** **Shiawassee NWR,** and the **Erie State Game Area.**

In Wisconsin, tundras stop over at **Crex Meadows, Necedah NWR, Lake Winnebago,** and the **Trempealeau NWR.**

18

A Closer Look: Passenger Pigeons, the Lost Phenomenon

(I offer this chapter as testament to what can still happen if we lose our vigilance. No one could then have imagined that the extinction of the most prodigious bird on earth could occur. What else might yet occur in these times that is thought unimaginable?)

Each spring the passenger pigeon, the most prodigious bird species the world has ever known, would fly northward, 4 billion strong, to nest in the great stands of oak and beech of the central and southern counties of Michigan, Wisconsin, and Minnesota. Their sky-darkening numbers seemed endless and inspired utter awe in those privileged to witness their flight. Aldo Leopold called them "a biological storm. … a feathered tempest [that] roared up, down, and across the continent, sucking up the laden fruits of forest and prairie, burning them in a traveling blast of life." One nesting area in Petoskey, Michigan, in 1878 was estimated to be 40 miles in length and 3 to 10 miles in width, covering some 100,000 acres of land. But that aggregation was dwarfed by the 1871 nesting in Wisconsin that covered a minimum length of 75 miles with a width of 10 to 15 miles and was conservatively thought to have blanketed an area of 850 square miles.

The passenger pigeon's colonial nesting habit, its laying of only one egg a year, and its phenomenal appetite for grains and nuts doomed the bird. Two billion birds required some 17 million bushels of mast a day, a number the lightly inhabited country could sustain in pre-Colonial days but not once the plow and ax of the proliferating European settler went to work. The main nesting area in 1871 was in the scrub-oak region of central Wisconsin, and newspaper accounts from towns like Kilbourn, Berlin, Watertown, and Fond du Lac vividly describe the extent of the nesting and the hunting slaughter that exploited it. A.W. Schorger, who wrote the book *The Passenger Pigeon: Its Natural History and Extinction*, conservatively estimated that this one nesting contained 136 million pigeons, of which he calculated at least 1,200,000 were shipped out to markets on the metropolitan East Coast that spring, a number not remotely close to the total number killed.

Schorger, in trying to describe the hunt, wrote in *Silent Wings* that he could do no better than quote from an 1871 article written by General Henry Harnden, an experienced hunter, who had gone to hunt the pigeons

from Kilbourn City on the Wisconsin River. I have drawn excerpts from
Harnden's extraordinary article as he hunts the roost.

The indescribable cooing roar produced by uncounted millions of
pigeons, as arousing from their slumbers they saluted each other
and made up their foraging parties for the day, arose from each
side, creating an almost bewildering effect on the sense, as it was
echoed and re-echoed back by the mighty rocks and ledges of the
Wisconsin bank.... . Our guide now told us to get into position
quick as possible as the large flocks would follow in rapid succession. ...

And now arose a roar, compared with which all previous noises
ever heard are but lullabies, and which caused more than one of the
expectant and excited party to drop their guns, and seek shelter
behind and beneath the nearest trees. The sound was condensed
terror. Imagine a thousand threshing machines running under full
headway, accompanied by as many steamboats groaning off steam,
with an equal quota of R.R. trains passing through covered bridges—
imagine these massed into a single flock, and you possibly have a
faint conception of the terrific roar following the monstrous black
cloud of pigeons as they passed in rapid flight in the gray light of
morning, a few feet from our faces.... . The unearthly roar continued, and as flock after flock, in almost endless line, succeeded each
other, nearly on a level with the muzzle of our guns, the contents of
a score of double barrels was poured into the dense mist.... . The
slaughter was terrible beyond any description. Our guns became so
hot by rapid discharges, we were afraid to load them. Then, while
waiting for them to cool, lying on the damp leaves, we used, those
of us who had [them], pistols, while others threw clubs.... .

Leaving the rest of the party, we drove off a few miles further
into a high wooded ridge where nests were located. Every tree contained one to four hundred nests. The young pigeons (squabs) were
hardly able to fly, and could be caught easily, when once ousted
from the nest. Here of course were hundreds of thousands of single
birds (probably the females) which could be shot one or two at a
time, as fast as the hunter could load and fire. We saw more than a
hundred trees that had fallen, by reason of the numbers of nests built
upon [their] branches. Many of the young pigeons were dead in their
nests; their mothers probably have been killed, and their young
starved.... .

It is estimated that not less than 100,000 hunters from all portions of the Union have visited the roost during the season.... .

The chief foods of the passenger pigeon were acorns and beechnuts, though they would eagerly consume all the newly sown grain on a farmer's field or pull up the sprouted grains once they were an inch high. The farmers were not heard to object over the loss of the pigeon.

Killing one adult meant the desertion of the nest. The male and female took turns incubating the egg and feeding the squab, so it was impossible for the egg to remain fertile, or for the young to be adequately fed and kept warm if the parent birds were killed. The squabs were taken right from the nest if still alive and killed too.

The last known wild passenger pigeon was killed by an Ohio boy with a BB gun in 1899, and the last pigeon in captivity died in 1913. A monument to the passenger pigeon was dedicated by the Wisconsin Society for Ornithology in 1947 in Wyalusing State Park, Wisconsin, at the confluence of the Mississippi and Wisconsin Rivers.

The time is very near when there will be no human being left on Earth who has seen and heard the biological storm once called the passenger pigeon.

April

Notes

19

Sandhill Crane Count

It's happened every spring since 1981. At 5:00 A.M. on a mid-April morning, nearly 3,000 people watch the sun rise over a marsh somewhere in Wisconsin and listen and scan for sandhill cranes. If the god of April feels kind, the dawn sky stains to a deep salmon and then to gold as the sun gradually rises over the wetlands, setting the marsh mists to a shower of color. And somewhere from within those mists rises a trumpeting call that shakes the marsh serenity right down to its muck, the male uttering a single note followed immediately by two notes from the female, the notes so close together that they are heard in unison. That's what everyone has come to hear and to mark, for this is the annual sandhill crane count day, a time when Wisconsin formalizes its gratitude for the return of a species once thought to be on the edge of extirpation from the state.

In 1936 only 25 sandhill crane pairs were estimated to survive in Wisconsin, and as the education coordinator of the crane count has written, "sandhill crane sightings were almost as rare as Santa sightings in the first half of this century." During this period Aldo Leopold wrote of the crane's demise in hopes of stirring the conservation passions of Wisconsin citizens: "Amid the endless mediocrity of the commonplace, a crane marsh holds a paleontological patent on nobility, won in the march of aeons, and revocable only by a shotgun."

The cranes hung on, and as the land use and abuse practices of ditch digging and marsh draining changed and conservation laws were implemented, the sandhills gradually came back, until in 1993 the census totaled 11,000 sandhills. Now the count is a combined wonder: first, that so many cranes now populate the state; and second, that so many people care enough about them to get up well before dawn on an April morning to count them.

The crane count is one of the largest single-species surveys in the world, but we in the United States are not the only people to revere cranes. Crane counts take place in other countries, too. Japanese children count red-crowned, white-naped, and hooded cranes, and Eurasian cranes are counted in France, Germany, Russia, Spain, and Sweden.

Wisconsin's crane count began as a high school study project in 1975 in Columbia County. At that time the Wisconsin Wetlands Association sponsored the event, and finally in 1981 the International Crane Foundation in Baraboo began organizing the counts. Now nearly every county in the state

In mid-April, nearly 3,000 people go out at dawn to count sandhill cranes in Wisconsin. Photo by the International Crane Foundation.

has a coordinator who pulls together volunteers and trains them to count at every site in that county likely to harbor cranes. Over the years, some 1,500 sites have been surveyed in 70 counties.

The count takes place in mid-April, because it falls after migration has taken place and before nesting occurs. In northern Wisconsin that means we've counted cranes in a foot of snow while skiing around marshes. We've been battered with high winds, drowned in pea-soup fog, and every so often blessed with gorgeous sunrises and calm, sunny mornings. The weather is part of the experience; the cranes are out there surviving, too. Tough weather only heightens a counter's appreciation for the hardiness of cranes.

Sandhills migrate early and rapidly in the spring, usually only spending a week at any stopover site to rest and feed. The territorial and nesting imperative is upon them, and the instinctual urge to breed propels them forward to their nesting areas. Southern counties may see cranes by as early as mid-February. By early April in the northern counties, even if the snow remains heavy on the marshes, they are there, courting and dancing in one of the most exquisite courtship rituals of any bird on earth. The dancers bow, jump, and "stick-toss." When the dancing occurs in a flock, first one bird begins slowly, then increases the tempo until the excitement of the dance spreads to the others, who join in dancing at the same time. Few more spectacular and elegant animal behaviors are ever observed by wildlife watchers.

To join in the Wisconsin count, call or write the International Crane Foundation near Baraboo, (608) 356-9462, for details of when the count is to take place and who the county coordinator is in your area.

Hot Spots

In Wisconsin, the **White River Marsh Wildlife Area** in Green Lake County has good accessibility and often has 200 cranes in a 5-mile stretch of marsh in spring. From Princeton, take County Road D north to White River Road. Turn right (east)—White River Road bisects the marsh.

The **Grand River Wildlife Area** in Green Lake and Marquette Counties and **Germania Wildlife Area** in Marquette County usually support large springtime flocks of sandhills. For all three areas, call (715) 524-2934 for current information on where the cranes may be located. To get to Grand River Marsh, take Hwy. 22 north from Pardeeville to County Road B. Turn right (east) and follow B along the south end of the marsh. Germania Marsh is located farther north, off Hwy. 22. Take Eagle Road to the right (east) off 22 into Germania.

The 14,500 acres of the **Navarino Wildlife Area** have wildlife blinds from which to view cranes (or sharp-tailed grouse, for that matter). Access to the wildlife area is 9 miles south of Shawano on County Road K, or 30 miles northwest of Green Bay on Hwy. 156.

Visit the **International Crane Foundation,** the world center for the study and preservation of cranes both to see a variety of crane species in captivity and to take advantage of educational programs. The foundation is open from May through October and offers guided tours every day from Memorial Day to Labor Day. Tours are only offered on weekends in May, September, and October. From just south of Wisconsin Dells on I-90/94, take Exit 92 (Hwy. 12) south. Turn left (east) on Shady Lane Road to reach the foundation facility.

20

Sharp-Tailed Grouse
Courtship Dance

One mid-April morning I watched seven male sharp-tailed grouse strut their stuff at Crex Meadows Wildlife Area in northwestern Wisconsin, and I was moved from astonishment to head-shaking laughter. The males put on a show that I would think only the most hardened female grouse could resist. Like the prairie chicken, male sharp-tailed grouse inflate a sac on the side of the neck (violet-colored for the sharpies, yellow-gold for the chickens). They also lift their tails, flare their yellow "eyebrows," push their heads forward, and often engage in flutter-jumping and the clashing of wings with other territorial males. Simultaneously they make a series of unusual calls, from deep-throated coos to a *chilka-chilka* to gull-like cries.

The sharp-tailed grouse is one of four grouse species in the Upper Midwest, the prairie chicken is another, along with ruffed grouse and spruce grouse. For my money, their courting dance has no equal (though the prairie chicken's comes awfully close). Some avid observers go so far as to describe watching the dance as a religious experience. Part of the magic is being in a blind well before sunrise and watching the morning gradually come to life. But the rest of the magic resides in the behaviors, colors, and calls of the sharpie, as the grouse is nicknamed.

The peak of the display occurs when the male "dances." He hammers his feet on the ground as fast as he can, like the fatigue drills athletes go through, stretches his wings out and down, inflates his purple sac, cocks his tail, and proceeds to spin around in a circle while vibrating his tail feathers. The feathers make a sound like an industrial sewing machine to me; others describe it as a rattling or clicking sound. Usually many males perform the dancing display in synchrony, and I have often watched five or more spinning slowly about in their spectacular attempt to lure a disinterested female from her hiding spot.

They never did get a female to wander in, but it was April 15, and maybe the females knew another week of waiting for warmer weather might help their chances of successful nesting. Because my feet were frozen after a few hours in the blind, I could understand their practical reluctance. (A tip for the uninitiated: Prairies are cold places in April, and blinds are cramped—wear winter clothes.)

The males displayed for over two hours, often getting so close to the blind that I couldn't see what they were doing out of my little portholes. In fact, I fully expected several to come right on in under the canvas (the temporary canvas blinds are often staked several inches off the ground), but none chose to join me on my wooden bench. In the meantime, sandhill cranes bugled, northern harriers soared, geese and various ducks flew overhead, and an eagle or two passed by. Certainly the sharpies are the lead actors, but the supporting cast is darn good too.

Sharp-tailed grouse belong to the brush prairie, vast grasslands dotted with clumps of hazel and aspen, and occasional tall, solitary trees. Traditionally, these areas in the North Woods are called pine barrens, and in the South they are known as oak savannas. They are a landscape between the prairie and the forest, and they once brimmed with wildlife, and in particular with sharp-tailed grouse. But with the growth of agriculture and the success of Smokey Bear in reducing wildfires, these lands either became agricultural fields or grew up into young forests. Now, in Wisconsin, only 50,000 acres of this habitat remains, most in isolated pockets too small to maintain healthy sharptail populations, which studies show require a minimum of 10,000 acres of barrens in which to nest and spend the winter.

As a consequence, sharptails are in substantial decline throughout the Upper Midwest. Wisconsin may have no more than 1,000 birds, and Michigan has very few left in the Lower Peninsula and only remnant populations in the Upper Peninsula. Only Minnesota can boast of a good population, but those numbers are clearly declining as well. Habitat can only be maintained through intensive controlled burning, mowing, grazing, or periodic farming, and neither monies nor land are usually available in sufficient quantities to get the job done right. Large clear-cuts provide temporary grounds for the sharptails to populate, but regrowth into forest pushes the birds out in a few years.

As sharptail numbers continue to decline, its spectacular courtship dance becomes all the more valued and memorable. The bird is not spooked easily around the blind and will put on a territorial clash and a hormonal bash that will keep you on the edge of your seat. One writer has described the birds dancing in their circles as looking like "little wind-up toys sold by street vendors." Although heavy populations still thrive in the Dakotas and the prairie provinces of Canada, the Upper Midwest grasslands may have difficulty supporting these birds for much longer.

Hot Spots

In Wisconsin, blinds are available free by reservation, except where noted here, from mid-April to mid-May in these five locations:

Namekagon Barrens in Burnett County: (715) 635-4091
Pershing Wildlife Area in Taylor County: (715) 532-3911
Sandhill Wildlife Area in Babcock: (715) 884-2437; (A $10 fee is charged, and hip boots are required.)
Crex Meadows Wildlife Area in Burnett County: (715) 463-2896
Wood County Wildlife Area: (715) 884-2437

Other Wisconsin sites with known sharptail populations include **Riley Lake Wildlife Area** in Price County. The area is found in the **Chequamegon National Forest** and is managed in clearings for sharp-tailed grouse. Take Hwy. 70 east from Fifield for 12 miles to Forest Road 137 and turn south (right). Forest Road 137 borders the western edge of the wildlife area. Take Forest Road 136 to the left to cover the south end, and turn left onto Forest Road 505 to head north and cover the east side.

The **Moquah Barrens** in Bayfield County, located within the Chequamegon National Forest, covers 8,696 acres of managed brush prairie–savanna. It was originally set aside by the U.S. Forest Service as sharp-tailed grouse habitat, and although they are not common, sharp-ies may be seen with effort. The Barrens are located off Hwy. 2. Go north 5.5 miles from Ino on Forest Road 236 to the intersection with Forest Road 241. The brush prairie begins here, and the wildlife area extends for 6 miles to the west.

The **Thunder Lake Wildlife Area** in Oneida County is prime sharp-tail habitat. Take Hwys. 32 and 45 north 1.1 miles out of Three Lakes and turn west (left) on a road with a sign pointing to the Thunder Lake Wildlife Area.

The **Dunbar Wildlife Area** in Marinette County is a 4,500-acre tract managed by the Wisconsin DNR through controlled burns. Several hundred acres are kept in open grassland. The area is located just north of Hwy. 8, midway between Dunbar and Goodman. The sign for the entrance is 4 miles east of Goodman on Hwy. 8.

The **Ackley Wildlife Area** in Langlade County is burned periodically to maintain grasses and sedges, but sharptails are barely holding their own. Take Hwy. 64 west out of Antigo for 12 miles to several parking areas along Hwy. 64.

For more information about sharptails in Wisconsin, write the Wisconsin Sharp-Tailed Grouse Society: P.O. Box 1115, Cumberland, WI 54829.

In Minnesota, the sharptail population is clearly declining, almost certainly due to the decline in brush prairie habitat. Still, these birds are huntable in Minnesota and are not on any state list of threatened birds. Free blinds are available, by reservation only, at a host of sites. Call or write the following offices for their current information:

Rice Lake NWR: (218) 768-2402
Eveleth DNR Office: (218) 749-7748
Cloquet DNR Office: (218) 879-0883
Aiken DNR Office: (218) 927-6915 (An expert birder friend told me that Aiken was the single best site in Minnesota for sharptails.)
Hinckley DNR Office: (612) 384-6148

Contact the Minnesota Sharp-Tailed Grouse Society, P.O. Box 3338, Duluth, MN 55803, for more information on Minnesota sharpies.

In Michigan, the **Fletcher Sharp-Tailed Area** is the last known sharp-tailed grouse area in the Lower Peninsula, and the birds are rarely seen. Numerous unmarked trails run throughout the area, and visitors are free to walk where they like. From Grayling, take I-75 south to the 4 Mile Road exit (Exit 251). Go west on 4 Mile Road for 3 miles and turn south on Military Road. Travel 4 miles and turn right (west) onto Fletcher Road. Drive 7 miles on Fletcher Road and turn left (south) onto a sand track called the Garfield Truck Trail, which takes you onto the Fletcher Sharp-Tailed Area. Go 1.7 miles to another sand road and turn right (west) and go 0.5 mile and park. The dancing round is a few hundred yards to the north. Call the Michigan DNR at (616) 775-9727 for more information.

The **Baldy Lake Sharp-Tailed Area** is a large expanse of open country in the Upper Peninsula and includes upland sandpipers and sandhill cranes. Take Michigan 28 south for 3 miles out of Munising to Forest Road 13. Go 7 miles to Forest Service Road 2268. Head west for just over 3 miles and take Forest Service Road 2269 south. Go for 2 miles to trails leading east to the area.

21

First Flowers of Spring

Spring can never come too soon for most Upper Midwesterners (except for die-hard skiers, who are a species unto themselves). Absence does truly make the heart grow fonder. The first spring flower blossoms dazzle senses too long suppressed by winter's white and cold. We await these floral pioneers like a baseball team gathered to pound the back of the winning runner.

The first flowers seldom come in large sizes or fancy shapes and colors. The struggle to survive late spring frosts asks too much to allow them to invest much energy in spectacular beauty. Their evolutionary strategy has been that it is better to stay short to avoid the drying winds and to grow stems covered in hairs to wear as a warming cape. Still, in the context of human hearts and minds that haven't experienced a wildflower in five or more months, their demure beauty is so appreciated that one wonders if anything more dressed up would be too much.

Where and when to go to find the first spring flowers requires some background. Wildflowers can be grouped arbitrarily into three seasonal categories: spring flowers, which bloom from about April 15 to June 15, with a mid-May peak; summer flowers, which bloom from about June 16 to August 15, with a mid-July peak; and autumn flowers, which blossom from about August 16 to early October, with a peak around September 10. These dates range widely, because Michigan, Wisconsin, and Minnesota each stretch north and south over 400 miles, creating a minimum four-week, and sometimes six-week, difference between the first blooms in the south and the first blooms in the north. The growing season is about 160 days in the southern counties, but usually less than 100 up north. More precisely, the growing season where I live in the northern Wisconsin town of Manitowish is often only 70 days—the last frost of spring usually occurs around June 10, and the first frost of autumn usually comes around August 20.

Thus, flowering dates must be adjusted for latitude as well as for other factors like soil type, the direction a site faces, and proximity to the Great Lakes. Living next to Lake Superior means spring will be cooler because the water takes so long to warm up, but autumn will be more moderate because it takes time for the water to lose its summer heat. Growing seasons along the big lakes are often more extended than inland—Houghton, Michigan, on Lake Superior, has a 140-day growing season even though it's about as far north as one can get in the Upper Midwest.

The first wildflower of spring anywhere in the Upper Midwest is skunk cabbage, which has the remarkable ability to generate its own heat through respiration in the wetlands it inhabits. To gain the honor of being the first spring flower, skunk cabbage melts a hole for itself through the snow, which often allows it to bloom with snow all around it. But skunk cabbage is neither pretty to look at nor to smell (as the name aptly conveys). I doubt too many folks would drive any distance to see one.

The first prairie flower of the year is the beautiful pasqueflower *(Anemone patens)*, which may bloom anytime from early April to early May, and which is worth driving to see. *Pasque* is the French word for Easter, given in accordance with the flower's expected blooming date and possibly due to its floral symbolism of resurrection after the long winter.

Every year amid the last snows of winter and the first warm days of spring, pasqueflowers, covered with long silky hairs, push up through the open prairie landscape. Look for pasqueflowers on dry thin-soiled prairies, or on south- or west-facing glacial ridges. The five to seven silky flower petals (sepals in this case, but only botanists care to make the distinction) may be pale purple, blue, or white, with a core of golden stamens surrounding a grayish center that will become plumed fruits in summer. Often the petals sweep upwards in a cup that resembles a tulip or crocus.

Early-blooming wildflowers like pasqueflower hug the ground in apparent deference to the power of April weather, which may as soon offer snow as provide sun. Prairie flowers in the early spring are seldom taller than 5 inches, while flowers on the same site that bloom in September average 18 inches in height. If you've found pasqueflowers, look also for pussytoes *(Antennaria neglecta),* prairie buttercup *(Ranunculus fascicularis),* rock cress *(Arabis lyrata),* and prairie-smoke *(Geum triflorum),* all of which bloom after the pasqueflower. But pasqueflower almost always wins the award for the first flower of spring (excluding our friend the skunk cabbage) in the Upper Midwest.

Hot Spots

In Wisconsin, two sites owned and managed by the Wisconsin Nature Conservancy have good showings of pasqueflowers: **Schluckebier Sand Prairie** in Sauk County, a 23-acre remnant of dry prairie containing more than 158 prairie plants; and **Black Earth Rettenmund Prairie** in Dane County, a 17-acre, dry to moist prairie remnant. Contact The Nature Conservancy in Madison for directions as well as information on how each site is currently being managed: (608) 251-8140. The Nature Conservancy limits visitation to many of its sites to prevent damage caused by trampling, so check to see if exploration is permitted on these sites during the times you wish to visit.

The **Greene Prairie** and the **Curtis Prairie** at the University of Wisconsin Arboretum in Madison are both restored prairies with public access. Contact the McKay Visitor Center at (608) 263-7888 for classes and current hours, or write the UW Arboretum, 1207 Seminole Highway, Madison, WI 53711. The arboretum is located in the center of Madison. Take Fish Hatchery Road north off of Hwy. 12/14/18/151. Fish Hatchery Road turns into Wingra Road. Take Arboretum Drive to the left into the arboretum and follow it to the McKay Center. You must get a key to enter Greene Prairie.

Several preserves managed by the Wisconsin DNR's Bureau of Endangered Resources (BER) also have excellent pasqueflower blooms. As with the Nature Conservancy sites, areas managed by the BER are usually quite sensitive, so please contact them at (608) 264-6031 for current visitor regulations prior to making a visit. **Rocky Run Oak Opening SNA**, a 285-acre site made up of an original oak opening and old fields, has more than 100 prairie-related species. From the intersection of State Hwys. 16 and 22 just south of Wyocena, proceed south on Hwy. 22 nearly 2 miles to the Rocky Run Fishery Area parking lot. Walk west and south on a dirt road for 0.7 mile to the area. **Muralt Bluff Prairie SNA**, a 40-acre dry ridge-top bluff in Green County, has outstanding displays of pasqueflowers and other dry prairie species, as does the **La Crosse River Trail Prairie SNA**, a 22-acre dry-mesic prairie established on the abandoned Chicago and Northwestern Railroad right-of-way. Muralt Prairie is reached by traveling 2 miles southwest from Albany on Hwy. 59, then northwest on Hwy. 39 for 1.8 miles to a parking lot at the north end of the area. The far east end of the La Crosse Prairie is most easily found by taking County Road U east from Rockland Village to Cypress Avenue. Turn east onto Cypress and follow it until it crosses the abandoned railroad track, then hike the track west.

Walking Iron County Park, a 5-acre prairie remnant just outside Mazomanie, offers scores of pasqueflowers.

Though pasques are the very first flowers of spring, mid-April has a lot more to offer than just these wonderful prairie flowers. Spectacular April wildflower sites can be found in far southeastern Michigan, particularly in Berrien and Cass Counties. Four sites stand out above the rest for the earliest and most bountiful wildflowers of the spring: **Dowagiac Woods, Warren Woods Natural Area, Trillium Ravine Plant Preserve**, and **Love Creek County Park and Nature Center**.

Dowagiac Woods may be the largest moist virgin-soil woodland left in Michigan. The 220-acre tract has over 400 identified plants and 50 species of spring wildflowers. Nine species of plants and animals found here are endangered. Owned by the Michigan Nature Association, the area's top attraction is the abundance of blue-eyed Mary, which begins blooming in early April and lasts for six weeks. The Michigan Nature

Pasqueflowers herald the coming of spring on the prairies. Photo by WDNR.

Association says it has found only one other woods in all of Michigan with such a quantity of wildflowers—the Timberland Swamp Nature Sanctuary (see chapter 25). If you tire of the flowers at any point, look up—nearly 50 species of trees are found in Dowagiac Woods.

From Dowagiac go west on Michigan 62 for 4 miles to Sink Road. Turn south (left) and go 1 mile to Frost Road. Turn east (left) and go 1 mile to a parking lot on your left, or stop about 0.25 mile short of the parking lot at a little trail in the far southwestern corner of the woods, which often has flowers blooming several weeks ahead of other flowers in the woods.

Love Creek County Park demonstrates that even small county parks can be treasures. Love Creek has 100 acres of diverse habitats, including a beech-maple climax forest, open meadows, a marsh, and lowland forests. Five miles of trails and many naturalist activities provide ample opportunities for flower lovers to get spring back in their blood, and winter out. Look for bloodroot, hepatica, and trout lily at their peak in mid-April. Just east of Berrien Springs on Hwy. 31, take Pokagon Road southeast for 2 miles to Huckleberry Road. Turn north (left) and go 1 mile to the park entrance.

Trillium Ravine Plant Reserve is only a 14-acre site, but it has two rare "toad" trilliums whose ranges barely extend into southern Michigan—prairie trillium *(Trillium recurvatum)* and toadshade *(Trillium sessile)*. Both usually bloom by April 9, though even in southern Michigan spring weather can look similar to winter weather. The flowers sit directly on the mottled leaves without a stalk and have petals of maroon red. Seven trillium species may be found in Michigan, and all may be seen on sites owned by the Michigan Nature Association. No trails run through Trillium Ravine, and one feels almost guilty walking anywhere because of the number of flowers that can be crushed. Please exercise extreme caution in exploring this site.

Take Hwy. 31 south from Berrien Springs to the Walton Road east exit. Turn left (east) and then take the first right onto East Geyer. Turn right onto East Riverside and follow it until you see the preserve sign on your right.

Warren Woods Natural Area is a 200-acre tract of climax beech-maple forest, southern Michigan's last such area, and so outstanding that it has been designated a Natural National Landmark. Most of the area has never been disturbed, though many of the huge beech trees have been engraved by vandals. Two trails enter the woods, one from the north side on Warren Woods Road, and another from a picnic area and parking lot on the south. Entry is easiest from the south, and the size of the beech trees here will astonish you. This site is well known for warblers in May, so consider several visits. From I-94, take Hwy. 12 (Pulaski Highway) east for 4 miles into Three Oaks. Turn north (left) on Three Oaks Road (also called Elm) and go to Elm Valley Road. Turn left (west) and go 0.5 mile to the parking lot on your right.

22

Sturgeon Spawning

Possibly the most remarkable and awe-inspiring fish spectacle in the Upper Midwest occurs when 4- to 6-foot-long spawning sturgeon cruise the rocky river shorelines of the network of waterways in Wisconsin that make up the Lake Winnebago system. These armor-plated giants thrash the surface with their sharklike tails so close to the shoreline that one can almost reach out and touch them. Not only can you get to within a few feet of the biggest fish in all of the Midwest, but you also get to experience a living fossil.

Sturgeon arrived on the evolutionary scene 100 million years ago, at just about the time of the dinosaurs' extinction, and they retain fundamentally all of their primitive characteristics. They wear "armor" like a stegosaurus in the form of bony, shell-shaped plates arranged in rows that run the length of the body. Each plate comes to a peak with a sharp-pointed spur, but as a sturgeon ages, the spurs smooth over, and the plates become barely visible. Sturgeon for some reason have never evolved their plates into the common thinner, flexible scales of more modern fish.

The sturgeon's long tapered snout gives it a sharklike look. Four feelers, or *barbels,* dangle just in front of the mouth. These sensory organs alert the sturgeon to food sources like snails, insect larvae, leeches, and other invertebrates as it slowly cruises the bottom. Then it uses its tubular mouth and vacuums up the food, along with silt and gravel, which is expelled through the gills. The mouth is grotesque but effective, because sturgeon have no teeth. And on Lake Winnebago, famed for its incredible mayfly hatch, one shudders to think how many more billions of mayflies would darken the skies (and windshields) of the area if the sturgeon's prodigious appetite were not at work on the larvae living on the lake bottom.

The Lake Winnebago system in east-central Wisconsin has the world's largest concentration of spawning lake sturgeon. The sturgeon swim upstream from shallow Lake Winnebago to spawn on the rocky shorelines of the Wolf, Little Wolf, Fox, and Embarrass Rivers. The actual dates depend on water temperatures and levels, but usually the event occurs in late April to early May. Spawning begins when the water temperature reaches 53°F in high water, and 58°F in low water.

Males arrive ahead of the females, often in groups of eight or more, frequently cruising so close to the surface that their tails, backs, and snouts are out of the water. When a ripe female enters the group, spawning begins.

As she drops her eggs, the males swim alongside her and flail their tails as they release milt (sperm). The 1/8-inch-diameter fertilized eggs are sticky and cling to the rocks until they hatch some 10 days later.

Even though one female may produce from 50,000 to 700,000 eggs, sturgeon remain rare because the eggs are eaten by crayfish, redhorse, carp, and even the adult sturgeon. Or they are lost to dropping water levels, or to a fungus that can grow on the masses of eggs. Less than one in a thousand will survive to the 1/3-inch-long larval stage.

Sturgeon were once very common but declined rapidly in the United States with extensive settlement when they were harvested heavily for their roe (their eggs make a highly valued caviar), their delicious taste, and for a high-quality gelatin called *isinglass* taken from their air bladders. Sturgeon skins were even tanned as fine-grade leather and made into handbags, shoes, and belts that were sold on the East Coast and in Europe. The building of dams also greatly restricted their movement and eliminated their access to spawning habitat. Today aggressive law enforcement, progressive harvest regulations, pollution control, and habitat preservation and creation have contributed to the sturgeon's recovery.

It's been a particularly long road back to reasonable population figures for the sturgeon, because the females don't reach sexual maturity until they are about 25 years old and 55 inches long. And thereafter they only spawn once every 4 to 6 years (males mature at about 15 years and 45 inches in length, and most will spawn every year).

Females live longer than males and grow to astounding sizes. Ninety-seven percent of all sturgeons over 30 years old are females. A 152-year-old, 215-pound, 81-inch-long sturgeon was caught in 1953 in Lake of the Woods, Ontario. An article in the Warroad, Minnesota, *Plain Dealer* in the 1880s reported a 276-pound, 8-foot-long sturgeon brought in on the *Isabel* on Lake of the Woods. The Fond du Lac *Journal* in Wisconsin reported the capture of a 9-foot-long, 297-pounder in the spring of 1881.

They not only live long and grow to incredible sizes, but they swim enormous distances. A 5-foot lake sturgeon caught in a commercial fisherman's net in Saginaw Bay in November of 1994 was traced by its aluminum tag to Lake Winnebago, 450 miles by water from the spot in which it was caught, and had been tagged on October 20, 1978, by the Wisconsin DNR. It had navigated the lower Fox River, which has 14 dams and 17 locks, before reaching Green Bay and then wandered through Lake Michigan, the Straits of Mackinac, into Lake Huron, and finally down the east coast of the Lower Peninsula to Saginaw Bay. In those 16 years it had grown 8 inches, which is an average rate of growth for sturgeon. Another sturgeon was taken in Lake Erie five years after it had been tagged in Lake Winnebago, 850 miles away.

Although huge in size and sharklike in appearance, sturgeons are absolutely placid and have been known to swim with and among humans—they're "harmless as a wet log," says one writer.

The Ojibwa knew the sturgeon's importance. They called it *nah ma*—"king of fishes."

Hot Spots

In Wisconsin, the main sturgeon populations are found in the **Winnebago chain of lakes** and the **Fox River** up to the Shawano Dam, the **lower Wisconsin River** below the Kilbourne dam in Wisconsin Dells, and the **Chippewa, Flambeau,** and **Menominee Rivers.** Sturgeon are also currently being transplanted on the Wisconsin River upstream from the dam at Wisconsin Dells, and on the **Manitowish River** upstream from the Turtle-Flambeau Flowage Dam.

The Wisconsin DNR estimates 25,000 legal sturgeon (over 45 inches long) live in the 137,000-acre Lake Winnebago. The **Wolf River** is the best place in North America to watch the sturgeon during their spawning cycle. The sturgeon spawn at 50 sites along the Fox and Wolf Rivers. Hundreds of volunteers and DNR personnel line the riverbanks during spawning to provide protection from poaching.

Pfeifer Park in New London is an urban site from which to watch sturgeon. Take Hwy. 45 north and turn right onto Waupaca Street. Follow Waupaca to Embarrass Drive and turn left, which takes you to Pfeifer Park. Walk the south shoreline of the Embarrass River.

Also take County Road X west from New London for about 2 miles. Park in the **Mukwa Wildlife Area** parking lot and walk along the south shoreline of the Wolf River.

Just below the **Shawano Dam** on the Wolf River in Shawano is another excellent site. Take Hwy. 29 west through Shawano to the bridge crossing the Wolf.

Near **Shiocton,** along Hwy. 54 near "Bamboo Bend," where Old Highway 54 crosses the Wolf River, are overpasses and riverbanks that allow excellent public viewing.

Call the Wisconsin DNR at (414) 424-3050 for the current year's spawning dates—the department will put you on a list and call you when the run starts. Or contact the New London Chamber of Commerce at (414) 982-5822.

In Michigan, sturgeon are rarely encountered except in Lake St. Clair and a few inland lakes with landlocked populations. The **Prickett Dam on Sturgeon River,** 10 miles southwest of L'Anse, is one known spawning area, though it's very difficult to get to. The sturgeon spawn in a small set of rapids about 43 miles above the river's mouth—some spawn and move back down the river in as little as four days. Many of the adults return to Keweenaw Bay, some 100 miles from the spawning site.

In Minnesota, lake sturgeon live in the **Mississippi River** as far north as the St. Anthony Falls dam in Minneapolis, the **St. Croix River** and its tributaries, the **Red River** along the North Dakota border, and **Lake Superior.** The state's largest population swims in the huge **Lake of the Woods, Rainy Lake,** and the **Rainy River** and its tributaries.

23

April Shorttakes

Fish Spawning

The smelt run along **Minnesota's North Shore** attracts thousands of loons, grebes, mergansers, and gulls, as well as smelt fishermen. In Michigan, one-quarter million people dip-net spawning rainbow smelt along tributaries flowing into the Great Lakes. The best times are between 10:00 P.M. and 2:00 A.M. Try any public boat landing at a tributary stream along the Great Lakes in any of the three states.

Walleyes spawn in late April and can be seen at night moving onto their rocky, shallow spawning grounds. One excellent place to see hundreds of spawning walleyes is from the shorelines and an observation deck in **Lake of the Falls County Park**, Wisconsin. From Hwy. 51 just north of Mercer, take County Road FF west about 5 miles and turn left (south) into the park on the west side of the river (over the bridge). Take a powerful flashlight to see the eyes of the spawning walleyes.

Suckers run in April, too. Try the **Kewaunee River Egg-Taking Facility** to see them through a glass viewing window (see chapter 56 for directions). On northern streams, eagles perch in large numbers in trees to take advantage of the sucker run. Look up and down while the suckers are moving.

Bluebirds Return

Bluebirds return to the Upper Midwest in April, and bluebird boxes should be put out by the first of April (earlier for southern counties). Contact state ornithological societies for bluebird restoration information.

Migrating Raptors

Hawk migration comes into full swing by late April. Check these sites in Michigan: **Mackinaw City/Straits of Mackinac, Whitefish Point Bird Observatory, Brockway Mountain Drive** (see chapter 28). **Port Crescent State Park** on Saginaw Bay has 3 miles of Lake Huron shoreline where hawks are funneled over the dune ridges on updrafts and rest and feed there.

Nelson Dewey State Park along the Mississippi River in Wisconsin offers a great vista from the ridge in the park that is excellent for viewing migrating raptors from March through April. Take County Road VV north from Cassville to Nelson Dewey State Park.

A Closer Look: Amphibian Choruses, Frog Phenology

There are many harbingers of spring, but one I really look forward to is the calling of the male wood frog. The wood frog is the first of the early breeding frogs around my North Woods home to sing, softly "quacking" from temporary woodland ponds in his fervent desire to find a mate. What follows is a two-week frog debauch, the males so driven to reproduce that they will clasp just about anything that moves, including clumps of mud, other males, egg masses, even female spring peepers. The wood frog hibernates aboveground in rotting logs and in the humus and often freezes solid over the winter—so maybe his ardor can be excused after being incapacitated all winter. After two weeks of breeding activity the females have laid all their eggs, and both genders retire to their woodland homes, where they won't be heard from again until next spring.

Generally only male frogs call, and they primarily give their breeding call, which is specific in attracting females for breeding. Fertilization takes place externally, when the males clasp the females and fertilize the eggs as they are laid.

The chronology of frog calling is fixed, though the actual first dates vary significantly from year to year based on when the ice goes off woodland pools and permanent lakes and also on the moisture levels and temperatures that occur thereafter. Within days, and often hours, the wood frog's crooning for a mate is quickly followed by the overwhelming chorus of "sleigh bells," courtesy of the spring peepers, and the soft *crrreeeekkkk*ing of western chorus frogs. Leopard frogs follow one to three weeks later with their characteristic low-pitched snores, which have been likened to the sound of rubbing a finger over a wet balloon. The leopard frog also gives a guttural "chuckle" that appears to function more as a territorial call. By mid-May American toads trill for up to 30 seconds, each individual singing on just one note. Each toad finds its own note, though, so a chorus of sorts may be heard, though the drone hardly could be called musical.

A week or so later, in late May to early June, the eastern gray treefrog and the mink frog chime in. The gray treefrog gives a swift staccato burst of song of about a second's duration that one author calls a "musical trill ... the most beautiful of any species of Wisconsin frog." I disagree, but beauty is in the ear of the beholder. Gray treefrogs often call from up in trees, and many a novice naturalist has wondered what that bird is that sings at night from the trees. The mink frog has a fascinating call likened to horses' hooves on a cobblestone street, or the clinking together of ball bearings.

In early June the green frog begins his courting, luring females with his loose banjo-string twanging. By now all calling frogs do so from permanent lakes and rivers.

The last, biggest, and certainly most extraordinary call of the breeding frogs is the bellow of the male bullfrog, which sounds to me like someone blowing bass notes on a glass jug, but which is also heard by others as the drawing of a bow across a bass fiddle. The bullfrogs join the reproductive party by mid-June, and along with the green frog are most commonly heard into July.

By mid-July the lakes and rivers lapse into silence except for isolated calls of male frogs who apparently haven't quite given up on breeding yet, or maybe they're just unusually expressive.

I count frogs for the Wisconsin DNR three times a year in Vilas County, a practice that has gotten me some strange looks over the years. Since the early 1980s in Wisconsin, volunteers have done calling counts on specific routes in every county in the state (surveys take place in Minnesota and Michigan, too). Ten stops are made on each route. The same route is taken three times every year, and the same stops are made to listen for male frogs trying to entice females.

Concern exists over whether certain frog species are in decline, so in order to get a valid picture of the breeding population of frogs and toads in the state, a long-term database is needed so hasty conclusions aren't drawn. The leopard frog appears to be declining not only in Wisconsin but elsewhere in the United States and Europe. The wood frog and chorus frog have shown population declines, too. And the cricket frog has virtually disappeared from southern Wisconsin in the early 1990s. Its decline may indicate a broader failing of the ecosystems in which it lives. Frogs and toads are sensitive to changes in water quality and quantity, so their population trends can serve as an index of environmental quality. Loss of habitat, local droughts, pollution, acid rain, pesticide contamination, or higher ultraviolet light levels from our thinning ozone layer may be contributing to these declines.

Identifying frog and toad calls in the Upper Midwest is really pretty easy. Wisconsin only has 12 species—11 frogs and the American toad—and Minnesota has 14 species (add the Canadian toad and Great Plains toad). Because each frog breeds at specific times and has specific habitat preferences, the calls can be learned without much time investment. You may be pleasantly surprised to learn how many sounds that you were attributing to other creatures turn out to be frogs and toads. The Madison, Wisconsin, Audubon Society produces an audiotape entitled "Wisconsin Frogs," which covers nearly every frog and toad in Minnesota and Michigan, too (see the Appendix for the address and phone number).

May

Notes

25

Spring Woodland Wildflowers

The lush profusion of wildflowers that appears almost magically in May can be astonishing both in number and diversity. People who live where seasons don't change just don't know how good a month like May can feel. The ice often doesn't go off our lakes in the North Woods until the last week in April, and most northern woodland flowers seldom risk peeking through the soil until May has truly arrived.

But when spring comes, it often comes like a locomotive—if you don't get out and enjoy it, summer is here before you know it. Spring flowers come and go quickly because they're in a race to flower before the leaf canopy fills in and shades the woodland floor. Nearly 70 percent of woodland flowers blossom by June 15 in their haste to beat the shade. It's the most intense floral period of the year, and if the mosquitoes haven't hatched in droves, by far the most enjoyable.

Depending on latitude, soil type, and a variety of other factors, the wildflowers a person may see locally can be very different from those not that far away. My family and I live in the traditional pine forestlands of northern Wisconsin that still produce big pines in the sandy soils we are blessed with. But drive 20 miles north into an area of heavier clay soils and the flora changes remarkably. Around my home our wildflower communities have to tolerate sand, so we enjoy the beauty of trailing arbutus, barren strawberry, wood anemone, and gaywings, while our neighbors just to the north and south have trout lilies, bloodroot, Dutchman's-breeches, trilliums, and other flowers that do well in heavier soils.

It is difficult to generalize about what flowers may be seen where and when, particularly in one short chapter. There are flowers just about everywhere in May in thousands of areas. The sites listed here are renowned for their beauty. Call ahead to the area of your choice to find out what may be blooming when you visit. And go back again at different times of the year—the site will usually change dramatically as the weeks go by.

Hot Spots
In Michigan, **P.J. Hoffmaster State Park** holds a Trillium Festival in mid-May (the eleventh annual festival was in 1995) at the Gillette Sand Dune Visitors Center. From Grand Haven, take U.S. 31 north to the Pontaluna Road exit, head west toward Lake Michigan, and follow the signs to the park.

Trilliums are but one of hundreds of spring flowers that bloom in May after a long midwestern winter. Photo by Carol Christensen.

The **Pigeon River State Forest** (Jordan River Valley) in Antrim County is a beautiful meandering steep river valley that offers great scenic beauty. You can find stands of orchids and other wildflowers and, as in most of these sites, excellent birding opportunities. A good dirt road runs the length of the river valley and is considered one of the prettiest drives in the Lower Peninsula. A network of trails laces the area. Look in low cedar stands along the river for orchids. From Gaylord, take Michigan 32 west to U.S. 131 and turn left (south). Go 0.25 mile to the north entrance road on the right. Other entrances are from the southern and western boundaries.

Brockway Mountain Drive, the highest roadway above sea level between the Alleghenies and the Rockies, offers a variety of rare and endangered plants in its rocky soils. Visit later in May to be sure the snow is gone and the road is passable (see chapter 28 for directions).

Timberland Swamp Nature Sanctuary in Oakland County, only a few minutes from metropolitan Detroit and Pontiac, has spectacular spring wildflowers. Its 245 acres lie within an 800-acre backwoods wilderness area within Indian Springs Metropark and is the Michigan Nature Association's showplace sanctuary. Millions of spring beauties (peaking around April 25) and tens of thousands of large white trilliums (peaking around May 12) carpet the forest floor. From I-75 about 1.5 miles west of Clarkston, take the Dixie Hwy. South exit and go 1.25 miles to White Lake Road. Turn right (southwest) and travel 1.5 miles to Andersonville Road. Turn right and go 3 miles to Ware Road, which will take you to the northeastern corner of Timberland Swamp. There are two trails in the sanctuary. Take the Blue Trail shortcut if the ground seems quite wet.

Indian Springs Metropark, once part of what was called the Huron Swamp, is predominately marshland and swamp forest but also has upland habitats. Superb wildflower viewing occurs here from mid-April through June. Look for showy lady's-slippers, trout lilies, trilliums, sundews, and pitcher plants (use the same directions as given above for Timberland Swamp).

Colonial Point, a 297-acre peninsula of mature hardwoods, juts out into Burt Lake in the northern tip of lower Michigan. Purchased by the Little Traverse Conservancy and turned over to the University of Michigan Biological Station, and now designated as a United Nations International Biosphere Reserve, the May forest floor supports a shimmering of Dutchman's-breeches, jack-in-the-pulpits, violets, trilliums, and spring beauties, among others. Take U.S. 31 north from Petoskey and turn right (east) onto Brutus Road. Travel for 4.5 miles and go straight on the gravel road where the pavement curves north. The forest is a quarter mile ahead on your right. An adjoining 195 acres was purchased by the conservancy in 1993 to further protect this area.

The **Lefglen Nature Sanctuary** in Jackson County near Grass Lake supports nearly 700 species of native Michigan plant species, more than one-third of the native flora found in the state! Owned by the Michigan Nature Association, this 210-acre sanctuary covers a diverse array of habitats. From I-94, take the Grass Lake exit and drive 1 mile south. Turn right on Grass Lake Road and go 0.75 mile through Grass Lake. Turn left onto Wolf Lake Road and drive south 4.5 miles to just past the intersection with Rexford Road; park at the nature association parking lot. A trail starts here that leads through the southern part of the property.

Dowagiac Woods, Love Creek County Park, Warren Woods Natural Area, and **Trillium Ravine Plant Preserve,** all mentioned in chapter 21, about the first spring wildflowers, provide outstanding arrays of May wildflowers as well (see chapter 21 for directions).

Try the Waxwing Loop Trail for superb spring wildflowers at the **Sarett Nature Center.** The Gentian Loop Trail is spectacular for fringed gentians, turtleheads, and cardinal flowers in August and September. From Benton Harbor, take I-94 east to Exit 34. Follow I-196/U.S. 31 and turn left onto Red Arrow Highway. Go 1/8 mile to Benton Center Road and turn right (north) to the nature center entrance.

The **Dahlem Environmental Education Center** has wonderful trails for trilliums and other wildflowers in May. Head south on U.S. 127 out of Jackson, Michigan, and take the Monroe exit. Turn left (west) onto

McDevitt Street, go to the first stoplight, and turn left onto Hague Road. Turn right (west) onto Kimmel Road and then right again onto South Jackson Road to the center entrance. The site is owned by Jackson Community College.

The **Seven Ponds Nature Center** is located among diverse habitats and offers 5 miles of hiking trails with bridges, boardwalks, and towers. It is excellent for spring through early fall wildflowers. The center is owned by the Michigan Audubon Society. Go north of Almont on Michigan 53 and turn left (west) onto Dryden Road. Travel 7 miles to Calkins Road, and turn left, following the signs to the nature center.

The **Lloyd A. Stage Outdoor Education Center,** owned by the city of Troy, has 100 acres of diverse habitats that provide excellent wildflower viewing. From Detroit, head north on I-75 to the Crooks Road exit. Turn right (north) and drive to Square Lake Road. Turn left (west), and continue to Coolidge Road. Turn right (north) and proceed 0.75 mile to the park entrance.

Kensington Metropark, a 4,300-acre park with a wide array of habitats, supports 350 species of wildflowers. From I-96, 3 miles east of the intersection with Michigan 23, take the Kensington Road exit (#151) to the west entrance—the nature center is 1.2 miles past this entrance.

Pictured Rocks National Lakeshore supports a profusion of wildflowers in the spring. Try the trail to Miners Falls, which one Michigander I know claims has the best spring wildflowers in the area. Also consider hiking the Lakeshore Trail, a component of the North Country Trail, which runs along the shore the entire length of the park. From Munising, take Hwy. 58 to Miners Castle Road to reach the Miners Falls trail. Continue on Miners Castle Road to intersect at its end with the Lakeshore Trail.

Fred Russ Forest (also called Newton Woods) is 580 acres of nearly virgin oak–mixed hardwood forest that is owned and managed by Michigan State University. Spring flowers are abundant! From downtown Cassopolis, take Michigan 60 east for 2.5 miles to Decatur Road and turn north. Drive 6.7 miles to Marcellus Highway, turn east, and drive for 0.25 mile until you see the forest on the right side of the road.

The **Kalamazoo Nature Center** offers exceptional spring wildflower viewing. Take U.S. 131 north out of Kalamazoo and turn east on D Avenue. Drive 3.5 miles to Westnedge Avenue, turn south, and drive for 0.75 mile to the nature center entrance.

Aman Park in Ottawa County is a 200-acre woodland with a wonderful array of spring flowers. At the junction of Michigan 11 and Michigan 45 in Standale, take Michigan 45 west for 3.5 miles to the park entrance.

A carpet of trilliums graces the understory of a rich woods. Photo by Carol Christensen.

In Wisconsin, a tour of the many trails of the **University of Wisconsin Arboretum** in Madison should yield a broad range of wildflowers from diverse habitats. From prairie to wetlands to pine forest, even to boreal forest, the variety of ecological communities arrayed here are quite impressive (see chapter 21 for directions).

The Wisconsin Nature Conservancy owns and manages many wonderful older forests that have profuse bloomings of spring wildflowers. **Kurtz Woods** near Saukville in Ozaukee County is designated a State Natural Area and is used extensively by education and research groups. Although it is only 31 acres, the site supports thick stands of sugar maple and American beech, with an understory of hepatica, bloodroot, wild leek, and spring beauties. From the intersections of Hwy. 33 and County Road O in Saukville, take County Road O south for 1 mile to Cedar Sauk Road. Turn right (west) and go less than 1 mile to reach the access road. Turn right (south) on this road and travel 0.5 mile to the northeast corner of the woods. Park along the road—a trail leads into the woods from here.

Several sites in the unglaciated **Baraboo Hills** region harbor wonderful wildflower blooms. **Hemlock Draw** has 11 distinct vegetative communities in its 533 acres, including northern forest plants rare for such a southern site. From Sauk City, take U.S. 12 north for 2.5 miles and turn left (west) onto County Road PF. Follow Road PF for 12 miles to County Road C and turn right (northeast). Take Road C for only

0.25 mile and turn left on Hemlock Road in Leland to reach Reich Drive. Take Reich Drive north for 0.5 mile to the preserve entrance.

Baxter's Hollow contains southern Wisconsin's only undeveloped watershed on its 2,900 protected acres. Many major vegetation types can be found here: shaded cliff, hemlock relic, sand barrens, northern pine–hardwood forest, southern red oak forest, southern maple–basswood forest, and others. From Sauk City, take U.S. 12 north for 8 miles to County Road C and turn left (west). Take Road C for 1.5 miles and turn right (north) onto Stone's Pocket Road. Drive 2 miles and park at one of several turnoff parking areas. A trail begins at the end of the road. Both Hemlock Draw and Baxter's Hollow are owned and managed by The Nature Conservancy.

Parfrey's Glen State Natural Area is also located in the Baraboo Hills and features a deep gorge harboring northern flora. It is located 3 miles north of Merrimac. Take Bluff Road north out of Merrimac to the glen.

Chiwaukee Prairie, a 165-acre Nature Conservancy parcel of great importance, sports 25 shooting stars per square yard from May 15 to June 1 (see chapter 33 for directions).

Wyalusing State Park in the beautiful unglaciated hills of far south-western Wisconsin is well known for its migrating warblers (see chapter 26) but also supports lavish wildflower displays on 18 miles of trails that wind through the park from 500-foot bluffs over the Mississippi River to the heavily wooded floodplain forest. Take Hwys. 18/35 south from Prairie du Chien and turn right (west) onto County Road C. Road C merges with County Road X, but Road C soon turns north and takes you to the park entrance.

For a most unusual early May treat, try **Nugget Lake County Park** in Pierce County, where many thousands of snow trilliums may be seen until late May. Snow trilliums bloom right after the snow melts in mid-April. Look to see the way the leaves are attached by very short petioles to the stems. Snow trilliums are earlier and smaller than other native white trilliums. Take Hwy. 63 east from Ellsworth and stay straight on Hwy. 72 when 63 swings north. Ten miles later turn right (south) on South Rock Elm Road and go 3 miles to the 752-acre park. Only 10 of Wisconsin's 72 counties are known to harbor the unusual snow trillium.

In Minnesota, **Nerstrand Big Woods State Park** represents the largest remaining stand in Minnesota of the Big Woods, an area of hardwoods in south-central Minnesota that once covered 2 million acres and of which today only 1,000 acres remain. This is the only site in the world to see the Minnesota dwarf trout lily, a federally designated endangered species that blooms from late April to early May. The overstory is made up of big sugar maple, basswood, elm, and green ash trees, and under them in a race to bloom before the trees leaf out are hepatica, wild ginger, wood anemone, bloodroot, spring beauty, trillium, and marsh marigold.

Nerstrand is about 11 miles southeast of Northfield. From Hwy. 3, take Hwy. 246 southeast out of Northfield and follow the signs to the park.

Townsend Woods SNA is considered the finest example of a portion of the Big Woods left in Minnesota. A 50-acre remnant, it is located along a north-facing glacial ridge that was too steep to be farmed. From Morristown, go 3 miles west on Hwy. 60, then turn north on County Road 99 and go 3 miles through Sakatah Lake State Park to the parking lot.

Kilen Woods State Park has hardwood spring wildflowers like bloodroot and Dutchman's-breeches, plus prairie plants on the **Prairie Bush Clover SNA**. Kilen is located 9 miles northeast of Lakefield in Jackson County. The park entrance is on Jackson County Hwy. 24, 5 miles east of Minnesota 86.

Myre Big Island State Park offers a spring mix of oak savanna and woodland flowers like shooting star, prairie-smoke, pasqueflower, and puccoon in the grasslands, and trillium, Virginia waterleaf, hepatica, and jack-in-the-pulpit on the forested island. Myre State Park is located 3 miles southeast of Albert Lea on County Hwy. 38. Exits off I-90 and I-35 have signs directing visitors to the park. Exit 11 on I-35 is the most convenient approach to the park.

Lake Shetek State Park contains the largest deciduous woodlands in southwestern Minnesota, an area more commonly associated with prairies. About half of the park is woodlands, and the other half is in prairie, so this is a good place to get the best of both floral worlds. Try the Loon Island and Park Lake Trails for the most abundant blooms. Lake Shetek State Park is 14 miles northeast of Slayton in Murray County. Take County Road 38 north of Currie to the park entrance.

26

Warbler Migration

Magic might be the only word for it. Those few days in May when the warbler migration pulses through in what seems like waves—that's pure heaven if you have any love for birds at all.

By early May many birds have already returned to the Upper Midwest, but most warblers bide their time until the spring insect hatch can be counted on. And when the winds are right (from the south), the birds come as if a signal flag had gone down and the race to their northern nesting sites was on. Most warblers are among the last birds to return to the area, their arrival marking the final climax of the spring migration.

For many Neotropical warblers, the flight from Central and South America back to their northern breeding grounds covers enormous distances. Blackpoll warblers cover at least 2,500 miles, from northern South America to central and northern Canada. The long-distance flights are all the more extraordinary given the size of a typical warbler. They seldom stretch beyond 5 inches in length and weigh only a third to a half of an ounce, which seems barely sufficient to withstand a light breeze. Add to the distance factor the facts that virtually all of the migration takes place at night and that many birds fall victim to the vagaries of weather, TV towers, and predators, and the large numbers surviving the journey become all the more marvelous.

Most of the excitement about warblers centers around their wonderfully diverse coloration, and around the intricate songs of a few. No northern family of birds rivals the exquisite hues of the wood warblers; they have rightfully earned the title of "the butterflies of the bird world." And no warbler may be more intensely colorful than the Blackburnian warbler, as suggested by some of its nicknames: firethroat, torch bird, and fire brand. Blackburnians like to perch on the highest tips of a tree, and with the sun acting like a beacon, their necks and heads can appear to be flaming.

In the North Woods, significant numbers of warblers seldom arrive until the second half of May, while southern counties usually experience warbler arrivals by the first of May. Some warblers, such as the palm, pine, and yellow-rumped, arrive earlier in the south, often by mid-April. A few warblers, such as the Canada warbler, take the opposite approach, biding their time and then zipping through the Upper Midwest late in May on their way to their Canadian nesting grounds.

Migrating warblers may be seen anywhere and on any given day in May. But there occur certain days where the winds send waves of birds through, or days where warblers are trapped by poor weather and get "backed up." And there are places where the birds are forced into narrow corridors and thus are concentrated. A peninsula jutting out into one of the Great Lakes, a coastline, an urban park in the midst of an ocean of metal and asphalt, or an island convenient as a rest stop, all serve as geographic funnels to concentrate songbirds into a small area.

Minnesota and Wisconsin Points, at Duluth/Superior, are such areas, long famed as migration "traps." Songbirds coming north through much of Wisconsin are forced westward along the Lake Superior shoreline until they reach Duluth at the far western corner of the lake, and then they ordinarily fan northward. But if a northerly wind brings in cold and fog and rain, the small birds are forced into thick woods to wait it out. Thousands of birds can be grounded for several days, and although the weather is less than ideal for comfortable bird-watching, it is ideal for getting birds to stay put. Then warblers and other songbirds appear to be perching in every shrub and tree.

Watch your statewide weather channel, and get out when the first warm fronts from the south start pushing into your area. Remember also to call the birding hotlines in each state for advice and counsel—they'll usually point you in the right direction at the right time.

Some 23 species of warblers nest in the northern regions of the three states, so even if you miss the migration, many breeding birds will still remain to dazzle you. For the best possible viewing, go birding before the leaves fill out the woods canopy, usually before June 15. While you're at it, why not consider joining the International May Day Bird Count, even if you aren't an expert? Contact a birding club in your area or your state ornithological union for dates and details.

Hot Spots

In Wisconsin, **Wyalusing State Park,** at the confluence of the Wisconsin and Mississippi Rivers, is home to many "southern" songbird species such as Kentucky, cerulean, and prothonotary warblers; Louisiana waterthrush; tufted titmouse; and yellow-throated vireo. Here too, migrating songbirds are often seen in great abundance and diversity, including rarities like yellow-throated and worm-eating warblers, and white-eyed and Bell's vireo. All told, 30 species of warblers may be seen in Wyalusing in early May. The boat landing tends to be the most popular place for birders, but also consider birding the Sugar Maple Nature Trail, the Sentinel Ridge Nature Trail, and the Old Immigrant Trail. Traveling south from Prairie du Chien on Hwy. 18, turn left (south) on County Road C, then turn right (west) onto County Road CX and drive 1 mile to the park entrance.

Nelson Dewey State Park, south of Wyalusing and also along the Mississippi, offers excellent songbird opportunities in May, too. Look for rarities like Carolina wren, cerulean warbler, blue-gray gnatcatcher, and tufted titmouse. Take Hwy. 133 north from Cassville, turn left onto County Road VV, and Nelson Dewey State Park is 1 mile on your right.

High Cliff State Park offers spectacular views from its bluffs along the northeast shoreline of Lake Winnebago, Wisconsin's largest inland lake, and top-notch birding as well. The park is 1 mile long and divided into two strips. The upper park is a high ridge called the Niagara Escarpment, and from its top you can watch warblers coming by at eye level. The lower forest at the south end, which lies between the escarpment and the lake, can have spectacular warbler migrations too.

Warbler movement coincides with the Lake Winnebago mayfly hatch. The hatch is so abundant that the birds pay little attention to anything other than the meal at hand and so are easily observed. The flies will also land on any upright object, including local birders, and though they are absolutely harmless, they can be a nuisance. Try to bird during the week because this park receives many weekend visitors. Take Hwy. 55 south for 1.5 miles out of Sherwood to the main entrance. The park is located 10 miles south of the Fox Cities.

While you're in the vicinity of High Cliff State Park, try **Calumet County Park,** which is located just south of High Cliff on the east shore of Lake Winnebago. This park too can have remarkable warbler migrations when the flies are hatching. Take Hwy. 55 south from High Cliff State Park and turn right onto County Road EE. Follow it for 1.5 miles to the end.

Wisconsin Point can be a songbird mecca in May—look for peak warbler days around May 15. From just east of Superior on U.S. 2, take the Moccasin Mike Road exit and follow it to the first left onto Wisconsin Point Road. There are turnoffs all along the road, which eventually ends directly across from Minnesota Point, with the boating channel running in between.

For urban park environments, few can match the **University of Wisconsin Arboretum** in Madison for its enormous diversity of habitats, which provide nesting and resting sites for a wide array of songbirds. Take U.S. 12/18 west from I-94 to the Seminole Highway exit. Turn north, then right again at the arboretum entrance. The McKay Visitor Center offers many tours and programs worth attending.

The **Schlitz Audubon Center** in Milwaukee conducts a May Day Count, usually in mid-May at the peak of migration. Contact the center, or a local bird club, to join in on the count.

In Michigan, the coastlines of the four Great Lakes that border the state serve as funneling corridors for warblers as well as for waterfowl and hawks. On Lake Huron, one of the premier warbler sites is **Tawas Point State Park,** located on a sandy, partially wooded peninsula that curves south into Lake Huron, forming Tawas Bay. A total of 205 bird species have been counted here. During the spring warbler migration, 31 warbler species have been seen. Look in the bushes at the tip of the peninsula and around the lighthouse. The area is also excellent for shorebirds and waterfowl. From Tawas City take Michigan 23 and turn right (south) onto Tawas Beach Road. Go 2.5 miles to the state park entrance. The road ends at the Coast Guard station.

Also on Lake Huron, **Whitefish Bay** in Alpena County supports large concentrations of migrating warblers, shorebirds, ducks, and hawks, and is particularly good in late May. Great blue and black-crowned night heron rookeries are close by. Look for passerines along the tree edges and for shorebirds along the gravel beaches of East Shore. From the cement plant in Alpena, take Misery Bay Road east to the Lake Huron shore. Some 1.5 miles of shore can be scanned from your car along Misery Bay Road.

Along Lake Michigan extends the world's largest accumulation of sand dunes bordering fresh water (see chapter 42), stretching from the Michigan-Indiana border along Lake Michigan to the Straits of Mackinac. Songbirds avoid crossing Lake Michigan, preferring to fly along the shoreline instead, and the birding opportunities along the coast seem endless. **Leelanau State Park** is located at the tip of the little finger of Michigan's "mitten." Here warblers and hawks tend to pile up during spring migration. The 1,253-acre area includes Lake Michigan and Grand Traverse Bay shoreline, as well as woodland. From the village of Northport, take Michigan 201 for 1.7 miles to County Road 640. Follow 640 for 1.7 miles to County Road 629 and turn left. Head north on 629 for 5.5 miles to the park entrance.

Sleeping Bear Dunes National Lakeshore has nearly 40 miles of protected shoreline along Lake Michigan and is excellent for watching migrations. Try Otter Creek's diverse habitats, which include sand dunes, mature beech-maple woodlands, cedar swamp, and pine-oak forests. Varied habitats mean varied bird species both nesting and in migration. Take Michigan 22 for 6 miles north after crossing the Platte River bridge, then turn left on Esch Road. Take Esch 1.3 miles until it ends at Lake Michigan. Explore any direction from this point.

Also try **Stocking Scenic Drive,** which takes you through extensive sand dunes and beech-maple forests while offering spectacular scenery along the lakeshore. This narrow one-way drive has many pull-offs—explore any one of them. Take Michigan 22 north of Empire for 2.2 miles and turn left on Michigan 109. Proceed for 3 miles to the entrance of Stocking Scenic Drive on your left. A self-guiding brochure is available at the entrance.

Just south of Sleeping Bear Dunes lies **Point Betsie,** a narrow neck of land between Lake Michigan and Crystal Lake. Continue south on Hwy. 22 out of Sleeping Bear Dunes to Point Betsie Road. Turn right (west) and head out to the Point Betsie Lighthouse, where the road ends at Lake Michigan.

The **De Graaf Nature Center,** just off Lake Michigan in the city of Holland, offers 25 to 30 species of warblers in early May on their way to their northern breeding grounds. From U.S. 31 in Holland, go west on the 16th Street exit, which joins 17th and then becomes Southshore Drive. Turn left (south) onto Graafschap Road and go 5 blocks to the nature center.

Migrants like to stop to rest and feed in the forested or shrubby habitats of **P.J. Hoffmaster State Park.** The Gillette Visitor Center within the park offers outstanding programs on dune ecology and other topics, including birds. From Muskegon, head south on U.S. 31 to Pontaluna Road and turn right (west). Follow the signs to the park entrance.

Warren Woods Natural Area, just inland from Lake Michigan in far southwestern Michigan and part of Warren Dunes State Park, has preserved 200 acres of mostly untouched beech-maple forest (see chapter 21 for directions and more discussion). Broad paths wind through the woods and along the Galien River, providing one of the best warbler areas in the state, particularly for more southern species.

Grand Mere State Park, just 6 miles north of Warren Dunes State Park, offers great bird watching for many species rare to Michigan. It's also good for summer warblers that are unusual for this area, such as black-and-white, black-throated green, prairie, hooded, and Canada warblers. Take Exit 22 (Stevensville) off I-94 and head west for 0.5 mile into the park.

At **Muskegon State Park,** 200-plus species of birds have been observed, and May is excellent for migrating warblers anywhere along the 5 miles of shoreline. Muskegon Lake helps force even more songbirds to the coast. From U.S. 31, turn onto Michigan 120 and head southwest, following park signs to Memorial Drive, which ends at the park's south entrance, or drive south from Whitehall on Scenic Drive to reach the park's north entrance.

The small village of **Copper Harbor** and the surrounding area on Lake Superior can be excellent for migrating warblers because of its location near the end of the Keweenaw Peninsula. Visit Fort Wilkins State

Park at the end of Michigan 26 just north of Copper Harbor and try the picnic and camping areas along Lake Fanny Hooe. Take U.S. 41 from Houghton-Hancock directly to Copper Harbor or turn onto Michigan 26 from U.S. 41 for a shoreline drive along Lake Superior to Copper Harbor.

Metro Beach Metropark, a 770-acre tract on Lake St. Clair, is considered one of the best places in Michigan for migrating spring warblers. Watch the lake for waterfowl as well. Take I-94 to Exit 236 (Metropolitan Parkway) and head east for 2 miles to the park entrance.

The **Kalamazoo Nature Center** is located in a natural corridor along the Kalamazoo River for spring and fall migrations. One of the largest banding stations in the United States operates here, regularly banding 7,000–10,000 birds each fall. Take U.S. 131 north out of Kalamazoo and turn east on D Avenue. Drive 3.5 miles to Westnedge Avenue and turn south for 0.75 mile to the nature center entrance.

In urban areas, the **Nichols Arboretum,** a University of Michigan–owned plantation along the Huron River that is now maintained as a city park, is an excellent site for spring and fall songbird migrations, with good chances of picking up rare southern species such as summer tanager and worm-eating warbler in the spring. From Main Street in downtown Ann Arbor, take Huron Avenue, which turns into Washtenaw. Turn left onto Geddes and go 0.2 mile to Observatory. Go another 0.2 mile, turn right onto Washington, and park in a lot across the street from Mary Mackley Hall. The arboretum may only be visited by walking.

In the Detroit area, the **University of Michigan–Dearborn Environmental Study Area** provides diverse habitats for attracting extraordinary numbers and varieties of warblers, including many rarities and accidentals. Follow the trail around the lake to look for warblers—38 species have been seen! Take Michigan 39 to Michigan 153 (Ford Road—Exit 7) and go west 1 mile to the Evergreen Road exit. Take Evergreen Road south for 0.5 mile to the entrance of the university and turn right. Go 0.3 mile, turn left, and park at the visitor parking lot.

At the **Lloyd A. Stage Outdoor Education Center,** owned by the city of Troy, 200 species of birds have been seen, and spring migration is the best time for viewing the 100 acres of wildlands. From Detroit, head north on I-75 to Crooks Road exit. Turn right (north) and drive to Square Lake Road. Turn left (west) and continue to Coolidge Road. Turn right (north) and proceed 0.75 mile to the park entrance.

Thirty-six species of warblers have been recorded at the **Carl G. Fenner Arboretum,** including rarities such as Kirtland's and golden-winged warblers. From I-496 east in Lansing, exit at Trowbridge and take it to its end at Harrison. Turn right (south) and go to Mt. Hope Road (the first stoplight) and turn right again (west this time). Drive 1.5 miles to the arboretum entrance.

In Minnesota, **Frontenac State Park** in Goodhue County has long been a favorite place for birders to view the spring warbler migration. The St. Paul Audubon Club has sponsored a spring warbler weekend on the second weekend of May for the last 23 years. A total of 229 species have been sighted over this time, including 33 warbler species. Every regular warbler on the Minnesota list except the worm-eating warbler has been seen at least once. Check in particular the trail out to Sand Point, which fingers out into Lake Pepin, and the trails and road near an area of the lakeshore called Point-no-point. Nesting warblers occur in the park.

Frontenac rests on the western shore of Lake Pepin, a huge broadening of the Mississippi River, and is part of what is referred to as the blufflands of southeastern Minnesota. The bluffs stretch from Red Wing all the way to the Iowa border, and they offer some of the prettiest country one could ever want to see. Frontenac State Park is located on U.S. 61, 10 miles southeast of Red Wing.

Minnesota Point, as mentioned in the introduction, can be as good as Pt. Poulee, probably the most famous songbird area in the eastern United States. If the weather conditions are right, meaning rain or fog for several days to hold the birds tight, you may be able to view a number of different birds. Due to such ideal conditions, one expert birder described seeing 26 species of warblers over three consecutive days (May 21–23 in 1993). Take Lake Avenue from the corner of Superior Street and Lake in downtown Duluth past Canal Park, cross the Aerial Lift Bridge, and follow Lake Avenue (which becomes Minnesota Avenue) the entire length of the 6-mile-long peninsula. The peninsula is well populated, but the road eventually dead-ends at the Sky Harbor Airport and 2 more miles of trees and beach await your exploration. But before you head off from the airport, check the **Park Point** recreation area, considered by Minnesota birders to be the best single spot for migrants anywhere in Minnesota, including seabirds, shorebirds, and songbirds.

In the **Superior National Forest,** Lima Mountain Road (Forest Road 152), off the Gunflint Trail (County Road 12), has 22 nesting species of warblers by the end of May. Turn left (west) off the Gunflint Trail just south of the North Brule River and about 20 miles north of Grand Marais, onto Lima Mountain Road. Bird the first 2 miles of this road, whereupon the road splits—turn northwest if you wish (Forest Road 315) and loop back to the Gunflint 6 miles later.

27

Shorebirds

Migration has been a puzzle for humankind from the beginning. Birds leave, birds return. But where do they go? And how do they know where to return?

A Swedish archbishop, Olaus Magnus, in the middle of the sixteenth century believed birds hibernated en masse under lakes and seas. He said local fishermen sometimes pulled these torpid birds up in their nets, and when they thawed out, they would fly around.

Charles Morton, an Englishman, published a book in 1703 on migration. Based on his extensive research, in particular his reading of Copernicus, who had concluded that the moon had seas, mountains, and an atmosphere, Morton decided that birds left Britain in the autumn and spent their winters on the moon. Morton realized that the birds would starve on their six-week journey to the moon, so he logically deduced that birds must be able to fly in their sleep and that islands must exist in the sky along the way where birds could feed and rest.

Other early naturalists believed that birds changed into animals or slept through the winter in hollow trees or caves or under stones or wrapped in cocoons of dried mud.

Although we know much more today, all of the mysteries of migration will probably never be resolved. Good examples of the miracles of migration are the shorebirds. They seem to be traveling vagabonds, many rushing from their Southern Hemisphere wintering grounds to their Arctic nesting sites, mating, raising their young, and hurrying back in an attempt to maintain maximum food and light levels. The window of nesting opportunity in the Arctic, the time between ice-off and the snows returning in August, is slim, and the distances the birds must travel are long. Red knots winter in the Straits of Magellan and then fly to arctic Canada, a round-trip of about 19,000 miles. The lesser golden plover spends its winters on the Argentine pampas and then travels up through South and Central America, crosses the Gulf of Mexico, and then flies up the Mississippi Valley to the Arctic tundra, some 8,000 miles north of its wintering grounds. Watching shorebirds wade and feed could be likened to watching an exotic international bazaar, with travelers from everywhere in the Western Hemisphere briefly sampling the fare, then moving on.

Not all journey so far, of course. The American woodcock is considered a shorebird, and its travels only take it to the southern United States for the

Many shorebirds like these willets stop briefly in the Upper Midwest during their spring migration from South America to the Arctic. Photo by Carol Christensen.

winter, and then it flies back to its breeding grounds throughout the Upper Midwest.

No matter the distance, for most shorebirds the spring migration through our area unravels rapidly, but if you can catch some of it, the shorebirds are beautiful in their breeding plumage. Among the most impressive markings are those of the black-bellied plover and the lesser golden plover's pronounced black-and-white facial striping.

Because shorebirds spend most of their lives along the edges of mudflats and sandy shorelines, the locations of spring migrants often vary from year to year depending on local weather conditions. A flooded field may be every bit as good for birding as a national wildlife refuge. So be creative in your search—there may be excellent temporary sites quite close to home.

Hot Spots

In Minnesota, the **western prairie region** is the place for sheer numbers. During the last full weekend in April the Minnesota Ornithological Society takes an annual field trip to the western counties looking for flooded fields, and on May 1, 1994, they saw 25 species of shorebirds! But temporarily flooded fields are hard to direct anyone to. Three permanent lakes are near guarantees for excellent shorebird viewing. **Salt Lake** in Lac Qui Parle County, right on the South Dakota border, is the most alkaline lake in Minnesota, with often low water levels and exposed mudflats. In fact, the water is one-third as salty as seawater and smells very much like an ocean tidal flat. The lake can be 300 acres at high water and absolutely dry in a drought. If the water is low, you may see avocets, willets, marbled godwits, Hudsonian godwits, and even piping plovers, as well as nearly all other shorebirds possible in Minnesota. Three species of geese, 19 species of ducks, and tundra swans also stop here in migration. The extensive sago pondweed is a waterfowl favorite, and the abundant zooplankton feeds the shorebirds. Take Hwy. 212 west out of Dawson and turn north onto a dirt county road 1 mile east of the South Dakota border (see chapter 39).

Thiekle Lake in Big Stone County had nesting avocets in 1992 and is considered one of the best sites in Minnesota for observing western grebes. And not incidentally, 21 species of shorebirds were seen here on one day in early May by one birder I know. Take Hwy. 75 north from the outskirts of Ortonville and turn right (east) onto County Road 62 to reach the lake (see chapter 39).

Mud Lake, really a broadening of the Bois de Sioux River (and eventually the Red River), is considered one of the best western lakes for migrant shorebirds (and waterfowl) in drier years. Reach the southern end of the lake (and the northern end of Traverse Lake) by taking Hwy. 117 west to where it crosses into South Dakota. Or scan from County Road 76 along the northeastern shore. From Wheaton, take Hwy. 27 west and pick up County Road 76 going north, or continue on and take Hwy. 117 west.

Zippel Bay State Park has 2 miles of sand beach along Lake of the Woods, near the largest breeding area remaining in the Great Lakes for the piping plover, a federally endangered species. Less than 50 breeding individuals have been counted on the four known breeding areas on the lake. Zippel Bay itself is one of the four nesting sites, though successful nestings are infrequent. About 6 miles east, **Pine** and **Curry Islands,** near the southeast corner of the lake, have the largest concentration of nesting birds. The islands are protected by The Nature Conservancy and the State Scientific and Natural Areas Program, and no landing is permitted on the islands during the breeding season. To reach Zippel Bay, take County Road 2 north out of Williams, and turn right (east) onto County Road 8, which will take you into the park.

And though I may seem to mention **Minnesota Point** (and Wisconsin Point) a lot in this book, there's no getting around the fact that this is a great area for shorebirds, too. Minnesota Point is a finger of land surrounded by water at the far southwestern base of Lake Superior. Shorebirds concentrate in large numbers on the beaches—200 ruddy turnstones may be flocked together here. Look also for red knots, plovers, whimbrels, and though they are rare, piping plovers may also stop over (see chapter 26 for directions).

In Wisconsin, **Wisconsin Point** offers the same opportunities as Minnesota Point. A good argument can be made for designating the Duluth-Superior area as the premier overall birding area in the entire Midwest (see chapter 26 for directions).

Fish Creek Marsh and **Whittlesey Creek Marsh** in Bayfield County are found at the mouths of Fish Creek and Whittlesey Creek, respectively, both of which empty into Chequamegon Bay on Lake Superior. Each has shallow sand- and mudflats that are exposed when the seiche (a surface oscillation) is out. Twenty-five species of shorebirds have been seen at Whittlesey Creek Marsh, including regulars like Hudsonian godwits, red knots, and long-billed and short-billed dowitchers. Fish Creek Marsh stretches for a mile or so along Hwy. 2, beginning at the Bayfield County line just west of Ashland. Bird from the highway or by walking along an abandoned road running north of the highway near the west end of the marsh. Whittlesey Creek Marsh is located just north of Fish Creek Marsh but is accessible only by walking the shoreline north from Hwy. 2 or by wading the creek from Hwy. 13. The shoreline route is tough walking due to muck. A canoe would work best.

Long Island, a spit of land jutting into Chequamegon Bay and part of the Apostles Islands National Lakeshore, is well known for its excellent shorebirding. Unfortunately for birders, it is accessible only by boat. One can launch from numerous boat landings along Hwy. 13 south and north of Washburn.

Along Lake Michigan, in **Manitowoc Harbor** about the third week of May, whimbrels and ruddy turnstones arrive in numbers up to 1,000. Take Maritime Drive south from Hwy. 42 to the harbor area, which also is the site of an impoundment where dredge spoils are being disposed— the exposed surfaces attract many birds.

In Oshkosh, on the **Lake Winnebago shore** near the zoo, ruddy turnstones have been observed in spectacular numbers. At the intersection of Menominee Drive and Hickory Street, turn into the Menominee Park area to look for the ruddy turnstones, which usually show up in time for the incredible lakefly hatch. The flies don't bite, but they will stain if you smush them on your clothing, so just leave them alone. They cover everything within a half-mile of the lake during their hatch, and the birds love them. Black turnstones, American avocets, and red-throated loons are a few of the more rare species that have been seen in this area.

Along the border of Iron and Vilas Counties, **Powell Marsh,** a 13,000-acre sedge-leatherleaf bog euphemistically called a marsh, is crisscrossed by Wisconsin DNR dikes that are used to manage water levels. If levels in any of the impoundments are drawn down, good shorebird populations arrive. Check for lesser golden and semipalmated plovers, greater and lesser yellowlegs, and various sandpipers, as well as sora and Virginia and yellow rails. Take Hwy. 51 north out of Minocqua to Powell Road (watch for the Wisconsin DNR sign on the left side), which is just south of Manitowish Waters. Turn left and proceed 4 miles to the overlook parking lot on the left.

In Michigan along the Lake Huron shoreline, **Nayanquing Point State Wildlife Area, Tobico Marsh State Game Area,** and **Fish Point State Wildlife Area** all offer superb shorebirding (see chapter 14 for directions). **Tawas Point** (see chapter 26) can be depended on to provide exceptional shorebird populations.

The **shoreline along Lake Erie** in southeastern Michigan contains many marshes and mudflats that are used extensively as stopover sites for shorebirds, among many other birds. Two areas are particularly well known for shorebirds. The **Erie Marsh Preserve** of the Michigan chapter of The Nature Conservancy is not only excellent in itself, but check the flooded fields along the roads leading to it (**Dean and Bay Creeks**), which are very attractive to shorebirds (see chapter 14 for directions).

Pointe Mouillee State Game Area, a peninsula jutting into Lake Erie, is considered the best shorebird habitat in the state. The Michigan DNR has built a series of dikes to control water levels that make for excellent hiking and biking. Six to 8 miles of dikes, 4 miles of Lake Erie marsh system shoreline, and a 3-mile-long dredge spoils island called The Banana all offer superb shorebird habitat. Call the Audubon Rare Bird Alert at (810) 477-1360 for information on current rare sightings that may be in the area.

Along Lake Superior, the beaches at **Wilderness State Park** are superb for migrating shorebirds, including red knots and black-bellied and piping plovers. Piping plovers nest here as well—please observe the posted limits to prevent any disturbance to nesting birds. From Mackinaw City, go west on Wilderness Park Drive for 11 miles to the entrance to the park. Follow the road for another 8 miles to its end at Waugoshance Point.

Along Lake Michigan, the **Garden Peninsula** attracts migrating birds, which can be seen crossing Lake Michigan from Wisconsin's Door County to land here. Look not just for shorebirds but also for hawks and passerines as well. From the town of Cooks (between Manistique and Escanaba) take U.S. 2 southwest for 3 miles to Michigan 183. Turn south onto Michigan 183 and traverse the 23 miles around the peninsula. Check back roads that lead to the shoreline wherever possible.

28

Spring Hawk Migration

For the human spirit, May offers miracles aplenty in the landscape's transition from five months of winter white into the lush greens of spring, but there's much more. The northern movement of raptors, or birds of prey, began back in March and reaches a crescendo usually in the first two weeks of May. Michigan seems particularly blessed, containing within its borders three exceptional convergence points raptors funnel through before they cross the Great Lakes in their spring journey. The action at all three sites on peak days often exceeds several thousand hawks, which can almost be maddening because of the internal debate that ensues as to which hawk to focus the binoculars on.

Hot Spots

The farthest northern point on the mainland of Michigan is the **Keweenaw Peninsula,** a 45-mile-long rugged strip of forest that juts way out into Lake Superior. Near its tip is **Copper Harbor,** and here on a following wind migrating raptors pass through in great numbers, sometimes reaching the point and turning around, awaiting the right wind to cross Lake Superior to Canada. Three roads can bring you to Copper Harbor, but the 8-mile-long Brockway Mountain Drive offers the perfect ridgeline for hawks to ride the thermals up and over, much as they do at Hawk Ridge in Duluth in the autumn (see chapter 51).

Brockway Mountain Drive is advertised as the highest road between the Alleghenies and the Rockies, and its scenic vistas are arguably the best the Midwest has to offer. There are wonderful rock-walled turnouts for hawk-watching, though sometimes birders have to look down into the valleys below to see a rough-legged hawk passing by. More often though, the hawks are near eye level or just overhead. On a clear day with a south wind pushing the birds ahead of it, the stream of raptors going by is simply spectacular, and the proximity makes observations very personal.

Mother's Day may be the best weekend for Brockway's hawks. More than 100 hawks an hour have been recorded on good days every spring, and usually there are several days that total over 1,000 hawks a day. Broad-winged, sharp-shinned, and rough-legged hawks dominate the counts, but red-tailed hawks, goshawks, and turkey vultures are common also. Rare sightings of peregrine falcons, golden eagles, and merlins

A red-tailed hawk, up close and personal. Photo by Bruce Bacon.

occur, too. All told, 15 species of birds of prey have been observed. The Copper County Audubon Club has volunteer hawk counters up on the ridge every spring.

Even though raptors may begin migrating through in April, it's wise to wait until early May to drive up to observe the migration because Brockway Mountain Drive is not plowed in the winter. If you're unaware, the Keweenaw Peninsula gets more snow than anywhere in the Midwest, averaging 270 inches every winter. Often the road is closed even in early May, but check with the locals to be sure. Be prepared to walk the road to the top if the road is truly impassable. Remember warm boots and winter clothes.

From Eagle Harbor take Michigan 26 north for 3 miles to the right turn up Brockway Mountain Drive. Continue 5 miles to the top lookout—a circle drive to your right allows you to park at the face of the hill up which the hawks ascend.

Please note: The fall migration is slim to none given how the funneling of birds heading south works out—the Keweenaw just isn't on that autumn highway.

Paradise Found might be the appropriate birding title for **Whitefish Point,** because the last town you go through to reach the point is Paradise, Michigan. If the spring migrators haven't leapt over Lake Superior at the Keweenaw Peninsula, they almost invariably drift east to the next large peninsula jutting into the lake, and that's Whitefish Point. The

Whitefish Point

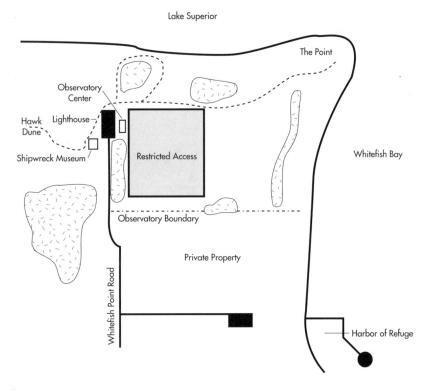

Whitefish Point Bird Observatory was established here in 1978 to count, monitor, and band birds, and to educate visiting birders as well.

The actual point is the prime area to watch migrating waterfowl, but just a few hundred yards to the west is Hawk Dune, an observation platform built high up on the dunes to make the hawk-watching all the more remarkable. The crossing to Canada is only 17 miles from here, but only eagles and falcons seem willing to tackle the journey. Most raptors continue to follow the shoreline while looking for an easier crossing.

Broad-winged hawks are the most abundant buteo, soaring by in large kettles, sometimes with over 100 birds circling together. Red-tailed and rough-legged hawks push through in good numbers also, nearly all using the thermals along the shoreline to effortlessly sail by. Sharp-shinned hawks use another approach, usually flying low and scattering over the entire area of the point. Fifteen to twenty thousand raptors will pass by here in any given spring. Sharpies number as high as 14,000 and broad-wings may number around 6,000. A record 35 peregrine falcons were recorded here in the spring of 1992.

The raptor migration begins in mid-March, but birding the point in subzero temperatures with the usual numbing wind isn't recommended. By late April the migration is peaking, and the first big waves of raptors—3,500 sharp-shinneds on one day, for instance—start coming through.

As a side note, but not one of insignificance, early May usually serves up thousands of common loons (9,284 were counted in the spring of 1994), as well as several hundred red-throated loons. And Whitefish Point is very well known for its northern owl migration. Eight species of owl have been caught here, including a record 163 boreal owls in the spring of 1988, though saw-whet owls are usually most common. Check for a current schedule of programs run by Whitefish Point Bird Observatory biologists. Morning programs for the public often show off a few of the owls caught on the previous evening. Bird at dusk when the owls leave their roosts for the best viewing opportunities.

To reach Whitefish Point, take Michigan 123 62 miles north from the Mackinac Bridge to Paradise. Continue north on Whitefish Point Road for 11 miles to the headquarters building of the Whitefish Point Bird Observatory. If visiting the point in early May, make advance hotel reservations, because accommodations are usually in short supply then.

The **Straits of Mackinac** are commonly visited by tourists interested in crossing the extraordinary Mackinac Bridge or by those wanting to be ferried over to Mackinac Island. Most have little idea that the straits are a natural funnel for hawks in May. Although it would be ideal to have an observation platform right on the Mackinac Bridge, a good vantage point for watching hawks is along Wilderness Park Drive (County Road 81), to the west of Mackinac City. Park your car about 2 miles west of the city, where Central Avenue turns left to become Wilderness Park Drive, near an old field called locally Pierce Field. Hawks often land in the old trees left standing in the field. Or observe anyplace convenient to you along the roadside. Wilderness Park Drive continues for another 9 miles until it reaches the entrance to Wilderness State Park. See chapters 27 and 31 for further information on Wilderness State Park.

29

May Shorttakes

Bison Calving

The only semiwild herd of buffalo in the Upper Midwest lives in **Blue Mounds State Park,** Minnesota, the result of three buffalo acquired in 1961 from the Fort Niobrara National Wildlife Refuge in Nebraska. Today, out of the 45 adults in the herd, 20 breeding females calve in May following a $9^1/_2$-month gestation. At birth the calves weigh between 30 and 70 pounds and are clothed in a bright tawny to buff-colored pelage, which they retain until they are three months of age, gradually replacing the coat with the dark brown of an adult. The cows and calves are inseparable for the first two weeks; the cows are highly protective of their young during this period. Many of the calves are sold at auction in October to keep the herd at carrying capacity—monies earned go to the improved management of the herd (see chapter 33 for directions).

Morels

Morels are the caviar of the mushroom world, sending mushroom hunters into great agitation when they begin to appear. No self-respecting morel gatherers will tell you where they pick their delicacies, but there is a Morel Mushroom Festival in mid-May in **Muscoda,** Iowa County, Wisconsin, and one in **Boyne City,** Charlevoix County, Michigan.

Woodcock Flights

The aerial courting display of the male woodcock takes place at dusk and at dawn throughout most of May. The male call is a nasal *peent,* which he makes from the ground in an open area while bobbing his head and strutting around. Then he flies up in a spiraling ascent, twittering musically all the way, stalls about 200 feet in the air, and then, calling with liquid chirps, drops like a zigzagging leaf right back onto the spot he started from. He starts *peent*ing again almost immediately if a female hasn't been drawn in by his performance, and thus it goes. **Seney National Wildlife Refuge** in Michigan is considered by some to be the best woodcock habitat in the United States (see chapter 37 for directions).

This bison calf and mother are part of Blue Mound State Park's herd of semiwild bison, the only such herd left in the region. Photo by Carol Christensen.

Western Grebes

The courtship displays of the western grebe are a magnificent sight to behold, particularly the "rushing" display, in which the pair moves rapidly across the water side by side, moving their feet so quickly that their erect bodies are completely out of the water, their necks arched and their bills pointed skyward. Western grebes nest in colonies of hundreds of pairs on some lakes. In Minnesota, **Lake Osakis** in Todd County, **Agassiz NWR**, **Swan Lake** in Nicollet County, **Big Stone NWR**, and **Lake Traverse** in Traverse County along the Minnesota and South Dakota border have breeding colonies.

30

A Closer Look: Spring Ephemerals

Most woodland wildflowers run a race in spring to blossom before the trees leaf out above them and take away the sunshine. The overarching tree canopy can be like a giant curtain pulled over the sky, creating a shaded understory dimpled with flecks of sunshine here and there but without enough sunlight for many plants to carry on energy-intensive flowering and fruiting. Forest flowers have evolved adaptations to contend with the fleeting period of full sunshine that the trees permit them. The adaptation most used is simply to move fast and strike when the sun is hot. Some wildflowers, like trailing arbutus, don't even wait until all the snow is gone, apparently preferring to risk blooming in the cold rather than to languish in the shade of an early spring.

"Ephemeral" aptly describes the life cycle of most of our woodland flowers. Leaves and flowers burst rapidly, remain only a few days to a few weeks until they're pollinated, then on come the fruits, the leaves die back, and where several thousand spring beauties or trout lilies had gloried in May, by June little evidence of their existence may remain. The speed at which they come and go usually means that by mid-June, even in the North Woods, about three-fourths of all flowering plants have completed their blooming. Marsh plants and roadside wildflowers take the stage as summer comes on. If you take a walk in the woods in July, you may wonder at the nearly complete absence of flowers, thinking that maybe some ecological catastrophe occurred, but the evil force is merely shade. The May flower-watcher is the one who catches the spectacle.

Many flower lovers want to know when to look for certain species. The science of phenology, the study of the march of observable biological events, can help predict dates of things, such as when the first robin returns or when blackberries come ripe. Though actual dates in any given year will vary according to a number of factors, such as amount of moisture and variances in temperature, you still can predict with relative accuracy when the major floral display in your area will happen. Keep a diary over the years, and you may be surprised at the regularity of biological events where you live.

Another way to predict when a flower will bloom in your area is to use Hopkins' Law. It says that the march of biological events varies at the rate of 1 day for each 15 minutes of latitude, 1.25 days for each degree of longitude, and 1 day for each 100 feet of elevation, being later northward, eastward, and upward. To put this into useful terms, recall that there are 60 minutes in every degree of latitude, and one degree of latitude equals about 69 miles. So spring can be said on level ground to move north at the rate of about 17 miles per day (69 divided by 4).

Here's an example of how to use the formula. I live 250 miles north of the Illinois border. So if a trillium blooms on April 20 directly south of me on the border, it should bloom in my area in southern Iron County about 15 days later (250 divided by 17). That's not quite accurate though, because the elevation difference between where I live in the northern highlands (about 1,600 feet above sea level) and the farm country along the border (about 1,000 feet above sea level) adds an additional six days. So I can look for trilliums or robins or bloodroot about 21 days after they appear over the Illinois border. For my area then, spring moves north at about 12 miles a day.

Although we don't think there is much elevation in the Upper Midwest, in Wisconsin the difference of nearly 1,400 feet from the state's highest point to the lowest point makes 14 days of phenological difference.

The climatological effects of the Great Lakes throw a wrench into the accuracy of this formula, as well. Spring comes much slower along the big lakes because the cool water temperatures moderate the land temperatures. So if you live along the Great Lakes, spring probably crawls your way at about 9 miles per day.

Hopkins' Law applies only to the spring. Autumn-flowering species may bloom first in the north due to more rapidly declining light and colder temperatures.

Microclimates also influence when a flower may come into bloom. For instance, a shaded north slope warms up much more slowly than does a sunny southern slope, so flowers on opposite sides of the same hill may vary by many days in their blossoming times. Likewise, prairies adjacent to forests warm up much more quickly than do the woodlands because of their complete exposure to the sun and wind—the ground may thaw three weeks earlier in the prairie adjoining a woodland.

Thus, it's beyond the capability of any book to give exact blooming dates for flowers in any area. Half the pleasure in wildflower-watching is the process of personal discovery anyway. The spring woodland wildflower explosion occurs within a brief window of time and then dies back to await another cycle of seasons until the next miracle of spring. Don't miss it.

June

Notes

31

Orchids

Orchids are usually placed upon the highest aesthetic pedestal of all our northern flora. Their remarkable shapes, startling color combinations, and appealing fragrances excite more flower lovers than any other plant family. Exotic names like ram's head lady's-slipper, dragon's mouth, fairyslipper, and rattlesnake plantain further add to the mystique.

Orchids richly deserve their exalted reputation because of their unique botanical characteristics. All orchids have three petals, three sepals, and leaves with parallel veins, but what distinguishes them is their "lip." The lip is a modified petal that has evolved into unusual structures such as the pouchlike moccasin of the lady's-slippers or the fringed landing pad of some of the rein orchids. Usually the lip is placed below the other petals, but in the case of the grass pink, the lip is above.

Orchids often produce millions of dustlike seeds that are nearly microscopic in size and can float for astonishing distances—up to 1,200 miles! Germination is another matter, however; most orchids require very specific habitat conditions and the presence of specialized fungi for their roots to team up with symbiotically. It's little wonder that many species are rare. Blossoms may take another dozen or more years to appear after initial germination. The showy orchid, Minnesota's state flower, rarely blossoms until it's 20 years old. Once established, though, orchids, like the showy, may live 100 years or more.

Propagation from seed is exceedingly slow and unreliable, and commercial growers have had little success in creating nursery stock for sale. Thus, be very cautious in purchasing orchids—many are dug from the wild and then labeled as nursery-propagated. Even if they are nursery-grown, most orchids have very specific habitat requirements that most gardeners find very difficult to duplicate. It is to be hoped that the futility of transplanting will dissuade future raiding of our wild orchid populations. Orchids are most beautiful when found as an unanticipated gift in a natural habitat.

Minnesota supports 43 native orchid species, Wisconsin 42 species, and Michigan 58 species. Although many orchids may be found on a variety of sites, others are highly specific in their habitat requirements. The western prairie region has only 11 orchid species, and so little of the native grassland habitat remains that many of the prairie species are quite rare.

Some generalized habitats in which to search for orchids are the sandy pine woods in central and northern counties of all three states that are home to the pink lady's-slipper *(Cypripedium acaule).* June is their flowering time and, rather remarkably, they can be found not only in dry sandy uplands under pines but also in sphagnum swamps. The common elements of the two habitats are acidic soil, shade, and lack of nutrients.

Look for yellow lady's-slippers *(Cypripedium calceolus* or *pubescens)* in richer hardwood forests, where they may be found growing in large multiflowered clumps.

Bogs are home to the grass pink *(Calopogon tuberosus),* the rose pogonia *(Pogonia ophioglossoides),* and the dragon's mouth *(Arethusa bulbosa)* in June.

Prairies serve up the diminutive small white lady's-slipper *(Cypripedium candidum)* in late May to June, prairie white-fringed orchids *(Platanthera leucophaea)* in late June through July, and common ladies' tresses *(Spiranthes cernua)* from mid-August through September.

Though orchids have the reputation of living only in undisturbed forests and not coping well with change, there are some species that colonize recently disturbed habitats. Certain members of the coralroots, twayblades, and ladies' tresses help to pioneer new sites. In fact, orchids probably occur in every county in the three states, and in every habitat type. Still, the orchids as a whole remain difficult to find, continue to decline in number due to habitat loss and collection, and are worthy of celebration and protection once they are discovered.

Hot Spots

In Wisconsin, the **Ridges Sanctuary,** a National Natural Landmark along Lake Michigan in Door County, has preserved nearly 1,200 acres of land that supports over 25 species of native orchids. The ridges, for which the sanctuary is named, are a series of 17 ancient Lake Michigan shorelines that are now parallel crescent-shaped embankments separated by marsh swales. Many hiking trails follow the crests of these ancient sand dunes, and naturalist-led tours are available twice daily during the summer. Large numbers and a high diversity of orchids grow here in part because of the boreal-like climate that is created by the cold moist winds off Lake Michigan. Of the more than 500 plants known to grow in the Ridges Sanctuary, at least 13 are endangered or threatened plant species.

Ridges Sanctuary is located near Bailey's Harbor on the northeastern shore of Lake Michigan. Take Hwy. 57 north out of Sturgeon Bay, and just north of the town of Bailey's Harbor turn right on County Road Q. The sanctuary entrance and parking lot are very soon on your right.

Chiwaukee Prairie (see chapter 33 for directions), a Nature Conservancy preserve in southeastern Kenosha County near the Illinois border,

Ridges Sanctuary

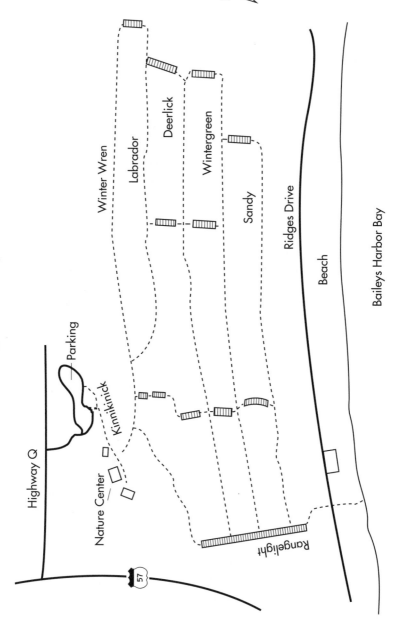

Highway Q

Parking

Nature Center

Kinnikinick

57

Rangelight

Winter Wren

Labrador

Deerlick

Wintergreen

Sandy

Ridges Drive

Beach

Baileys Harbor Bay

N

hosts one of the largest populations of rare prairie white-fringed orchids in the world (though they usually don't bloom until early July). Chiwaukee is home to more than 400 native plant species and is an old beach ridge complex with swales between the ridges similar in some ways to the Ridges Sanctuary.

For pink lady's-slippers, the **Trout Lake Nature Trail** in the **Northern Highlands State Forest** usually produces several hundred along the trail and near a boardwalk leading over a bog. From Boulder Junction, take Hwy. M south for 3 miles to the Wisconsin DNR nature trail sign on the right. Take the trail to the left to reach the lady's-slippers within a few minutes. Look both in the upland sands under the jack pines and in the bog.

In Michigan, **Isle Royale National Park** hosts 34 varieties of orchids (see chapter 37 for directions), providing a good excuse, if one could possibly be needed, to visit this wilderness island preserve.

Estivant Pines Nature Sanctuary is best known for its old-growth pines, but it also supports 13 species of orchids and 23 species of ferns. Take either Michigan 28 or U.S. 41 to Copper Harbor, then briefly follow U.S. 41 for 0.2 mile toward Fort Wilkins State Park. Turn right (south) toward Lake Manganese and follow the signs to the sanctuary. After 2.3 miles turn right onto Burma Road and go 0.6 mile to the parking entrance.

Wilderness State Park has a large population of wild orchids, including rose pogonia, grass pink, calypso orchid, showy ram's head, dragon's mouth, and various lady's-slippers within the 8,035-acre park. The Sturgeon Bay Trail south of Big Sucker Creek is particularly good for stemless (pink) lady's-slippers and grass pinks, ram's head can be found very close to the contact station, and green adder's-mouth may be found along the Red Pine Trail. From Mackinaw City, go west on Wilderness Park Drive for 11 miles to the entrance to the park. Follow the road for another 8 miles to its end at Waugoshance Point.

In Minnesota, more than 2 million orchids spring up every June along a 75-mile-long "wildflower corridor" **from Greenbush to Baudette along Highway 11.** Called the **Borderland Trail,** the highway ditches support over 800,000 showy lady's-slippers, the Minnesota state flower. Although we like to think of orchids as occupying only the most sensitive and undisturbed habitats, here it is possible to "orchid-watch" at 55 mph along a state highway. The highway doesn't offer continuous orchids along its entire length, though. Try just west of Williams for thousands of showies and yellow lady's-slippers in the swale between the railroad grade and the road on the north side of the highway. Other hotspots (look for the road signs reading Wildflower Route) are west of Baudette, west of Warroad, west of Roseau, and east of Greenbush. Self-guiding wildflower maps may be picked up from the area information centers or by calling the Borderland Trail Area Chamber at (800) 351-3474. Showies bloom from mid-June to early July, and because local conditions can cause variation in blooming periods, call ahead to make sure the corridor is at its peak.

The woodland trails of **Itasca State Park** are a good place to find striped coralroot *(Corallorhiza striata),* a saprophytic (lives off decaying organic matter) orchid that looks positively "nonorchidy" at first glance but that has its own unique appeal.

Small white lady's-slippers bloom from late May to mid-June in what's left of Minnesota's once vast prairie

Lady's-slipper orchids can be seen in the tens of thousands along Minnesota's Borderland Trail. Photo by Carol Christensen.

region, now only 1 percent of its original size and still decreasing. Once sold by the wagon load to markets in Minneapolis, Milwaukee, and Chicago for pennies a bouquet, the small white lady's-slipper is listed as a species of special concern in Minnesota (it's listed as threatened in Wisconsin, where only about 30 populations still survive). Still, Minnesota is the only place where one can still stand in a native moist prairie and see thousands of small white lady's-slippers in one sweep. **Coteau des Prairies** ("highland of the prairies") contains southwestern Minnesota's largest population of small white lady's-slippers. A Minnesota Scientific and Natural Area, the 327-acre remnant prairie stands 200 feet above the flat landscape in a highlands that looks like a range of blue mountains from a distance.

To reach **Prairie Coteau State Natural Area,** take Hwy. 23 northeast from Pipestone for 10 miles to the parking lot on the left (north). At the base of the steep hillside next to the parking lot lies a little sedge meadow—look here for a glimpse of how the small white lady's-slipper might have appeared in the days of intact native prairies.

Small white lady's-slippers may also be seen at **Western Prairie North,** a 476-acre state natural area leased from The Nature Conservancy and compressed between agricultural lands on all sides. To reach the site from

Lawndale in Wilkin County, take Hwy. 52 for 2.5 miles north to County Road 188. Turn right and go 1 mile to a large wooden Minnesota DNR sign reading Richard M. and Mathilde Rice Elliot SNA. No trails exist here, so simply wander out carefully into the grasslands to explore for orchids and other prairie flowers.

Western prairie fringed-orchid *(Platanthera praeclara)* is listed as endangered in Minnesota yet may still be seen in substantial numbers at the end of June and into the first week of July in several northwestern prairie preserves. Considered equally as large and spectacular as the showy lady's-slipper, the prairie fringed-orchid is also Minnesota's most threatened orchid. To find the prairie fringed-orchid, try the **Pembina Trail Landscape Preserve,** an integrated network of protected prairie lands located near the edge of North America's original tall-grass prairie. Within the preserve are **Pembina Trail Preserve State Natural Area, Crookston Prairie State Natural Area,** and **Foxboro Prairie State Natural Area,** all areas where the prairie fringed-orchid has been seen (see chapter 16 for directions).

32

Loon Chicks Hatching

In mid-June loon chicks are first seen on northern lakes, often hitching a ride on the backs of their parents. The chicks, usually two to a clutch, hatch one or two days apart, and then the chicks are escorted by their parents to their "nursery," usually a secluded cove where the water is shallow and calm and where small fish are numerous. Within a few days the chicks can eat small minnows fed to them by the parents. The youngsters can dive, but they tend to pop right back to the surface because they're more feathers than body at this point. Within 10 to 13 days, though, they are able to sustain a dive, though their fish-catching success rate is dismal. One study showed that even at three weeks of age, a loon chick only captures fish in 3 percent of its attempts.

So the adult loons play a very important role in the survival of their chicks. One of their tasks is to haul the young chicks around on their backs. In their first week of life, the chicks spend over half their time being carried.

For wildlife observers, witnessing the loon taxi service can be a memorable experience, but the adult loons have more in mind than a pleasant piggyback ride for their chicks. The youngsters may suffer mortality from cold and fatigue or may be eaten by predators like snapping turtles, big fish like musky and pike, and eagles or hawks. Among other waterfowl, only grebes provide this ferrying of young as a common practice.

The chicks have big appetites, requiring eight times the energy of the adults, says one study, and another study with yellow-billed loons showed the adults feeding the chicks 73 times in a single day. The chicks beg for food by pecking at the base of the adult's bill.

This high level of parental care is the secret to catching and banding loons. One of the adult pair will nearly always remain with the flightless chick(s), regardless of the perceived danger of a situation, and banders count on this fidelity. By slowly motoring up to a family at night, playing a tape of a wailing loon, and holding a searchlight on the adult, researchers can get close enough to the loons to capture them by net. Since 1993 this method has been used to band adults and chicks, and a great deal of information is currently being confirmed about loons that was only assumed before.

Adult loons may also accept orphan chicks. And they will perform distraction displays to draw away intruders, much like a killdeer does with its broken-wing act. If the eggs fail to hatch or are eaten by a predator, loons

Common loon populations are currently stable, but increasing shoreline development threatens their success. Photo by Carol Christensen.

very often renest, hatching their young in mid- to late July rather than mid-June. Juvenile loons with this late a start have been known to get caught in rapidly forming ice in November.

The loon-family support system does have some limitations. The chicks may engage in sibling rivalry to the extreme. Observations of a dominant chick driving its sibling away from the parents and precipitating its starvation have been made. And the chicks engage in pecking fights early on to establish dominance. The adults offer food to the first chick that appears, so the dominant chick in a poor fish year will survive, while the subordinate one will not. *Siblicide* is the word for it, and although it is uncommon, changes in food availability due to acidification of lakes or overharvest of fish may increase the importance of the rivalry among loon chicks.

Loons prefer islands or secluded bays for their nests, usually returning to the same site year after year. Although it's usually understood that loons mate for life, the female appears to mate more with the lake than with a male. If another male forces her mate from the lake, she will usually mate with the new male.

The nest must be built on the water's edge because of how far back the loon's feet are set on its body—a loon can't walk on land and literally has to push itself forward on its chest.

Usually two eggs are laid in mid-May, one day apart. The parents share the task of incubating the eggs for about one month. Many predators are desirous of the eggs—raccoons, eagles, gulls, ravens, and crows, among others, have been observed eating loon eggs.

Loons are counted in Wisconsin and Minnesota every five years by volunteers, or "loon rangers," through the Loon Watch program. Loon Watch is an education and research program coordinated by the Sigurd Olson Environmental Institute of Northland College, which works to protect and preserve common loons and their aquatic habitats in the Upper Midwest. Call the institute if you wish to participate.

If you observe a nest or chicks, please stay as far away as possible to reduce disturbance to the loon family. And in particular, help educate boaters to the need for a no-wake zone on lakes with incubating loons. Waves can easily wash eggs out of the water-level nests.

Hot Spots

In Minnesota the loon population was estimated at 12,039 in a 1989 count. The 1994 count estimated the summer population at 12,048, a remarkably similar number to 1989, indicating a stable loon population at the present.

The **Boundary Waters Canoe Area Wilderness** (BWCAW) is the finest wilderness in the Midwest and the only lakeland wilderness in the United States. The 1.25-million-acre wilderness extends for 200 miles along the Minnesota-Canada border and includes nearly 1,200 miles of canoe trails. Better yet, if that's possible, the BWCAW is bordered on the north by the million-acre Quetico Provincial Park, on the west by Voyageurs National Park, and on the south by 2 million more acres within the Superior National Forest. In the BWCAW alone it would be possible to spend a lifetime of canoeing and not see it all.

Several thousand lakes studded with islands pockmark the rocky boreal landscape, and hundreds of thousands of canoeists a year come here to lose themselves, and to gain themselves. Entry permits are required from May 1 to September 30, and quotas have been established to protect the sense of experiencing true wilderness. Eighty-six access points to the BWCAW exist. Detailed topographical maps and a compass are absolutely essential for paddling here.

Need it be said that no finer area in this country can be explored to view and hear common loons? Outfitters and guides galore make initial adventures here easier to consider if the size and scope of the area are daunting. The BWCAW is located north of Duluth in the Superior National Forest, and the town of Ely is the stepping-off point for many visitors. To reach Ely, take Hwy. 61 north out of Duluth through Silver Bay to Hwy. 1. Follow Hwy. 1 into Ely.

More than 30 lakes dominate **Voyageurs National Park.** Many of the lakes are enormous—Rainy Lake covers 350 square miles, for instance. Although the park totals 218,000 acres, over one-third (84,000 acres) of that is water. Islands dot the waterscape, and bogs and wetlands along the miles and miles of lakeshore provide excellent nesting habitat for loons (and great blue herons—10 percent of Minnesota's great blues nest here). The only real way to experience this park is by boat, either motorized or canoe. Even most of the hiking trailheads are accessible only by water. The westernmost edge of Voyageurs is located 12 miles east of International Falls on Hwy. 11. Otherwise, to reach the main visitor center, approach the park from Hwy. 53 north. Turn right (north) on County Road 122 and take it to the visitor center. County Road 23 from Orr leads to Crane Lake at the park's east end.

In Michigan, the last loon survey took place in 1991, and 493 breeding pairs were found. The total population, including nonbreeders, is estimated to be around 1,800. There were 269 breeding pairs in the northern Lower Peninsula, 217 in the Upper Peninsula, and 7 in southern Michigan.

The **Sylvania Wilderness and Recreation Area** occupies a total of nearly 24,000 acres of lakes and old-growth forest in the **Ottawa National Forest** and is managed with special camping and fishing requirements in order to maintain the pristine nature of the area. Motorboats are permitted on only two lakes, and no wheeled vehicles may be used in the interior. Sylvania is perhaps Michigan's best imitation of the Boundary Waters Canoe Area, though certainly a miniature version. Sylvania lies on the continental divide between the Lake Superior and Mississippi watershed drainages, a geographical setting that greatly contributes to the extraordinarily clear water of the 36 named lakes in this area (18,327 acres are designated as wilderness). My family and I have camped here many times over the years and invariably have listened at night to some of the most holy loon serenades imaginable.

The Sylvania tract is located just southwest of Watersmeet in Gogebic County. About 3 miles west on U.S. 2 from Watersmeet, turn left (south) on County 535 to reach the check-in building.

In Wisconsin, the 1990 Wisconsin Loon Survey estimated the common loon population to be 2,790, plus or minus 235. The 1985 survey's estimate was 2,829, plus or minus 248, so it's safe to say Wisconsin has between 2,600 and 3,000 loons, and the loon population appears stable.

The **Turtle-Flambeau Flowage** has 22 pairs of loons nesting on it. See chapter 37 for directions.

The **Northern Highlands State Forest** in Vilas, Oneida, and southern Iron Counties has the highest numbers of loons anywhere in the state. Vilas has 54 lakes with nesting loons, according to a 1992 count, and Oneida has 41 lakes with nests. Contact the Wisconsin DNR area headquarters in Woodruff for information on lakes where loons can be observed without significant disturbance.

33

Prairie Blooming

On a prairie in June, you can see blooming showy lady's-slipper, small white lady's-slipper, lead plant, puccoon, prairie rose, prairie-smoke, golden alexander, spiderwort, alumroot, pale beardtongue, prairie phlox, larkspur, blanketflower, and maybe most remarkable of all, prickly pear cactus, though the list goes on and on.

One seldom thinks of cacti as being present in the Upper Midwest, but two species of prickly pear cactus are residents of the dry prairies of Wisconsin, Michigan, and Minnesota. They grow where little else will, in the sandiest and thinnest soils, and usually on slopes or bluffs that help maintain the extreme dryness. The June blossoms have 8 to 12 showy yellow petals that are often tinged with red at their bases. These beautiful flowers emerge from around the edges of the cactus pads, which project needlelike spines that can pierce a thin leather shoe. Watch out also for the short, fine multibarbed hairs that grow on the pads—these will work their way into your skin in no time.

Prickly pears tend to grow in small colonies about a square yard in size. The pads, if broken off by an animal, will produce roots of their own, reproducing the plant wherever the pad roots.

The September-ripening fruits are rather remarkable too. They are berries but appear like a fleshy, many-seeded purple plum. And they taste good—if they were more common, one could make a fine jelly from them.

Cactus rustlers are threatening the very existence of most of North America's 268 native cacti, and though we think of this as a problem in America's Southwest, it is a concern in the Upper Midwest as well, because there are so few sites containing cacti. If you visit a site with cacti, be sure not to disturb these plants in any way.

But where should you go to see the finest prairie wildflowers? Once I spent a week in mid-June visiting every prairie site I could find in Minnesota, and I learned that each site has its own personality, which is expressed at different times and in different ways. Prairie soils vary from dry to moist to wet, and many prairie wildflowers are very choosy about specific moisture levels. Further, some require certain soil types, like sands or limestone or organic peats. So generalizations about what wildflowers you will find on "prairies" is tough, because prairies vary so much in character. Because any prairie is spectacular from May through September, you simply can't lose

Cactus in the Upper Midwest? Yes! The prickly pear cactus can be found in numerous dry prairie sites. Photo by WDNR.

going at any time in the flowering year. My advice is simple—go when you can, and as many times as you can, because the prairies keep changing in a wondrously diverse way. I can tell you of the prairies I found most beautiful to start you on your way to discovering other prairies throughout the growing year.

Hot Spots

If you can only visit one prairie, go to **Blue Mounds State Park** in far southwestern Minnesota. The combination of ridge-top scenery; the only buffalo herd left in the Upper Midwest; substantial numbers of prairie-nesting birds like dickcissels, western meadowlarks, and bobolinks; tall prairie grasses; a fine network of trails; and the abundant prairie flowers make this site a must-see. Approximately 1,500 acres of prairie are contained within the park, most of which sits atop a ridge outcropping of Sioux quartzite. The panoramic view was described by Philo Hawses in 1867: "I could see all the way to Iowa, with the prairies green and not a tree to be seen except for those along the Rock River."

Prickly pear cactus grows in the rock outcrops along the ridges—I found them in rocky crevices on the Upper Mound Trail. For overall diversity of grasses and flowers, hike the Upper Cliffline Trail and the Upper Mound Trail. The Lower Mound Trail takes you right along the fence line of the buffalo herd, which numbered 46 adults and 19 calves in 1995. They're semiwild, meaning that even though they are fenced in, the enclosure is many hundreds of acres in size and the bison roam freely within this area.

Blue Mounds is located 6 miles north of I-90 and Luverne. Take Hwy. 75 north from Luverne and turn right (east) on County Road 20, which leads right into the park. An interpretive center with limited hours is located on the southern edge of the park. Take County Road 8 east off of Hwy. 75 to reach it.

The **Big Stone National Wildlife Refuge** has some remnant tall-grass prairie, and prickly pear cactus may be seen in bloom in early June. Try the Rock Outcrop Hiking Trail and stop 11 of the auto tour. From Ortonville, take Hwy. 75 south 2 miles to a railroad crossing where a small sign directs you to turn right onto the refuge auto-tour route.

The Crookston area offers some of the most extensive prairies left in Minnesota (see page 68). The **Pankratz Memorial Prairie,** a Minnesota Nature Conservancy parcel, contains 320 acres of varying prairie landscape. The **Tympanuchus WMA** has 840 acres of dry to moist prairie with a brush-aspen component. Walk the ridges for the dry prairie wildflowers, which can be quite different from those just 50 yards away but downslope. To find Tympanuchus, continue south on County Road 46 from Pankratz Memorial Prairie and turn left (east) onto County Road 45. Go 1 mile to reach the northwestern edge of the unit—a small sign will identify the site. (See also chapter 16 for additional directions.)

The **Dugdale** (960 acres), **Burnham Creek** (400 acres), and **Chicog** (1,624 acres) **WMAs** are also highly recommended. To reach Dugdale, take U.S. 2 east from Crookston to Hwy. 32, and turn right (south). Go 6 miles to the parking lot entrance.

To reach Burnham Creek, continue on Hwy. 32 south from Dugdale about 1.5 miles to the first gravel road, and turn right (west). Go about 3 miles to an intersection and turn right (north). Go about 0.3 mile and park on the gravel road.

Chicog may be reached from Minnesota 102 by turning south on County Road 44 at Melvin.

These are large areas with few signed trails, so the exploring is left open to you.

Prairie Coteau Scientific and Natural Area offers what some consider the best stand of small white lady's-slippers in the state on the wet prairie near the parking lot. The higher elevations are dry prairie with puccoon, prairie-smoke, and other species growing on dry sites. Prairie Coteau is located 10 miles northeast of Pipestone on Minnesota 23.

In Wisconsin, **Chiwaukee Prairie** in Kenosha County is 580 acres of the richest known prairie in Wisconsin, of which 226 acres are protected. More than 400 plant species have been identified here, and at least 76 bird species. The site is an ancient beach of Lake Michigan, which was underwater after the retreat of the last Wisconsin glacier some

Blue Mounds State Park

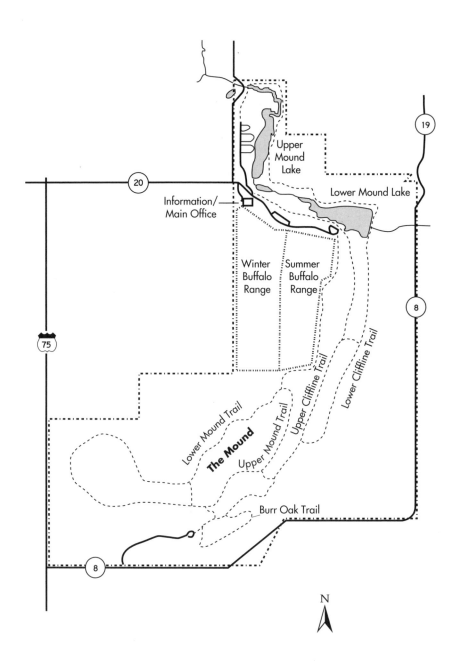

10,000 years ago. Lake Michigan was then 60 feet higher than today, and through a succession of lake-level drainages and drops, Chiwaukee Prairie was uncovered and became a beach and dune site. With the successive retreats by Lake Michigan, the site dried and became what is now called a *beach ridge complex*. The rippled topography and high water table produce a potpourri of microhabitats that support patches of quite variable wildflowers and grasses.

Set in the midst of farms and suburbs, Chiwaukee could easily be missed by the average traveler, yet no comparable site is left in the Upper Midwest that is as rich. Today it is protected as a National Natural Landmark and a State Natural Area. Look for shootingstars, 25 per square yard, in mid-May to early June and for prairie white fringed-orchids in mid-July. I visited in September, and fringed gentians were common in many areas of the prairie.

Chiwaukee is located just 0.25 mile off Lake Michigan in the most southeastern corner of Wisconsin 4 miles south of Kenosha. Take the Hwy. 165 (also called Hwy. 50) exit off I-94; go east on Hwy. 165 for 6.25 miles to Hwy. 32 (Sheridan Road), then south to Tobin Road (116th Street), then east on Tobin Road for 1 mile. Turn right on First Court (Marina Road) and travel 5 blocks to 121st Street and turn right. Go 1 block to 2nd Avenue and turn right onto 119th Street, which takes you to the The Nature Conservancy sign.

The 1,410-acre **Quincy Bluff and Wetlands Preserve** was acquired in 1990 by the Wisconsin Nature Conservancy, but in 1992 the Wisconsin DNR announced plans to purchase additional lands to total 10,500 acres, an expanse that would be Wisconsin's largest designated natural area. Here, 2 miles of sandstone ridges sandwich wetlands bordered by barrens and forest. The project area supports nine types of plant communities, and prickly pear cactus and the Karner blue butterfly can be found here. To reach Quincy Bluff, take Hwy. 13 north from Wisconsin Dells for 14.4 miles to County Road H. Turn left (west) and go 2.4 miles through White Creek. Turn right (north) onto 16th Avenue, then left onto Evergreen Avenue, and then right onto 16th Drive. Continue 2.2 miles to the Quincy parking lot on the right side of the road.

Spring Green Preserve, another Nature Conservancy parcel, is the largest tract of Wisconsin Desert, or dry prairie, in the state. Prickly pear cactus abounds here, providing food for the endangered ornate box turtle, Wisconsin's only terrestrial turtle. The site is situated on the ancient terraces of the Wisconsin River, which now lies 3 miles away. From Spring Green at the intersection of Hwys. 14 and 23, take Hwy. 23 north 0.5 mile to Jones Road. Turn right (east) and go 0.75 mile to a dirt access road just past a driveway. The unmarked dirt road leads to a parking lot.

In Michigan, **Algonac State Park** has 62 acres of original prairie in four scattered plots. Three hundred species of plants have been found here. The park's entrance is off Michigan 29 2 miles north of the town of Algonac.

Allegan State Game Area, better known for its fall migrating geese, is the best place in Michigan to see prickly pear cactus, but it's also considered the best place in late July to early August to see blazingstar and is good for wild lupine around Memorial Day and into June. Cruise Hwy. 89 starting at the Kalamazoo River bridge to look for lupines. From Allegan, take Michigan 89/Michigan 40 northwest and turn left (west) on Monroe Road, which becomes 118th Avenue after 5 miles. Continue west for another 1.5 miles to the area office.

Newaygo Prairie Nature Sanctuary, a Michigan Nature Association parcel of 110 acres, is divided by a road into two sections. Thirty acres of the southern 80-acre section are outstanding dry prairie, with prickly pear cactus, prairie-smoke, and other typical dry-prairie flowers. This prairie preserve is located just northeast of Newaygo. Take Croton Drive about 2.5 miles east out of Newaygo and turn left (north) on Poplar Avenue. The sanctuary will be about 0.5 mile on your right.

34

Kirtland's Warblers

It may be hard to believe, but Smokey Bear, after all his good work and heavy press, has a downside. Preventing forest fires has saved untold forest acres from destruction, but as the old saying goes, one person's loss is another person's gain. In this case, however, we're speaking not about humans but about birds. One of North America's rarest songbirds, the Kirtland's warbler, depends on regular forest fires for its survival, and Smokey's effectiveness has played a significant role in the Kirtland's decline. These blue-gray and yellow warblers, just a bit smaller than a house sparrow, rely on Christmas tree–sized, 8- to 20-year-old jack pines with low-hanging branches that touch the ground for their nesting habitat. Since jack pines will only release their seeds from their tightly sealed cones when a temperature of 116°F is reached, this usually means a forest fire has to occur. But as a result of our war against forest fires, this bird has been pushed onto the federal endangered species list and may only be seen in a small area of jack pine barrens in Michigan's northern Lower Peninsula.

Federal and state agencies have managed sections of this jack pine barrens since 1957 specifically to help the Kirtland's. Controlled burns; efforts to remove brown-headed cowbirds, which parasitize warbler the nests; and the planting of nearly 4 million jack pines in 1994 alone on over 2,000 acres of land have assisted in bringing the population up to 633 singing males in 1994, a large increase from 485 in 1993, and the highest number counted since the census began in 1951. The lowest number counted was in 1987, when only 187 singing males were found.

The entire worldwide population (less than 1,500 individuals) of Kirtland's warbler nests in this part of Michigan and nowhere else. The area measures 60 by 100 miles and lies mainly east of Grayling in the jack pine plains of Crawford, Oscoda, and Ogemaw Counties. A few pairs of Kirtland's also nest in Kalkaska, Iosco, Roscommon, and Montmorency Counties. Interestingly, and for unknown reasons, large tracts of burned-over jack pine exist in other areas of the UP, Wisconsin, Ontario, and Quebec, but Kirtland's warblers have not chosen to nest there, though individual singing males turn up now and again. For all the intense research that has been done on the Kirtland's, as many questions remain as answers exist related to their population dynamics. It doesn't seem as if the bird should be so rare, yet it is.

Kirtland's warblers arrive in early May and depart between August and October for their wintering grounds in the Bahamas. They can be heard singing from mid-May to mid-July, usually from the top of a pine or a high stub.

Hot Spots

Free guided tours of the nesting areas almost always turn up singing males (they stop singing in early July and are then very difficult to find). Tours are available from mid-May through July 4 through the **Michigan DNR in Grayling.** Call (517) 348-6371 for exact times.

Tours also leave from the **U.S. Forest Service (USFS) District Ranger Office** in Mio; call (517) 826-3252 for exact times. Be sure to take spotting scopes and binoculars for the best viewing—sightings are usually assured on these tours. And keep your eyes open for prairie warblers, upland sandpipers, clay-colored sparrows, and eastern bluebirds.

To reach the Michigan DNR office in Grayling, take the Business I-75 exit (Exits 254 or 259) off I-75 into Grayling, and turn east onto Michigan Avenue once in town. The office is past the hospital.

The Forest Service Ranger Station in Mio may be found by driving 32 miles east on Michigan 72 from Grayling. In Mio, turn north on Michigan 33—the station is immediately on your right.

If you prefer to try your luck on your own, the **Jack Pine Wildlife Viewing Tour** is a 48-mile auto-tour loop marked with special signs designating the route. Brochures are available in places of business in surrounding towns or by calling the Michigan DNR or USFS office. Listen for the clear, loud, and persistent song of the Kirtland's, which sounds like *chip-chip-chip-chery-reep.* The birds usually forage on the ground and low in trees looking for various insects and ripe fruits in season.

The **Kirtland's Warbler Festival** is held in Mio in June. Contact the Chamber of Commerce for Oscoda County, P.O. Box 426, Mio, MI 48647; (800) 826-3331 or (517) 826-3712 for more information.

If you've never heard a Kirtland's warbler, call the *Bird Watcher's Digest* Bird Information Line at (614) 373-2181 to hear a singing male (call between mid-June and mid-August).

35

June Shorttakes

Breeding Bird Surveys

Surveys of the types and numbers of breeding birds in each state take place in June. Join in by contacting the ornithological society in your state. Amateurs are as welcome as pros—it's a very good way to learn birds and birding if you're still in the novice category.

Bog Walks

June is a great time to muck around in a bog because most bog flowers bloom in May and June; the bog orchids in particular are most prevalent in June. Organized botanical and birding trips are usually led at nature centers in all three states. If you do explore a bog, be sure to vary the paths you use—bog vegetation is easily trampled into permanent trails. Save your old sneakers for use in the bogs, or wear tall rubber boots. Exercise great caution anywhere close to where the bog meets open water.

Dragonflies and Damselflies

Large hatches of predatorial dragonflies and damselflies occur in June, and their numbers can never be too many, given their efforts as mosquito-eaters. Dragonflies and damselflies crawl out of the water, often attaching themselves to pier posts, shoreline rocks, and tall grasses and rushes along the water's edge, to emerge from their larval bodies as flying insects. Their metamorphosis is every bit as remarkable as that of any butterfly. Look for the empty brown husks of the aquatic larvae in among shoreline vegetation and pier posts.

36

A Closer Look:
The Song of the Loon

Loons and the North Country are synonymous to most people. Various writers have designated the common loon as the voice of the North and the spirit of the northern lakes, titles few would dispute. The loon's voice distills the essence of wildland into a long wail, the avian equivalent of the howl of a wolf.

Loons speak in four general voices: the wail, the hoot, the tremolo, and the yodel. Variations of each vocalization add further complexity to the language of loons. The hoot is a one-note, quiet call that sounds just like its name, though the "t" is spoken softly. The hoot acts as a simple "check-in" communication, usually used to maintain contact within a family group or socializing flock.

The tremolo, or laughing call, usually signals alarm or concern and is given as a territorial warning to any intruders. If an eagle or another loon flies over a loon family's territorial lake, the adult male will invariably begin to tremolo over and over again; the distress is evident even to human ears. Several subtypes of this call are given, from a low-level minimum alarm to a high-frequency intense vocalization that indicates a high degree of anxiety. Loons were thought for a long time only to give the tremolo call in flight, but they have been heard giving the yodel call in flight, too. Researchers hypothesize that a flying loon may be "testing the waters" by tremoloing to see what response he gets from a lake. Perhaps the loon can judge the quality of the response and determine if a territorial confrontation on the lake would be worth the effort. It is not atypical for "rogue" males to attack either the female or male of a family and to try to kill any chicks. A tremolo duet may occur when both a male and female call simultaneously to try to distract an intruder away from their nest or chicks. Tremolos are also given when a loon is swimming across the water in response to an invader coming into its territory.

The wail call is the one that is probably the most associated with loons. It serves as a general call to communicate with other loons on a large lake or nearby lakes, a sort of "I'm here, and where are you?" song, or an invitation to visit. Different subtypes of the wail call can be given, from a simple single-note call to one that jumps a note to one that jumps up again to a third note. A chorus of loons wailing at night may be the pinnacle of avian song experience.

The yodel call offers the greatest complexity. The call, given only by the male, begins on an introductory note, then leaps into a higher undulating phrase that repeats over and over again. A yodeling loon is expressing his aggressive territoriality. This call clearly says, "Back off, this is my place." Yodels are often accompanied by behavioral displays, such as the male lying flat with his neck stretched across the water or rising up into an upright posture and extending his wings.

Territorial battles between loons have resulted in the deaths of adults and chicks and are wildly ferocious. Loons will dive under the water and come up under other loons, grab other loons' wings with their bills, and even stab with the pointed bills. For longtime loon-watchers who often re- fer to the loons on their lakes as "our" loons, these battles can be terribly distressing to watch.

Every loon, like every human, has its own voice, and a sound spec- trograph can be used diagnostically to identify individual loons. This method was used for years to try to determine if specific loons were returning to the same lakes, or to identify just which loon was engaging in a particular ob- served behavior, but the recent successful banding of loons has helped re- searchers do their identification in the field at the time of the observed event.

The Upper Midwest once had loons nesting throughout its territory, but the common loon has been pushed northward onto lakes that remain unpolluted, relatively quiet, and that maintain island or wetland shore habi- tat suitable for nesting sites. As we continue to divide and develop lakefront property into the tiniest lots possible, we strain the tolerance of a species that epitomizes the reasons people come to the North Country in the first place. I hope we will not love our northern lakes so much that they become merely playgrounds for human recreation and yet more lost homes for the loons.

July

Notes

37

Extraordinary Wildlife Viewing

July is the best month overall to visit the sites listed below because of the lush flora growing at this time. Breeding bird populations are at their peak, and the young of most animals are active, too. Plus, it's warm, even hot at times, which is a fairly rare climatic condition in the northern half of these three states. This is the month to explore the wild luxuriance of these sites in comfort. Now, if only the mosquitoes would reduce their armies, we'd have a near paradise.

In Minnesota, the Agassiz NWR may be the richest of all sites in the Upper Midwest, in large part because it's located in the transition zone between the northern conifer forest, tall-grass prairie, and prairie pothole regions. Breeding birds include all five grebe species (red-necked, western, eared, horned, and pied-billed), several thousand black terns, more than 20,000 Franklin's gulls (likely the largest colony in North America), more than 10,000 pairs of breeding ducks (17 different species), large rookeries with black-crowned night herons (350 pairs), great egrets, cormorants, great blues, 45 pairs of sandhill cranes, colonies of Forster's terns, sharp-tailed grouse, and shorebirds like Wilson's phalaropes and yellow rails. The bird list totals 280 species, about half of which are breeders. Toss in about 1,000 loafing white pelicans, and add to this 250 resident moose, a resident wolf pack, and the only herd of elk (20 to 30) in the state at nearby Thief Lake WMA just 5 miles northeast, and the wildlife viewing opportunities appear endless.

An early July visit should provide numerous beautiful sightings of black-crowned night herons and great egrets, as well as hundreds of white pelicans and hopefully a moose or two. Scan any gull-like birds that fly over—a variety of terns and gulls should be commonplace.

The earlier in the month you visit, the better. The marsh vegetation can grow so high that viewing becomes difficult. Consider the fall, too (see chapter 57). Don't wait to visit in the winter unless you enjoy icy winds—Thief River Falls is often the coldest place in the lower forty-eight. Only 13 bird species spend the winter at the refuge.

In Michigan, the Seney NWR covers over 150 square miles, nearly two-thirds of which is wetland, and has 25,000 acres of federally designated wilderness. Common nesting birds of interest include Canada geese, American bitterns, black terns, common and hooded mergansers, ring-necked ducks, sandhill cranes, common loons, trumpeter swans (34!), yellow rails, black-backed woodpeckers, merlins, sharp-tailed and spruce grouse, ospreys, and bald eagles. This may be the best place in America to watch woodcock do their remarkable courtship flight (a May phenomenon). Forty-five mammals including wolves, black bears, bobcats, otters, and moose may be seen, if luck is with you.

A 7-mile self-guided auto tour has several observation decks equipped with scopes (try the auto tour on a mountain bike—a pleasurable way to experience this tour), or take to the 70 miles of gravel roads and do your own exploring. The auto tour is closed to all motorized traffic as of October 1, so bikes or your feet are the best way to travel through the refuge during the fall season. I biked the auto tour in October and in a 3-hour span saw only two other people and a lot of birds. Also consider canoeing the small Driggs River through the heart of the refuge.

In July, the auto tour should turn up numerous eagles and osprey, as well as trumpeter swans and a host of varying waterfowl. Seney is also well known for its yellow rail population, a small, secretive marsh bird that few people ever see. Check the NWR's headquarters for summer programs led by refuge biologists.

Because no waterfowl hunting has occurred in Seney since 1935, no lead shot is present in the pools and wetlands, providing a true refuge for nesting and migrating waterfowl.

Isle Royale National Park offers isolation, solitude, and beauty and is the only island national park in America. Situated in northwestern Lake Superior, the park is accessible only by boat and seaplane, and once on the island, explorable only by foot, sea kayak, canoe, or motorboat. People come here to experience wilderness, and the offerings are plentiful. Isle Royale was designated part of the National Wilderness Preservation System in 1976 and a Biosphere Reserve by the United Nations in 1981.

The main island is 9 miles wide and 45 miles long, with 160 miles of hiking trails, and is characterized by a series of rugged ridges and valleys interspersed with lakes and bogs. The more than 200 outlying islands and islets create wonderful habitats for common loons, goldeneyes, and mergansers (none of which are all that common to most birders). Typical inland birds of spruce-fir boreal habitats breed here, such as golden-crowned kinglets, red-breasted nuthatches, and Swainson's thrushes, while aspen–white birch forests are home to ovenbirds, American redstarts, red-eyed vireos, and chestnut-sided warblers.

There are many species missing from the mammal population. This is explained by the theories of "island biogeography," which state that many species never reach islands, and those that do often fail to thrive due to a lack of a larger gene pool and an inability to repopulate if a crash in population occurs. So you won't see deer, black bears, raccoons, skunks, porcupines, cottontails, or chipmunks. But most visitors don't come for those, they come to see moose and wolves. Moose swam to the island in the early 1900s and, without a predator on the island, increased in numbers dramatically. Wolves arrived on the island by crossing the Lake Superior ice in the winter of 1948–1949. Since then, a complex interaction between these two species has taken place, which has been the subject of intensive pioneering wildlife research. As of the winter of 1995, wolf numbers have temporarily stabilized at 14.

In July, moose sightings are relatively common, but the wolves are seldom seen. Keep one eye on the ground as wolf tracks can often be seen, and when a wolf track overlaps a moose track, you can imagine the possible ensuing confrontation. Wolves are only successful around 8 percent of the time in conflicts with moose, so the result of such a battle is not a foregone conclusion.

In Wisconsin, the Turtle-Flambeau Flowage supports 11 pairs of bald eagles, 21 pairs of common loons, and 18 pairs of ospreys—the richest assemblage of these glamour species on one body of water anywhere in Wisconsin. Merlins and black terns also nest here, contributing to the total of 124 nesting species of birds. Twenty-nine species of mammals occur here, including timber wolf, bobcat, otter, mink, fisher, pine marten, black bear, and an occasional moose. A dam built in 1926 backed up the Flambeau River, creating 14,300 acres of big water with 314 islands and 327 miles of shoreline, 95 percent of which is in public ownership.

In July, sightings of loons, osprey, and eagles should be commonplace, particularly if you explore early in the day.

The best way, and really the only way, to see the flowage is by canoe or small motorboat (the flowage is very shallow and harbors stumps still left over from the original flooding). My favorite launching site is Murray's Landing, at the far eastern end of the flowage. Get a good topo map if you wish to venture on the water any significant distance from the landing, because it's very easy to get turned around. The flowage is arguably Wisconsin's best attempt at duplicating the Boundary Waters Canoe Area, though it's a miniature copy at best, and it allows motors.

Crex Meadows WMA in Burnett County is 30,000 acres of marsh, brush prairie, and forest. Eighteen miles of dikes were constructed to create 27 flowages that impound over 6,000 acres of marsh. Brush-prairie restoration work totals over 6,000 acres. Over 265 bird species have been recorded in the wildlife area, and there are 40 miles of roads within the boundaries to drive. I've heard a few expert birders claim this area harbors the best birding in Wisconsin, though making those sort of claims usually just gets you in trouble.

In July, look especially for the several pairs of breeding trumpeter swans and their cygnets. Nonbreeding flocks of sandhill cranes may be seen in the sedge marshes, and pelicans and Caspian terns often turn up on the larger flowages. And don't forget to do some prairie-watching too, though June is usually the peak for prairie wildflowers. Look for big bluestem grass as it begins to dominate the prairies in July, along with various goldenrods, asters, lupines, and prairie sunflowers.

Phantom Flowage may be the richest site in this area—1,800 acres of wetland with nearly every bird counted. Nesting birds include black terns, sandhill cranes, common loons, sora and Virginia rails, ospreys, American bitterns, and great egrets. Spring and fall migrations may bring white pelicans; western, red-necked, and horned grebes; common terns; and Bonaparte's gulls.

Hot Spots

Minnesota's **Agassiz NWR** is an eye-opening spot to visit in July. The only difficulty with this 61,449-acre (40,043 acres of wetland!) refuge is that access is limited. A 4-mile self-guided auto tour with a 0.25-mile hiking trail is the best, and just about only, access available, other than along County Road 7. A 100-foot-high observation tower and a 14-foot-high observation deck offer good overviews, but the refuge is so enormous that they don't begin to give you a sense of what's all out there. Through prearrangement, it may be possible to be given a key to some of the gated dikes, which will allow you to get a much better feel for this remarkable refuge. Write, call, or visit the Agassiz headquarters to ask permission to explore the dikes, though the refuge personnel look out first for the needs of the resident wildlife, and second for the needs of visitors. And that's the way it should be. And don't forget nearby **Thief Lake WMA,** just 5 miles northeast of Agassiz NWR. From Thief River Falls, take Hwy. 32 north to Holt. Turn right (east) on County Road 7 and go about 1 mile to the refuge headquarters.

To get to the **Seney NWR** from the Mackinac Bridge, drive 65 miles west on U.S. 2 to Michigan 77. Turn right (north) on 77 and go 13 miles to the entrance of the refuge, which leads to the visitor's center and the start of the auto tour.

Isle Royale lies 18 miles from Minnesota and 56 miles from Michigan (only 13 miles from Ontario). Ferry service is available from Houghton and Copper Harbor, Michigan, and Grand Portage, Minnesota. Seaplane service is available in Houghton. No wheeled vehicles are permitted on the island, but consider transporting over a canoe or sea kayak, if you are an experienced paddler, to explore the rugged coastline and inlets.

To get to Isle Royale from Houghton, Michigan, a 123-passenger vessel operates from June 2 to September 12, leaving at 9:00 A.M. on

Agassiz National Wildlife Refuge

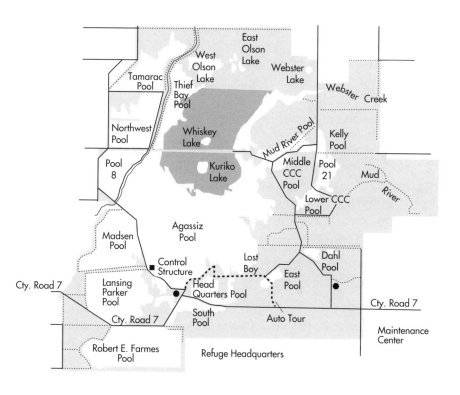

East Olson Lake

West Olson Lake

Webster Lake

Webster Creek

Tamarac Pool

Thief Bay Pool

Northwest Pool

Whiskey Lake

Kelly Pool

Mud River Pool

Pool 8

Kuriko Lake

Middle CCC Pool

Pool 21

Mud River

Lower CCC Pool

Agassiz Pool

Madsen Pool

Control Structure

Lost Boy

Dahl Pool

Lansing Parker Pool

Head Quarters Pool

East Pool

Cty. Road 7

Cty. Road 7

South Pool

Auto Tour

Cty. Road 7

Maintenance Center

Robert E. Farmes Pool

Refuge Headquarters

N

Refuge Wetlands
Refuge Uplands
Wilderness Area

Tuesday and Friday. For reservations and information contact: Isle Royale National Park, 87 North Ripley Street, Houghton, MI 49931; (906) 482-0984.

From Copper Harbor, Michigan, a 57-passenger vessel operates from May 11 to September 30. Contact: Isle Royale Ferry Service, Copper Harbor, MI 48918; (906) 289-4437.

From Grand Portage, Minnesota, a 150-passenger vessel operates from June 11 to September 5, and a 49-passenger vessel operates from May 7 to October 31. Contact: Grand Portage–Isle Royale Transportation Lines, 1332 London Road, Duluth, MN 55805; (218) 728-1237.

To get to **Murray's Landing** at the **Turtle-Flambeau Flowage,** take Hwy. 51 north from the little crossroads of Manitowish for 0.25 mile. Take a left onto Murray's Landing Road and follow it for 5 miles to the landing.

Crex Meadows WMA is reached by taking Hwy. 70 east from the St. Croix River bridge for nearly 5 miles. Turn left (north) onto Hwy. 48/87, and proceed into the small business district. Turn left (west) at the Post Office, go 1 block, and turn right (north) on Oak Street. Turn right (east) at the "T" intersection, and then left 1 block later onto County F. Shortly after, turn right onto County D, and the Crex Headquarters is on your left.

38

Rookeries—Herons, Egrets, and Cormorants

On a misty dawn morning, the sight of a great blue heron emerging from the fog over a lake, wings slowly beating, can stir the heart and mind as powerfully as any wildlife experience. The majesty of large and graceful birds is difficult to surpass and seldom fails to draw lengthy oohs and aahs from wildlife-watchers. Yet the pinnacle of heron-watching may not be in sighting the individual but rather in watching the nesting rookeries that resemble great airports as the adults wheel in and out with food for gaping juvenile mouths.

Many novice birders are surprised to learn that most herons nest in substantial colonies, building large stick nests usually in a cluster of dead trees. These rookeries can be quite small, but large rookeries may include many hundreds of nests and several heron species. In the Upper Midwest, the heron family includes the herons—great blue herons, black-crowned night herons, green-backed herons, and yellow-crowned night herons (rare in the area); the egrets (though egrets really are herons that were given the name for the long plumes they wear during breeding)—cattle egrets and great egrets; and the bitterns—American bitterns and least bitterns. Of these birds, only the bitterns and green-backed herons are not colonial nesters, instead nesting individually near the water surface in marshes and bogs. In large rookeries, several of the other species often come together to live in tightly packed neighborhoods and are frequently joined by double-crested cormorants.

Many nests are often placed on limbs of the same tree, and given the substances that might fall out of the nests (herons regurgitate indigestible food in pellet form, for instance), the lower nests, I would suppose, constitute the "low rent" housing for the neighborhood. Recently dead trees caused by beaver flowages and areas of flooding are choice sites for building rookeries, though colonies may also be built in live trees. One colony I know of on the Turtle-Flambeau Flowage in northern Wisconsin is on an island, in thriving red pine trees. Another rookery, Cathedral Pines (described later in this chapter), is in the top of old-growth white pines.

Rookeries come and go as the dead trees topple due to wind, decay, and ice shear, so traditional sites may not have long histories or stable futures.

Double-crested cormorants nest on telephone poles put up in Green Bay by the Wisconsin DNR. Photo by John Bates.

They may also be abandoned for reasons unknown, then rebuilt in another area, or forgotten altogether.

Herons eat mostly small fishes, only a small portion of which are game fish. Eating small fish has the effect of culling a population of fish so numerous that growth is stunted. Other foods include the delectable wetland smorgasbord of crayfish, frogs, salamanders, snakes, aquatic insects, and rodents.

Herons return to their nesting colonies early in the spring, and the incubation of the eggs takes less than a month. Young fledge in about one and a half to two months. During this period it is imperative that human watchers do not intrude upon the colony but remain a respectful binocular range away. In July the young are of good size, and it's a full-time job for the adults to keep them fed, so a constant progression of birds is on the wing back and forth. By August the young fledge and the colonies are usually abandoned until the next spring.

Rookeries should under no circumstances be entered while birds are present for the obvious reasons that this will disturb feeding and care of the young. Adults will abandon entire colonies if there is too much disturbance, so stay well offshore from island colonies or concealed by trees near inland colonies. If birds appear to be flushing due to your presence, get away from the area.

Hot
Spots

In Wisconsin, the eastern end of **Berkhahn Flowage** in the **Mead Wildlife Area** has a large rookery with 80 pairs of great blue herons, 400 pairs of double-crested cormorants, and numerous black-crowned night herons. Five active osprey nests are in the area around the rookery. Hike the dike road from the Wisconsin DNR headquarters for 3 miles to the end of Berkhahn Flowage. Although the rookery is closed during the breeding season, viewing with binoculars from the dike trail is still excellent. Mead Wildlife Area Headquarters is located on County Road S 2.5 miles south from the junction of County Roads C and S. Or take U.S. 10 west from Stevens Point off Hwy. 51 and go north on S for 7 miles to the refuge headquarters. The Mead is nearly 30,000 acres of wildlife area with diverse habitats and an enormous variety of wildlife.

Also within the Mead Wildlife Area, **Teal Flowage** has a rookery with cormorants and black-crowned night herons. Teal Flowage is 0.75 mile north on County Road S from the wildlife area headquarters. Hike the dike trail down the south side of the flowage.

Several islands in the southern end of **Green Bay** have large colonies of cormorants, great blue herons, and black-crowned night herons. These can only be reached by boat. Launch from the boat landing at the mouth of the Fox River where it empties into Green Bay.

Horicon Marsh NWR (see chapter 57 for directions) offers the largest freshwater cattail marsh in the country, and as one would expect in the midst of so much water, herons thrive here. **Fourmile Island SNA** has the largest great blue heron and great egret nesting colony in Wisconsin. It can be viewed from a canoe along the west branch of the Rock River in the adjacent Wisconsin DNR–owned **Horicon Marsh State Wildlife Area** (no canoeing is allowed in the refuge), but the island itself is closed to entry.

The **Cathedral Pines** old-growth forest within the **Nicolet National Forest** (see chapter 8) has a most unusual great blue heron rookery with 80 nests in the tops of some of the old white pines. A hiking trail takes you close by the rookery. From Lakewood, take Hwy. 32 0.9 mile to Archibald Lake Road (Forest Road 221). Turn south and proceed to Cathedral Drive. Turn right (west) and go 0.4 mile to the hiking trail.

The **Cranberry Flowage** in Monroe County is a large reservoir next to Hwy. 21 that supports a great blue heron rookery of over 100 nests and a few pairs of cormorants and great egrets. The rookery can be seen from the highway on the northern edge of the reservoir. From Wyeville, take Hwy. 21 west for 2 miles to the reservoir. Or exit from I-94 onto Hwy. 21 and go east for 1 mile to the reservoir.

Grettum Flowage, a part of the **Fish Lake Wildlife Area**, is a 500-acre reservoir that was first flooded in 1973, and by 1974 great blue herons and double-crested cormorants had established a rookery on it.

In 1975, great egrets nested in the rookery, possibly the northernmost nesting site for this species in Wisconsin. Soon after, black-crowned night herons, American bitterns, and green-backed herons moved onto the flowage as well. Look for ospreys and eagles nesting here as well as 14 nesting duck species. Grettum Flowage is south of Crex Meadows (see chapter 37). Take Hwy. 48/87 south out of Grantsburg for 4.5 miles to the Grettum Dike Road. The flowage can be viewed from Hwy. 48/87 and from the dike road that crosses it.

Black Brook Flowage, within the **Amsterdam Sloughs Wildlife Area** in Burnett County, contains a great blue heron colony at the north end of the flowage, along with a few cormorants and great egrets and several active osprey nests. Take Hwy. 35 south from Webster for 2 miles and turn right (west) onto County Road D. Go nearly 4 miles, and the rookery is easily viewed from the dike trail just south of County Road D.

In Minnesota, **Lake of the Woods** has over 1,000 cormorant nests on **Crowduck Island.** Unless you have a good motorboat or enjoy big-lake canoeing, the island is inaccessible, but cormorants may be seen fishing at a host of locations along this enormous lake. Check **Zippel Bay State Park** (see chapter 39); **Morris Point; Wheelers Point;** the **Warroad Marina,** 1 mile north of Warroad along County Road 74 on the north edge of Warroad; and the public-access boat landing off County Road 12, 2.5 miles east of Hwy. 11.

The island in **Long Lake** in Kandiyohi County has one of the largest heron rookeries in Minnesota—some 2,300 nests of cormorants, great egrets, cattle egrets, and great blue herons. Scan the lake along its north shore from County Road 27. From Wilmar, take Hwy. 71 north and then turn left (west) onto County Road 27. The island is over a mile out into the lake, so consider putting a canoe in at the boat landing on County Road 27 or using a good spotting scope. Regardless of how close you may or may not get, the herons will be constantly on the move and easily seen flying to and from their foraging areas.

Lake Johanna in Pope County has a large rookery on the south end of the lake that provides nesting sites for great blue herons, cormorants, great egrets, and black-crowned night herons. Little blue herons and cattle egrets have bred here, too, the first recorded breeding sites for either species in Minnesota. The only real access is at the boat landing on the north end of the lake. Take Minnesota 104 south to County Road 8 and turn left (east). Go 0.9 mile and turn right onto a dirt road with a sign reading Public Water Access. The lake can't be adequately viewed from here, so put a canoe in for a remarkable birding experience. Even though you must stay a good distance away from the rookery, it is very exciting just to be a part of the general hubbub.

Egret Island, a 34-acre island owned by The Nature Conservancy on Pelican Lake in Grant County, supports thousands of nesting great blue herons, black-crowned night herons, great egrets, and cormorants. A boat landing on the western shore provides good viewing, though the island is still a mile offshore. From I-94 take Minnesota 78 north 1.7 miles to the boat landing. Additional summer sightings in this area have included snowy egret, cattle egret (which may nest here), little blue heron, tricolored heron, and yellow-crowned night heron.

Lac Qui Parle WMA in the Minnesota River valley serves as an important corridor for migrants in the fall (100,000 geese stop here), but its three major water impoundments also provide great habitat for nesting herons. A large heron rookery can be seen just southeast of the hamlet of Odessa. About 7 miles south of Ortonville on Hwy. 7, take County Road 21 to the right (south). After passing Odessa on your right (it's just a few houses), the road goes up a hill and makes a 90-degree sweep to the left. Just past this curve look out to your right to view the huge rookery down in the river valley. Binoculars or a spotting scope are very helpful because the rookery is a good distance away. Continue on this road (1 mile total from Odessa) to the second gated road on the right with a sign reading Public Hunting Area. Take this road to the dead end at the dam and walk out onto the dam for a great view of the rookery. Expect white pelicans to be feeding at the dam as well.

Voyageurs National Park has double-crested cormorant rookeries on islands in Rainy Lake, a common tern rookery on an island in Kabetogama Lake, and is home to 10 percent of all Minnesota's great blue herons.

And finally, Pigs Eye Lake in St. Paul has what may be the only rookery of yellow-crowned night herons in Minnesota as well as the largest colony of black-crowned night herons. Cormorants, great blues, and great egrets also nest here.

Swan Lake in Nicollet County and Heron Lake in Jackson County are also known to be exceptional heronry sites, but viewing access to them is well nigh impossible. Keep them in mind if in the future the public gains access (Swan Lake does have a boat landing but no public shoreline to scan from).

Other easy-to-spot rookeries are Kabekona rookery, southwest of LaPorte on Minnesota 64; Madden's rookery, north of Brainerd on County Road 77; and Pigeon Lake rookery, south of Dassel on Minnesota 15.

In Michigan, the Maple River Wetlands within the Maple River State Game Area is the largest contiguous wetland complex in middle Michigan. A large heron rookery is easily visible in the tops of flooded trees just west of U.S. 27 in Unit A of the four-unit wildlife management area. From Lansing, take U.S. 27 north. After crossing the Maple River there is a sign for the parking lot on the east side of the road. Call the Michigan DNR for more information: (517) 373-9358.

The **West Bloomfield Woods Nature Preserve** has an active heron rookery with more than 200 individuals that is easily seen from the west end of the greenway trail. The site is located in a suburb only 20 miles from downtown Detroit. From Detroit, head north on I-75 to West I-696. Head west to the Orchard Lake Road exit and turn north. Travel 6 miles to Pontiac Trail and turn left (west). Drive for 1.5 miles to Arrowhead Road, turn left (south), and go 0.5 mile to the park entrance.

The 4,500-acre **Rifle River Recreation Area** has a great blue heron rookery that can be seen from the hiking trail along Skunk Creek. Trumpeter swans may also be seen in this area. From Rose City in Ogemaw County, take F-28 east (also called the Rose City Road) nearly 5 miles to the entrance to the recreation area on the right (south) side of the road.

Gene's Pond DNR Forest Campground in the UP has a great blue heron and cormorant rookery in the trees near the campground. From Felch on Michigan 69, go west 0.5 mile to County Road 581 and turn right (north). Drive 5 miles and turn left (west) at the sign reading Public Access. Go 1 mile to the parking area for boat access in order to view the rookery from the water. To reach the campground on the north side of the pond, take Leeman Road (County Road 422) to the signs for Gene's Pond Forest Campground.

39

White Pelicans

The first time I saw white pelicans they were flying in a long white V out of a pure blue sky onto Upper Red Lake in northwestern Minnesota. They silently flapped their wings as a group a few times and then glided for 5 or 10 seconds, then flapped again and glided. For birds so large (8-foot wingspan, more than 15 pounds), they flew with remarkable grace. As they came down to land on the shallow waters of Upper Red Lake, they appeared like transport planes gliding over the surface before lowering their huge webbed feet and gently settling onto the lake. There they swam in groups among the other anglers, whose motorboats and high-tech gear seemed not to impress them in the least.

Pelicans are remarkable fliers and often forage 100 to 150 miles away from their colonial nest sites. In flight, pelicans pull their heads back onto their shoulders, partially resting their enormous bills on their folded necks. The stubby white body, black wing tips, and orangish bill and skin pouch leave little doubt as to the white pelican's identity.

On the water, white pelicans feed by plunging their heads underwater and scooping up fish. They often fish cooperatively in groups by swimming close together in a semicircle facing shore and "herding" the fish ahead of them into shallow water, where they are more easily harvested. And they need to be good fishers. An adult pelican requires about 4 pounds of fish a day, the major portion being fish like carp, catfish, and chubs.

The enormous skin pouch holds about 3 gallons of water that may be scooped up while fishing and that is squeezed out the corners of the mouth before food is swallowed. The pouch holds two to three times more than the stomach of a pelican, inspiring the Dixon Lanier Merrit limerick that begins: "A wonderful bird is a pelican,/ His bill will hold more than his belican."

After a fish is caught, it may be carried in the esophagus (never in the pouch) and then fed, partly digested, to the young.

White pelicans used to be a western Minnesota specialty, but several colonies have moved east, particularly along the Mississippi River and onto the southwestern shores of Green Bay in Wisconsin. White pelicans are known to nest in only two sites in Minnesota as of this writing—Marsh Lake in the Lac Qui Parle State WMA, and Lake of the Woods—but are clearly expanding their range and may be nesting elsewhere by the time you read this.

Because pelicans are highly gregarious nearly all year-round, with flocks of both sexes and all ages socializing together, the likelihood of seeing a large number of pelicans together is very good. Although their beauty will capture your eye, don't expect an equal dose of singing ability. Adult pelicans are most often silent or may utter piglike grunts, and the young may offer a whining sort of grunt or piercing scream, none of which sounds like music to our ears.

Hot Spots

In Minnesota, **Marsh Lake,** a flowage formed by a dam on the Minnesota River in Lac Qui Parle County, is the site for some 1,500 nesting pelicans. There are several areas to scan for them. The Hwy. 75 dam, though not on Marsh Lake proper, is perhaps the easiest site from which to see pelicans—they tend to sit, along with cormorants, just below the dam gates. Many people fish the pool below the dam, sharing the resource with the pelicans, who often feed within a cast-length of the fishermen. A road runs along the top of the dike for most of its length and provides scanning opportunities of the big water. The pelicans are most active from May through July and disperse in August after the fledging of the young.

Take Hwy. 7 west from Appleton to Hwy. 75, and turn left (south). After crossing a bridge over a portion of the river, the dike will rise up on your right. A one-way road runs from south to north along the dike, so pass the first road leading onto the dike with the sign reading Do Not Enter, go to the second road at the dam itself (2 miles from the turn onto Hwy. 75), and double back along the dike.

The **Marsh Lake dam** can be reached by taking Hwy. 119 south out of Appleton. Just as you are leaving town, a sign for the dam reading Marsh Lake Flood Control Dam directs you to the right onto County Road 51. Follow County Road 51 until it makes a 90-degree sweep to the right—go straight here instead, taking the road marked Minimum Maintenance Road (why there isn't a sign here for the dam is a mystery). The first road to the right then will have a sign for the dam; follow this road directly to the dam (you cannot cross the dam, so you will have to retrace your route to go back). Pelicans should be feeding right below the open gates. A parking lot, outhouses, and picnic tables here may make your visit more enjoyable.

One other dirt road crosses the west end of the lake. Take Hwy. 7 west from Appleton for approximately 9 miles to an unnamed road (it's called Louisburg Road locally), which has a small sign reading Public Water Access, and turn left (south). This road takes you through a marshy area that provides limited open water to scan but that still usually turns up pelicans, along with a host of marsh birds (yellow-headed blackbirds galore). The culverts that allow the water to flow through here are a good place to stop and watch for terns and cormorants as well as pelicans, which may be seen flying back and forth.

Lake of the Woods has 14,000 islands, 65,000 miles of shoreline, and 1 million acres of water (300,000 acres within American borders). And within this vastness, white pelicans nest and may be seen feeding. **Zippel Bay State Park** provides the largest public ownership along Lake of the Woods. From Hwy. 11 in Baudette, take Hwy. 172 north to Minnesota 8 and turn left (west). Turn right (north) on Minnesota 34 (there will be signs for the park) and go a little over 1 mile to the park entrance. Park roads lead to three different access points to the lake, one on Zippel Bay itself. Each site may turn up pelicans, but also scan the shorelines for shorebirds and the lake for cormorants, four species of tern, Franklin's and Bonaparte's gulls, and other waterfowl. The endangered piping plover nests in this area, and may sometimes be seen feeding along these shores.

Because white pelicans forage over 100 miles from their nesting sites, they may be seen on any lake or marsh in this area that offers good fishing. Try the auto tour at **Big Stone NWR,** just to the northwest of Marsh Lake. Pull off at stop 4 and climb the granite outcropping for an overlook of a flooded valley of the Minnesota River. The road between stops 4 and 5 offers further viewing opportunities.

Just to the north of Big Stone NWR, **Thielke Lake** provides habitat for large numbers of various waterfowl, including pelicans (I saw over 60 here one morning). Take Hwy. 75 north from Ortonville to County Road 62. Turn right (east) and go 1.5 miles to the lake, where the road follows the south shore. A small bay to the south of the road often packs in pelicans, common egrets, cormorants, and great blue herons. Scan the lake to the north for pelicans and breeding western grebes.

Agassiz NWR and **Thief Lake WMA** are both loafing sites for nonbreeding pelicans. The auto tour at Agassiz (see chapter 37) should turn up pelicans, along with a host of other bird life. Thief Lake harbors large numbers of pelicans, too. Try the observation mound on the south shore a mile east of the Minnesota DNR Thief Lake office. See chapter 37 for directions.

Lake Johanna in Pope County, like Thielke Lake, concentrates various herons and waterfowl. Take County Road 8 east from Minnesota 104 for 0.9 mile and turn right at the dirt road that leads to the boat landing (a small sign reading Public Water Access will identify the turn). Unfortunately, this is the only spot where one can get any view of this exceptionally rich lake. Take along your canoe for the best viewing opportunities. (See chapter 38 for more information.)

Salt Lake in Lac Qui Parle County (see chapter 27) usually has for-aging pelicans, as does **Upper Red Lake** in Beltrami County. Vistas of Upper Red Lake are hard to come by, but try the public beach area on the north end of Waskish. From Hwy. 72 north, turn left at a small sign reading Waskish Beach Day Use Area. There also is a public-water access site just north of here at the crossing of the Tamarac River. Put a canoe or motorboat in here to explore this vast shallow lake. The pelicans seem acclimated to the passing of anglers in motorboats, so close-up views of them are possible.

Farther south and east, **Minnesota Lake** in Faribault County may be a new nesting site for white pelicans. The best views are from its east side along County Road 21 south of the town of Minnesota Lake. Also check the north shore along County Road 20 west of town. From I-90, take Hwys. 109 and 22 northwest to the town of Minnesota Lake.

Along the border of Minnesota and Wisconsin, the **Upper Missis-sippi River National Wildlife and Fish Refuge** has harbored increasing numbers of white pelicans during the summer. Scan pools 4 through 8 near La Crosse for the best viewing opportunities. Call or write the ref-uge headquarters for maps of this area. Farther north, hundreds of peli-cans may be seen at **Weavers Bottoms,** above Winona (see chapter 62 for directions).

A final site in Wisconsin has become a hot spot for white pelicans. **Green Bay's southwestern shore** has recently attracted hundreds of peli-cans. Try the **L.H. Barkhausen Waterfowl Preserve** there. Barkhausen is reached by taking the Lineville exit east off Hwy. 41/141 just north of the city of Green Bay. Turn left (north) onto Lakeview Drive and go 0.5 mile to reach the preserve and the West Shore Interpretive Center. Or launch a boat or canoe from the boat landing at the eastern end of Lineville Road to explore the bay.

40

Butterfly-Watching

The butterflies of the Upper Midwest are a widely diverse group, including arctic species of northern bogs, western prairie species, and even a few migratory subtropical species. Around 150 species may be seen in this area, of which 120 or so breed here. The majority are specialized, living in limited areas that meet their exacting ecological requirements. The minority are widespread generalists able to thrive in disturbed habitats that we humans are so good at creating.

As with all faunal groups, many butterfly species are now rare. For instance, seven species are listed as threatened or endangered in Wisconsin, all of which are associated with barrens or prairies, two habitats found in little more than postage-stamp-size areas in the state. Illustrative of a rare specialist is the regal fritillary, which appears to require large areas of prairie with a continuous bloom of prairie flowers to provide nectar.

Butterfly-watching and bird-watching have a lot in common. Indeed, some writers view butterflies as the warblers of the insect world. Butterflies come in all sizes for watching, from smaller than a thumbnail, like the eastern tailed blue with its 3/4-inch wingspan, to the giant swallowtail, whose wingspan exceeds 5 inches.

Binoculars are necessary for viewing at a distance—most butterfly-watching isn't done with a net in hand, as it once was. If approached very slowly from behind, many butterflies allow people to get very close—often to within inches. For best success avoid sudden movements, casting a shadow on the butterfly, or becoming silhouetted against the sky within the butterfly's line of view. Butterflies are prey species to a host of predators, so they are often quite wary. Try to carry a pair of binoculars that can focus up close, to within 15 feet or less if possible.

The best viewing often takes place during two periods: early in the day when butterflies are basking in the sun's heat in an attempt to raise their body temperatures, and later in the day while they're focused on feeding. Many adult butterflies are very limited in what they eat, as are their larvae. Some butterflies will only lay eggs on one type of plant, the most well-known example being monarch butterflies, who use only milkweed as the host for their eggs. So if you can get to know which butterfly is attracted to what plants, the searching becomes much easier. Butterflies are seasonal, too, much like wildflowers. They "bloom" within specific time frames, so it's important to know when to look.

Like birds, butterflies live in varied habitats. By visiting a host of habitats in different parts of the Upper Midwest, you will greatly increase your chances of seeing a diversity of species. Most butterflies prefer sunny locations, so look on sunny trails throughout woodlands, near puddles, in farm fields, open wetlands, and sunny flowering fields. Although most butterflies feed at flowers, other species may feed at mud puddles rich in minerals, or even in animal droppings, an equally rich site. Roadside depressions filled after a rainstorm may be every bit as good an area as wildflower meadows for finding butterflies.

Butterflies carry on most of the behaviors we are used to seeing in mammals and birds, such as courtship, aggressive territorial defense, socialization, evasion of predators, migration, and basking in the sun. The more you observe, the more you may be surprised at how easy it is to get hooked on butterfly-watching.

The North American Butterfly Association (NABA), a nonprofit organization formed to educate the public about the joys of nonconsumptive recreational butterfly observation, coordinates butterfly counts usually around the Fourth of July, though the counts can take place anytime from mid-June to late July. Novice counters are welcome to join many of the counts, and in fact a significant number of counts are set up to help inexperienced butterfliers develop their identification skills.

Based on the methods used in the Christmas Bird Count (see chapter 67), a butterfly count takes place within 15-mile-diameter circles that have been established over the years and that are revisited every year at the same time in order to develop a database for a specific area. After years of accumulating information, biologists can then begin to see population trends and make specific management recommendations. The count takes the "butterfly pulse" of an area, and from its results the area's environmental health may be gauged.

I know of no better way to gain an understanding of and appreciation for butterflies than to go butterfly-counting for a day with knowledgeable people. By joining in, not only will you grow in your wisdom and appreciation, but you will also be assisting in an important biological survey.

Garden butterfly-watchers are also needed, much like the Christmas Bird Count's feeder-watchers. If you have spent time trying to attract butterflies to your property, you may join the count right from your backyard if you live within one of the count circles.

The NABA publishes a quarterly magazine called *American Butterflies,* which provides information on how to attract butterflies to your garden, where to find butterflies, how to identify butterflies, as well as interesting natural histories of specific species.

A note on collecting butterflies: A good 35-mm camera and a macro lens can give you much better clarity and richness of detail than can holding a dried specimen in your hand. Consider purchasing a 100-mm focal length macro lens that focuses to life size without an adapter. These days collecting is best done by photography, both from an educational standpoint as well as a conservationist ethic.

For more information on butterflies in general, contact the following organizations:

> The Lepidopterists' Society, 3838 Fernleigh Avenue, Troy, MI 48083-5715
>
> Wisconsin Entomological Society, 7119 Hubbard Avenue, Middleton, WI 53562
>
> The Xerces Society, 10 Southwest Ash Street, Portland, OR 97204
>
> Young Entomologists' Society, Department of Entomology, Michigan State University, East Lansing, MI 48824-1115
>
> Midwest Monarch Project, 3116 Harbor Drive Southeast, Rochester, MN 55904
>
> Journey North, 125 North 1st Street, Minneapolis, MN 55401 (tracks monarch migration north in the spring on the Internet)

Butterfly booklets specific to Wisconsin may be purchased through the Madison Audubon Society, 222 South Hamilton Street, Suite 1, Madison, WI 53703. *Butterflies of Southwestern Wisconsin* and *Butterflies of Northwestern Wisconsin,* both by Ann Swengel, are available at a cost of $3.50 each ($2.50 plus $1.00 postage).

Hot Spots

In Wisconsin, **Nelson Dewey State Park** along the Mississippi River in southwestern Wisconsin offers varied habitats, such as rich hardwood forests and dry prairies, for finding a wide array of butterflies. Take County Road VV north out of Cassville to reach the park. **Dewey Heights Prairie,** within the park, has six species of butterflies that may soon earn threatened status if they are not properly protected.

Point Beach State Forest, on Lake Michigan's shoreline, supports sand barrens along the shore and woodlands and wetlands in its interior, all of which combine to offer diverse habitats for a wide range of species. Migrating monarch butterflies (see chapter 47) may be seen in large numbers here in August and September. From Two Rivers, go north on County Road O, which runs through the heart of the forest.

Scuppernong Prairie SNA, a 185-acre prairie in the Kettle Moraine region, is only one of two areas in Wisconsin that now supports the Powesheik skipper, a state-designated endangered butterfly. From Eagle in Waukesha County, go west on Hwy. 59 for 1 mile and turn right on County Road N. Take N for 1.5 miles to a parking lot on the left.

Muralt Bluff Prairie, a 62-acre state natural area in Green County, has a healthy population of the regal fritillary. From Albany, go 2 miles south and west on Hwy. 59 to Hwy. 39. Turn right (north) on 39 and go 1.8 miles to a parking lot on the left—a tiny roadside sign indicates the driveway.

Butterfly counts are held at **Wehr Nature Center** in Franklin, **Riveredge Nature Center** in Newburg, **Havenwoods Environmental Awareness Center** in Milwaukee, **Crex Meadows Wildlife Area** near Grantsburg, **Retzer Nature Center** in Waukesha, the **Southern Unit** of the **Kettle Moraine State Forest** near Eagle, and **Bong State Recreation Area** near Kansasville.

In Michigan, the Gillette Visitor Center in **P.J. Hoffmaster State Park** hosts Great Spangled Butterfly Days for a week in early July. Contact the park naturalist at 6585 Lake Harbor Road, Muskegon, MI 49441; (616) 798-3573. The park may be reached by taking Michigan 31 south from Muskegon and exiting west onto Pontaluna Road, which ends after 3 miles at the entrance to the park.

Counts are held at the **Chippewa Nature Center** in Midland, the **University of Michigan Dearborn Environmental Study Area** in Dearborn, and **Whitefish Point Bird Observatory** near Paradise, and others may well be established by the time you read this book.

In Minnesota, counts are held at **Jay Cooke State Park** in Duluth, the **Deep Portage Conservation Reserve** in Deep Portage, and **Itasca State Park** near Douglas Lodge.

Contact the North American Butterfly Association, 4 Delaware Road, Morristown, NJ 07960, (201) 285-0907, for other counts that might be taking place in areas of interest to you.

41

July Shorttakes

Blueberry Picking

Some of the best blueberry picking occurs in barrens, areas that are regularly burned by state, federal, or private agencies to manage for fire-dependent species like jack pines. In Wisconsin, the **Moquah Barrens** in the **Chequamegon National Forest** grows some very big wild blueberries. Take Hwy. 2 west from Ashland to the little crossroads of Ino, and turn right (north) on Forest Road 236. Go 6.2 miles to the intersection with Forest Road 241 and turn left (west). The barrens stretch about a mile west here on either side of the road. Or continue north on Forest Road 236—the barrens will be on your left for another mile. The **Necedah NWR** in Juneau County produces a leaflet showing the best blueberry-picking areas in the refuge.

In Michigan, the **Baraga Jack Pine Plains,** a part of the **Baraga State Forest,** encompasses thousands of acres of jack pine forest and provides excellent blueberry picking in the latter half of summer. From U.S. 41 at Alberta, turn west on Baraga Plains Road. As you follow this road, watch the habitats change from northern hardwoods to mixed conifers to pure jack pine. The blacktop ends at a prison camp, but continue on the well-traveled sand road to the left and into the extensive jack pine stands. The **Seney National Wildlife Refuge** also offers great berry picking off the 80 miles of gravel roads that traverse the refuge.

In Minnesota, the **Tofte Ranger District** in the **Superior National Forest** offers a blueberry- and raspberry-picking guide that will lead you to all the best areas of the year. The Forest Service has begun developing blueberry management sites dedicated to increasing wild production, and many of these are designated with signs.

Hungry Black Bears

Black bears are particularly mobile in June and July as they become active reproductively. With the closing of open landfill sites throughout the Upper Midwest, bear-watching has become pretty difficult—the dumps were a near guarantee for seeing bears, but what a dismal place to watch them! Black bear populations are strong in the northern counties east of Roseau, Minnesota, although only at an average of one bear per square mile. Adult male bears normally range over an area of about 10 to 27 square miles, while females stay closer to home, ranging over some 4 to 5 square miles, so it is nearly impossible to predict where bears may be seen. Bears are generally shy and secretive but are known to gorge on berries in July and August. Look for bears in open wooded areas with dense undergrowth—they're quite active during the day in the summer. Look also for wild cherry trees with broken branches later in July and August, sure signs of hungry bears.

Among the best places to watch for bears are backyard bird feeders in the evening. Black bears seem to have discovered a taste for sunflower seeds, much to the destruction of bird feeders, and the number of people who watch bears at their feeders has increased enormously in recent years.

42

A Closer Look: Dune Ecology

From Indiana Dunes National Lakeshore all the way up the west coast of the Lower Peninsula of Michigan to the Straits of Mackinac lies the world's largest accumulation of sand dunes bordering fresh water. Carl Sandburg wrote about this national and global treasure, comparing the sand dunes of Lake Michigan to what the Grand Canyon is to Arizona and Yosemite is to California, and suggesting the dunes constituted eternal signatures of time upon Earth.

The dunes extend as far inland as 2 miles, rolling in a variety of forms—some naked sand, some lightly colonized with grasses and stubby shrubs, and those farthest inland deeply forested. They form complex structures that ecologists have classified, such as platforms, domes, blowouts, bowls, and parabolas. A few climb as high as 400 feet above Lake Michigan, mountains of sand that dwarf more renowned areas like North Carolina's Outer Banks, where the highest dunes reach only 140 feet.

Their size and scope are marvels, but no more so than their shifting movement: The dunes leapfrog their way forward, the front moving to the back over and over again. Eventually a stand of vegetation takes hold, usually a beach grass like marram that can survive the sterility and searing sun of the dune. The grass collects a mound of sand around it, and soon sand collects on the back side of the tiny mound, interrupting more wind, forcing more sand to drop out. Ultimately a ridge may form in a long slope toward the lake and with a steep drop over the back edge. The roots of the beach grasses burrow and surface, cloning again and again to colonize the dune, acting like a giant hand to hold on to what has formed. Bury marram grass and it sends up new sprouts, refusing the shifting gravesite the dune attempts to cover it with.

When vegetation doesn't prevent the sands from following an itinerant lifestyle, great "walking dunes" can move many feet in a year. One walking dune buried an entire abandoned fishing village in Michigan; another in 1992 enveloped a cottage on the Indiana lakeshore.

Though they are remarkably hardy, beach grasses can be trampled into oblivion by dune lovers, the resultant paths creating avenues for sand to move and grow, eventually building a kind of saddle through which sand can blast and become what is known as a blowout.

For most of us, our study of geology in school was an exercise in ancient time-traveling, but on a dune geologic forces work in periods of days, even hours, to sculpt new landforms. One can see geology at work in the here and now in addition to biological principles of plant succession that could hardly be better mapped for the student of terrestrial ecology. The marram grass colonizes a bare dune on its windward side; on its lee side may be found sand reed grass and little bluestem; farther back a patch of cottonwoods pioneers the sand, somehow eking out a living in the ever so slightly richer sands along with wild grapes and sandcherry; and another hundred feet back jack pines struggle to hang on in the still-minimal "soil" that is more sandbox than garden quality. Often one encounters a "ghost forest," skeletons of cottonwood, jack pine, or oak that were overwhelmed by the accumulating sands.

Here is one of the richest diversities of plants per acre that one can find anywhere. The variety of landforms and microclimates supports plants both from southern and northern ecosystems that ordinarily wouldn't be found in these latitudes—arctic bearberry may grow next to prickly pear cactus. Dune country may help provide a visual definition for the word "dynamic."

About 40 percent of Michigan's dune ecosystems are protected in state, local, or federal parks and preserves, but nonetheless, they remain susceptible to being loved to death by the incredible array of uses we humans wish to subject them to—dune-buggying, hiking, beach volleyball, not to mention sunbathing and swimming. Development of virtually every piece of privately owned duneland has taken place, though laws now exist to prohibit construction on the steepest slopes, opening up a political can of worms where people sue the government for "taking" their property. Sandburg wrote about the signature of these dunelands. Let us write our signature as best we can on these fragile sands in invisible ink.

Hot Spots

Sleeping Bear Dunes National Lakeshore is a 40-mile stretch of northwestern Lower Peninsula coast with dunes perched over 400 feet above the lake, 326 bird species, and observation platforms overlooking the dunes and lake. **North and South Manitou Islands** contribute another 30 miles of shoreline. From Traverse City, drive west on Michigan 72 to the park headquarters in Empire.

Warren Dunes State Park contains a 2-mile stretch of massive sand dunes—some are 240 feet high. The area is heavily used in summer, so consider a visit in the spring and fall, when solitude and study might be more easily possible. From I-94, take Exit 16 and follow Red Arrow Highway south to the park entrance. **Grand Mere State Park** is nearby, with almost 1,000 acres so unique that it has been designated a National Natural Landmark. From I-94, take Exit 22 and head east on John Beers Road. Turn left (south) onto Thornton Road, which will take you to the park entrance.

Saugatuck Dunes State Park in Allegan County has 2 miles of dunes from 20 to 180 feet high, has set aside a 290-acre nature area, and requires a 20-minute walk to reach the beach from the parking lot. From I-196 just north of the town of Saugatuck, take Exit 41 west onto Blue Star Memorial Highway and then turn immediately right onto 64th Street. Go north for 1 mile and turn left (west) onto 138th Avenue, which will take you to the park entrance.

P.J. Hoffmaster State Park near Muskegon offers 2.5 miles of forested dunes. The Gillette Visitor Center provides outstanding programs on dune ecology. Like many of these dune sites, Hoffmaster is an excellent location from which to watch migrating songbirds in May. From Muskegon, head south on U.S. 31 to Pontaluna Road and turn right (west). Follow the signs to the park entrance.

To get away from the hordes of beachgoers, try **Nordhouse Dunes Foot Travel Area** in the **Huron–Manistee National Forest,** a backcountry camping site with miles of sand dunes. This is the only nationally designated wilderness area in the Lower Peninsula, and though it is only 3,450 acres, you can certainly get the feel of wilderness here. Nearly 3 miles of beach are overlooked by dunes that reach as high as 140 feet. From Hwy. 31 about 12 miles south of Manistee, turn west on Town Line Road. Go 2.5 miles to Quarterline Road and turn right (north). Take this road for 2 miles and turn left (west) onto Nurnberg Road. Go 6 miles to the parking lot at the trailheads.

The **Big Knob Forest Campground** on Lake Michigan contains rare plants including Huron tansy, Houghton's goldenrod, pitcher thistle, and dwarf lake iris. The dune and swale habitat constantly changes with the effects of wind and water. From Naubinway (between Manistique and St. Ignace), continue on U.S. 2 for 7.5 miles to signs for Big Knob Forest Campground.

At **Ludington State Park,** walk the Skyline Trail for magnificent views of Lake Michigan and high dune ridges, or explore the 1,699-acre Wilderness Natural Area. Take Michigan 116 north from Ludington to its end at the park entrance.

Kitchel–Lindquist Dunes Preserve has a full sand dune ecosystem, from bare beach areas to climax dune forest. From Muskegon, head north on U.S. 31 to the Ferrysburg exit. Turn right (west) onto 3rd Street, which bears right and becomes 174th Avenue. From 174th turn left onto North Shore Road and go 2 miles to Lake Michigan, where the road veers south and becomes North Shore Drive. One mile south turn left onto Berwyck Street, and the entrance to the preserve will be immediately on your left. This is also an excellent site for fall hawk migration.

Lake Michigan doesn't have all the dunes, though it certainly has the most. **P.H. Hoeft State Park** near Rogers City has 1 mile of sand dunes along Lake Huron—preserving one of the best stretches of the Huron Dunes. These are low, rolling dunes without the grandeur of the Lake Michigan dunes, but they're worth exploring. Take Hwy. 23 northwest from Rogers City for 5 miles to the park entrance.

Pictured Rocks National Lakeshore along Lake Superior contains the **Grand Sable Dunes,** which stand 300 feet above the big lake and extend for 4 miles. From Grand Marais take Hwy. 58 west for 2 miles to Sable Falls, where you can begin your hike of the dunes.

August

Notes

43

Tall-Grass Prairies

When the first westward-bound pioneers left the forests of the East and reached the immense tall-grass prairies of the Midwest, they were stunned. P.F. de Charlevoix in 1761 described the Little Fox River region in Racine and Kenosha Counties in southeastern Wisconsin as "nothing ... but immense prairies, interspersed with small copses of wood, which seem to have been planted by hand; the grass is so very high that a man is lost amongst it ... ."

In 1835, Lieutenant D. Ruggles described the prairie around Fort Winnebago in Columbia County, Wisconsin: "'Rolling prairies' appear in undulation upon undulation, as far as the eye can reach, presenting a view of peculiar sublimity, especially to the beholder for the first time. It seems when in verdure, a real troubled ocean, wave upon wave, rolls before you, ever varying, ever swelling; even the breezes play around to heighten the illusion; so that here at near two thousand miles from the ocean, we have a facsimile of sublimity, which no miniature imitation can approach."

Though little is left today of those tall-grass prairies that once covered much of southern Wisconsin, southern and western Minnesota, and a small portion of southwestern Michigan, you can still find areas where the grasses swallow you up. Several prairie preserves in western Minnesota comprise over 2,000 acres. For the most part, though, the "miniature imitations" disdained by Lieutenant Ruggles must now suffice, a loss credited to pioneers who saw greater worth and utility in fields of domesticated grasses such as corn, wheat, and oats waving in the wind than in wild grasses like big bluestem and Indian grass. And who can blame them—filling empty stomachs has nearly always taken precedence over beauty or ecological integrity.

Whether their actions are understandable or not, today native tall-grass prairie is the rarest of all major North American biomes, virtually extinct as a natural functioning ecosystem. Of Wisconsin's estimated original 2 million acres of prairie, only 2,000 fragmented acres remain, representing about 1/10 of 1 percent of the original.

In Michigan, historical prairie may have covered 100,000 to 700,000 acres (no one is quite sure exactly how much), but now only about 400 acres are left. The estimate for tall-grass sites in Michigan is even lower—35 acres of the original estimated 45,000 acres remain. In all of Michigan, only 39 sites representing all the prairie types that existed prior to settlement have been identified.

Big bluestem on the Curtis Prairie often grow taller than 7 feet. Photo by Carol Christensen.

In Minnesota, much more has been preserved, but then much more was there to begin with. Less than 1 percent of the original 18 million acres of prairie is left, for a total of 150,000 acres. In western Minnesota you can spend a long time exploring prairie remnants, a dozen or more of which are 400 acres or larger in size because of the restoration and preservation efforts of the Minnesota Nature Conservancy and the Minnesota DNR.

How do we know what a prairie is so that we can recognize it? A prairie is defined as an area covered by 50 percent or more of native grasses, with less than one mature tree per acre. Prairies often progress into oak savannas, an area defined as having more than one tree per acre but with less than one-half of the total area in trees.

Not all true prairies are alike. For simplicity's sake, prairies are often divided into three types (though many individual grass species may be found in all three types):

1. Wet prairie. These have poor drainage, and the soils are often saturated. Common plant community members include switchgrass, sloughgrass, bluejoint, and marsh milkweed.

2. Moist (mesic) prairie. Mesic sites have good drainage and moderate water availability. Big bluestem, Indian grass, and prairie panic grass are dominant members.

3. Dry (xeric) prairie. Little water availability and shallow soils typify dry prairies. Little bluestem, needlegrass, pasqueflower, and sideoats grama grass are common constituents of the dry prairie.

Presettlement Range of Prairies

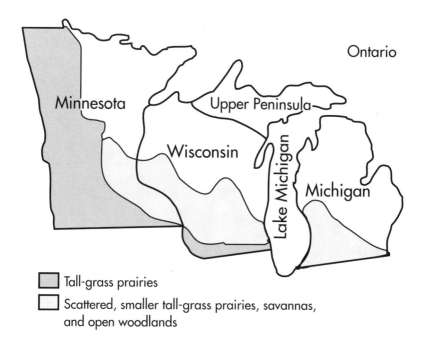

Tall-grass prairies

Scattered, smaller tall-grass prairies, savannas, and open woodlands

Tall-grass prairies are found on mesic sites, but mixed among the dominant tall grasses like big bluestem and Indian grass are many other short grasses like prairie dropseed, sideoats grama, and prairie panic grass, as well as hundreds of wildflowers. The tall-grass prairie came by its name honestly—in a good year grasses in a tall-grass prairie can reach 9 feet in height, though in an average year the grass usually stands 4 to 6 feet high.

Pioneers looked upon this unfamiliar landscape with trepidation, assuming that a place that couldn't grow trees wouldn't be much good for growing crops either. But they were astonishingly wrong. The deep black topsoil layer of the mesic prairies was rich in nutrients and thick with fibrous roots that withstood early plowing efforts. But in 1837, John Deere marketed the polished steel plow, and the end of the unbroken prairie sods became a certainty. The only question was how soon.

The pioneering task of domesticating the wild prairies still required enormous and indomitable effort, even with the advent of the steel plow. Who of us today would so willingly undertake so seemingly impossible task? O.E. Rölvaag in his classic book *Giants in the Earth* wrote of the pioneers throwing themselves "blindly into the Impossible" and accomplishing the "Unbelievable."

Indian grass in flower. Photo by Carol Christensen.

Like the cutting of the pineries of the North Woods, pride was measured in one's ability to break the prairie sod. And how do we measure pride now? We have come full circle to measure it in how much prairie we can save or restore. The sight in the early fall of a tall-grass prairie flowering with the golden plumes of Indian grass and the wine reds of big bluestem competes favorably with any fall sugar maple spectacle. With the swelling of a wind, the grasses flow into motion, a spectacle that Willa Cather in her book *My Ántonia* described, "as if the shaggy grass were a sort of loose hide, and underneath it herds of wild buffalo were galloping, galloping ... ."

A tall-grass prairie may contain 300 or more species of flowers and grasses, but it's more than the beauty of its flora. Tall-grass prairies also provide habitat for a diverse wildlife community, many of which are now threatened or endangered. Rare birds like prairie chickens, marbled godwits, chestnut-collared longspurs, and Sprague's pipits nest in the grasses, and a host of rare butterflies depend on specific prairie plants.

The largest remaining stand of tall-grass prairie in North America covers only 13 square miles—the Konza Prairie in Kansas—much too small to fill the definition of a complete ecosystem, which in the case of a prairie means the inclusion of buffalo and fire. Fire prevents the buildup of dead grasses into a thick choking thatch, converts dead grasses into readily available nutrients, and halts the ever-competing spread of shrubs and trees waiting in the successional wings. Buffalo, the other necessary component for any true prairie, randomly graze, reducing the buildup of dead grasses and thus helping to create an ever-shifting prairie mosaic of burned and unburned areas.

Minnesota tall-grass prairie sites include the **Felton area of Clay County**, the most significant prairie region in Minnesota. It is the only area in the state where one can find chestnut-collared long-spurs as well as the only site on which Sprague's pipits and Baird's sparrows appear with some frequency. The Felton area comprises 6,000 acres of high-quality prairie on public and private lands. Within this area is The Nature Conservancy's **Blazing Star Prairie**, 160 acres that for the most part were never plowed or grazed, although they were hayed annually. The site hosts nine species of plants and animals considered of significance, including three state-designated endangered prairie bird species—Sprague's pipit, Baird's sparrow, and chestnut-collared longspur. Marbled godwit and greater prairie chicken also nest here.

To reach Blazing Star Prairie, drive 7.1 miles west on Clay County Road 34, off of Minnesota 32, or go 4.3 miles east on County Road 34 from Felton. In either case, where Clay County Road 110 goes north, take the two ruts south on a wagon road (some books have called this an "improved township road") for 1 mile until you come to The Nature Conservancy sign. A gravel pit with mountains of gravel to the west presents an incongruous prospect in relation to this prairie but reminds the visitor what could happen without protection.

The Nature Conservancy–owned **Bluestem Prairie** is 2,458 acres in area, with 307 native plant species, of which 54 are native prairie grasses. This is the largest prairie owned by the Minnesota Nature Conservancy and is one of the finest stands of virgin sod left in western Minnesota. Bluestem Prairie was designated as a State Scientific and Natural Area in 1982. The adjacent **Buffalo River State Park** also has substantial tall-grass prairie within its boundaries and the same complement of native grasses and forbs.

Wildlife-sighting possibilities include upland sandpiper (listen for its lengthy "wolf whistle" and watch for its broken-wing act), bobolink, and even moose. Prairie chicken blinds are available for watching booming in the spring: Call The Nature Conservancy Bluestem office at (218) 498-2679. Three rare butterflies may also be seen—Dakota skipper, Poweshiek skipper, and regal fritillary.

The Bluestem Prairie is about 13 miles east of Moorhead. From Hwy. 10, go 1.5 miles south on Minnesota 9 to an unmarked gravel road. Turn east on the gravel road and drive for another 1.5 miles to The Nature Conservancy sign on the south side of the road—just a tenth of a mile farther is a parking area on the north side of the road. The road bisects the preserve, though most of the preserve is to the south.

The Nature Conservancy–owned **Pembina Trail Landscape Reserve** is 2,044 acres in area, and contains more than 200 native plant species, including 7 rare species, and 60 species of birds. Pembina Trail is primarily a mesic black-soil prairie located near the northwestern edge of the historical North American tall-grass prairie. **Crookston Prairie** and **Foxboro Prairie** are Minnesota Scientific and Natural Areas managed within the area's larger prairie complex. The Dakota skipper, a rare butterfly, can be found here, where it feeds exclusively on certain prairie plants. Look for marbled godwits, upland sandpipers, prairie chickens, western meadowlarks, and sandhill cranes in the extensive open grasslands, and keep an eye open for moose, which are occasionally seen crossing these prairies. Short-eared owls hunt the grasslands, and Wilson's phalaropes and yellow rails may be found in large areas of sedge meadow, marsh, calcareous fen, and shrub swamp within the preserve.

To get to Pembina Trail Preserve, take Hwy. 102 southeast out of Crookston to Polk County Road 45. Follow 45, a dirt road, east about 7 miles until you see a Nature Conservancy sign on the south side of the road. Another Nature Conservancy sign, on the north side of the road and across the railroad tracks, can be found farther east on 45 and identifies the Crookston Prairie SNA.

Blue Mounds State Park is an exceptional tall-grass prairie site and is particularly well suited to public use because of its extensive trail system (see chapter 33 for directions).

The **Zimmerman Prairie**, another Nature Conservancy parcel, is 80 acres of poorly drained virgin black-soil prairie dominated by big bluestem, Indian grass, and prairie cordgrass, all adapted to moist soils. Three significant animal species—marbled godwit, upland sandpiper, and greater prairie chicken—nest here. Zimmerman is located about 30 miles northeast of Moorhead or about 5.5 miles northeast of Ulen. Take Hwy. 32 north for 2 miles from Ulen and turn east onto a gravel road, Clay County Road 42 (which turns into Becker County Roads 18 and 16). Travel 5.3 miles east until you reach a Nature Conservancy sign on the north side of the road designating the site.

Western Prairie North in Wilkin County is in the heart of the Greater Prairie Chicken range in Minnesota. A mesic and wet tall-grass prairie with 120 plant species, the site has been affected very little by agriculture. Look for marbled godwit, upland sandpiper, greater prairie chicken, and 19 species of butterflies. From Lawndale go north 2.5 miles on Hwy. 52 to Wilkin County Road 188. Turn right (east) and go 1 mile to the southwest corner of the preserve and another 0.5 mile to a parking area on your left.

As with nearly all prairie sites, Western Prairie North is managed by prescribed burning. Volunteers are usually needed to help out. For more information, contact: Scientific and Natural Areas Program, Minnesota

DNR Section of Wildlife, Centennial Office Building, Box 7, St. Paul, MN 55155.

The Minnesota DNR published in 1995 *A Guide to Minnesota's Scientific and Natural Areas,* which gives descriptions of many more prairie sites and directions on how to find them.

In Wisconsin, the 60-acre **Curtis Prairie** in the University of Wisconsin at Madison Arboretum, is the oldest prairie restoration in Wisconsin and has wet, mesic, and dry prairie communities as well as an interpretive center for visitors. While on the campus, visit the 40-acre **Greene Prairie,** a restoration effort begun in 1943 containing a wet prairie and an oak opening (you will need to ask for a key to enter—Greene Prairie is preserved for scientific study).

The **Schluckebier Sand Prairie** in Sauk County contains over 158 species of prairie plants, including the rare bush clover *(Lespedeza leptostachya),* a prairie plant not seen in Wisconsin for 90 years until 1969. This site was once cultivated but was too sandy for good agricultural production. It was thus left fallow over 50 years ago, a hiatus that has allowed it to restore naturally into its native prairie community. Schluckebier is divided into two sections—the southern 14-acre prairie is located along the road with cornfields to the east and west and a hay field to the south. Little bluestem dominates, with Indian grass on the higher ground. I visited in September and found prairie gentians in flower. The northern section, only 8 acres, rests off the road between two cornfields (as one might expect, given that corn is the "tall grass" of the twentieth century). A short path must be followed through a narrow band of black locust woods to the site. Five- to 6-foot-high big bluestem, little bluestem, and Indian grass compete with other grasses for dominance in this very pretty stand, remarkable in part for its survival in the midst of so much corn.

The prairie is located west of Prairie du Sac in Sauk County. Take Hwy. 78 north out of Prairie du Sac and turn left (west) onto County Highway PF. Cross Hwy. 12 and continue west for 1.5 miles.

The **Avoca Prairie** is the largest virgin tall-grass prairie east of the Mississippi. Take Hwy. 133 east out of Avoca for 1.5 miles. Turn north onto Hay Lane Road, a dirt lane. Follow the road beyond Marsh Creek to a parking lot. The 1,885-acre site is dominated by little bluestem, northern dropseed, and Junegrass and is owned and managed by the Wisconsin DNR. Contact the Bureau of Endangered Resources for more information at (608) 266-7012.

Michigan tall-grass sites are few and far between. Try the **White Pigeon River Nature Sanctuary,** owned by the Michigan Nature Association, which offers an undisturbed prairie habitat. From the junction of U.S. 12 and U.S. 131 in White Pigeon, take U.S. 12 west for 2 miles to Burke Road. Turn south and drive 0.5 mile to the sanctuary.

The **Petersburg State Game Area** in southwestern Monroe County is a good place to see big and little bluestem, Indian grass, and other prairie plants. The area is 2 miles southeast of Petersburg and just west of U.S. 23.

Once prairie viewing gets under your skin, you will want to return again and again throughout the seasons to witness the variety of floral displays and to feel a sense of history where, as Donald Culross Peattie wrote, "a grass ocean filled the space under the sky … buffalo country, wide wilderness, where a man could call and call but there was nothing to send back an echo."

44

Fledgling Bald Eagles and Ospreys

By early August, young ospreys and bald eagles are often perched on the rims of their nests or along adjacent branches, preparing for their maiden flights. There's nothing childlike about these youngsters, though. They are *big*. In fact, bald eagles have one of the fastest growth rates of any bird in North America. In the three months after hatching, eaglets gain 10 pounds or more and grow from 3 to 36 inches tall. They often appear even a little bigger than their parents because their flight feathers are several inches longer.

Both bald eagles and ospreys usually fledge in early August. Immature bald eagles are poor flyers initially and need lots of practice, often ending up on the ground or perched in a tree and calling for help. Osprey young, on the other hand, seem to master flying the first day out and appear identical in flight to adults.

The chronology of nesting events for bald eagles goes something like this: return in mid-February, eggs laid on April 1 (average of two), eggs hatch on May 1, eaglets fledge on August 1. Bald eagles become sexually mature at four to five years old. In the meantime, the immatures will maintain brown mottled plumage with irregular white marks on the breast and wings. They will become progressively whiter on the tail and the head until they achieve the full adult plumage of a pure white tail and head at five years of age. An immature eagle's feet are yellow, like the adult's, but unlike the adult's yellow bill and eyes, an eaglet's bill and eyes are brown.

Immature bald eagles are often mistaken for golden eagles, but goldens do not breed in the Upper Midwest, though they can be seen overwintering here (see chapter 2). Immature bald eagles can be distinguished from migratory golden eagles by their white upper-wing linings—the adult golden eagle is uniformly brown underneath.

Adult bald eagles are easily identified by their white heads and tails. Males and females are identical in plumage, but females weigh 10 to 14 pounds while males weigh only 8 to 9 pounds. The wingspan ranges from 6 to 7.5 feet. And although it takes them a few years to mature, bald eagles may grow quite old by avian standards, living 25 to 30 years.

Bald eagles prefer to build their nests among the protective upper branches of large white pines. Their nests are used again and again and built onto every year. Several nesting territories in Wisconsin have been occupied for 40 to 50 years. One nest in Sawyer County, Wisconsin, is said to have been in use since 1918! Another in Vilas County is thought to date to the

Osprey are now experiencing much better nesting success due to artificial platforms built by Wisconsin DNRs. Photo by Bruce Bacon.

early twenties and is now 11 feet deep. Occasionally bald eagles will build two nests and rotate between them over the years.

The nesting chronology for ospreys is a bit different. They return from South and Central America in mid- to late April usually just before the ice is off the lakes, lay their eggs in early May (an average of two young), the chicks hatch in early June, and then fledge by early August.

Artificial nesting platforms support 80 percent of Wisconsin's osprey nests (ospreys on platforms have averaged a 70 percent nesting success rate, a much higher success rate than on natural nests). The platforms are built by cutting the top off the tallest live tree along a lake and bolting a flat platform to the stub. Ospreys like to be higher than anything around them in the landscape. The artificial platforms provide a much more stable and long-lasting site for nesting and result in a higher chick survival rate than natural nests. Although they are more desirable, natural nests are usually built in dead trees and are very susceptible to wind and ice damage—10 percent of all natural osprey nests blow down each year.

Nesting on the highest point in the landscape causes a good deal of mortality for osprey young. They are quite vulnerable to weather because their natal down feathers don't thicken into a warmer second natal coat, as in other birds of prey. The adult must remain at the nest to shield the chicks from sun, rain, and cold. Only one chick per nest on average lives to fledge every year.

Ospreys become sexually mature in three to four years and after migration, spend the balance of their first full year in South or Central America just growing up. About half will return in their second year, and by the third year most will have returned. The young osprey return to the same area they were fledged in to try to establish a nearby territory. Ospreys are "clumpers," meaning they seem to prefer nesting in the vicinity of other ospreys, and so a good deal of perfectly good osprey territory continues to remain vacant simply because the birds won't pioneer the new areas.

Unlike bald eagles, immature ospreys look very much like their parents, though the immature plumage is edged with a light buff. Adult females have a necklace of dark streaking, and the adult male is all white on the neck and chest.

Ospreys and eagles can be difficult to tell apart when they are high up in flight. Look for the osprey's characteristic long narrow wings, which are bent back at the wrist, compared to the bald eagle's flat, nearly straight wings.

Bald eagles and ospreys don't like each other—they often engage in territorial battles if one enters the other's territory.

And because ospreys are almost exclusively fish-eaters while bald eagles are opportunists that will eat almost anything, one researcher has noticed an interesting coincidence. On a large lake or flowage where both bald eagles and ospreys are present, ducks have a tendency to nest near ospreys, possibly having learned that the osprey won't tolerate any eagle intrusions, thus inadvertently protecting the ducks.

Bald eagles remain threatened on federal endangered species lists but may soon be delisted to a species of special concern on the state lists of Wisconsin and Minnesota. Ospreys are not on the federal lists but continue to be considered threatened in all three states.

In Minnesota, the recovery of bald eagles has exceeded its original recovery goal of 300 occupied nesting territories and continues to grow at a rate of 30 new nesting pairs per year. In 1973, only 115 occupied nest territories were active, and only 113 young were fledged. By 1993, 568 nest territories were active, and they produced an estimated 602 fledged young. If this rate continues, Minnesota could have more than 700 pairs of eagles by the year 2000. Eagles now nest even in southeastern Minnesota in the Lac Qui Parle Wildlife Area near Watson, and nested in 1988 for the first time in a hundred years along the Minnesota River valley in western Minnesota.

The Raptor Center at the University of Minnesota, which opened in the early 1970s to treat and release injured eagles, has treated more than 90 bald eagles every year. The poisoning of eagles, who became ill from eating sick and dead waterfowl that had shotgun pellets in their bellies, led to the banning of lead shot in all waterfowl hunting in Minnesota.

The bald eagle and osprey are listed as threatened species in Minnesota, but their continued dramatic increase will most likely lead to their removal from the state threatened species list.

Every year the Minnesota DNR transplants eagle chicks from northern nest sites into states trying to restore their eagle populations. New York, Pennsylvania, Tennessee, Missouri, Arkansas, and Georgia all now have eagle populations in part generated from Minnesota stock.

Hot Spots

The **Chippewa National Forest** has over 200 eagle-breeding areas and over 150 osprey pairs that are protected by buffer zones and seasonal limits on human activity. In fact, the Chippewa has the largest number of nesting bald eagles in the continental United States—more than 10 percent of the nation's breeding eagles nest here. In the last 20 years, the eagle population has nearly tripled. Stop at the visitor center on Minnesota 46 on the northeast end of Lake Winnibigoshish—usually an eagle can be seen sitting nearby. Or check out the **Leech Lake Dam** and **Winnie Dam.** Better yet, launch a canoe on one of the larger lakes like **Winnibigoshish, Cass, Leech,** and **Bowstring**—eagles often perch on islands in these lakes. Write or call for the Forest Service eagle-viewing map, which shows some of the best eagle sites that can be seen by road or by boat. Or contact the Forest Service district ranger stations in Black Duck, Cass Lake, Deer River, Marcell, or Walker for current locations of eagles.

Tamarac National Wildlife Refuge has 17 active eagle nests and is an excellent area for viewing nesting bald eagles. Contact the visitor center for current information. Or take the Blackbird auto-tour route. Stop 5 sits across Blackbird Lake from an eagle's nest. From U.S. 59 just south of Callaway in Becker County, take County Road 26 to reach the refuge headquarters and visitor center.

In Wisconsin in 1972, only 82 active breeding eagle pairs were found, and eagles were placed on the Wisconsin endangered species list. That same year, the federal government banned the use of DDT and other organochlorine pesticides in the U.S., and the eagles began a slow comeback. In 1995, Wisconsin boasted 590 pairs of bald eagles.

Vilas and **Oneida Counties** in the lake district of north-central Wisconsin support 82 and 63 active pairs of eagles, respectively (Oneida leads in ospreys, with 90 nests compared to Vilas's 44). The **Rainbow Flowage** in Oneida County, a 4,500-acre impoundment of the Wisconsin River, provides habitat for 16 ospreys and 4 eagle pairs. Take County Road D east from Lake Tomahawk to the intersection with County Road E at the Rainbow dam. Continue east on D for 3 miles to where it crosses Swamp Creek—an osprey nest is visible to the north.

Another good spot, though you'll need a boat, is the north end of the flowage. From just south and east of St. Germain, take County Road J south from Hwy. 70 to the public boat landing just over the bridge crossing the channel that leads to the Pickerel Reservoir. Osprey platforms line the eastern shoreline of the flowage.

The **Turtle-Flambeau Flowage** (see chapter 37) has the highest collective number of bald eagle and osprey breeding pairs on any piece of water in the state. The 10 active eagle nests and 21 active osprey nests are best reached by boat on this 12,000-acre flowage. By car, you can take the Northwoods Auto Tour, available at the Wisconsin Mercer DNR station, which leads you around some of the flowage. Stop 10 places you directly across a narrow channel from an osprey platform on Dead Horse Lake.

The **Willow Flowage,** a 7,300-acre impoundment of the Tomahawk River in Oneida County, supports 10 osprey and 8 bald eagle pairs. Access is really only by boat. Take Hwy. 51 south from Minocqua to County Road Y. Turn right (west) and follow Y to Willow Dam Road, which leads you to two boat landings on the eastern shore of the flowage. Topographical maps are a must for exploring all three of these flowages because of their intricate shorelines and numerous islands.

In Michigan, the eagle population hovered around 86 pairs through the 1970s, and ospreys were counted at 51 nests in 1965, but with protection both species began increasing in the early 1980s. The western UP has the densest eagle breeding numbers, while the eastern UP and the flowages of the northern Lower Peninsula have the greatest concentrations of ospreys. **Fletcher Floodwaters,** in the northern Lower Peninsula, has 25 osprey nesting platforms, the largest human-assisted osprey colony in Michigan. The large tripod platforms may be easily observed from shore or from a boat. The floodwater encompasses 9,000 acres along the Thunder Bay River. The Audubon Society owns 6,000 acres here and can provide a tour guide; call (517) 727-2877 for more information.

As is often the case, the best viewing is done from a boat. The public boat landing is off Jack's Landing Road. Go east from Hillman on Michigan 32 and turn right (south) on Jack's Landing Road. Follow it to the shoreline.

The **Dead Stream Flooding,** though it doesn't have the most romantic of names, offers 30,000 acres of wetlands (known as the **Dead Stream Swamp**), the largest semiwilderness area in the Lower Peninsula. Take a canoe, because this area may only be explored by nonmotorized craft. An active bald eagle nest is visible from the boat ramp, and five osprey platforms make osprey-viewing opportunities quite common. Extensive wild rice beds attract large numbers of waterfowl in the fall. From Michigan 55 just east of U.S. 27, turn north on Old U.S. 27 and go for 2.5 miles to County Road 300. Turn left (west) and proceed 1.5 miles to Michelson Road, where you will turn right (north) and continue on to the small parking lot.

45

Nighthawk Migration

Autumn songbird migrations test mightily the skills of amateur birders, who must then differentiate between birds no longer in their bright breeding plumage. The warblers are renowned for being tough to identify in fall, earning the moniker in bird guides of "confusing" fall warblers as well as several extra pages in an attempt to help the average birder sort them all out. There are some songbirds, though, that are easily identified and whose migrations are truly spectacular, too. One bird most amateur naturalists miss seeing in migration is the common nighthawk. It's missed mostly because nighthawks migrate in large numbers as early as mid-August, a time when most of us just refuse to believe that the summer is really over and birds are on the move. Major flight days occur from August 15 to September 5 in the north and a week later to the south. The flights occur usually between 3:00 P.M. and dusk. Situate yourself in an open area not far from water and you have a good chance of seeing the migration.

Nighthawk flights in the 1800s were likened in size to that of passenger pigeons; one writer in the 1850s observed nighthawks for two full hours in one continuous flock moving south. Today, tens of thousands of nighthawks still migrate along the north shore of Lake Superior. On August 26, 1990, a phenomenal 43,690 nighthawks passed by the Lakewood Pumping Station in Duluth in a two-and-a-half-hour period. Less extraordinary but still substantial record counts include 18,000 nighthawks estimated to have passed over Cedar Grove Ornithological Station in Sheboygan County, Wisconsin, on August 31, 1958, and 10,000 counted in a flight over Crex Meadows in Burnett County on August 20, 1963.

Nighthawks are among the first birds to leave in the autumn and the last to return in late May because of their total reliance on insects. To come any earlier or leave any later could tempt the frosty hand of fate and result in few insects to eat on the journey.

Nighthawks silently flutter south in what appears almost haphazard, if not random, fashion. But the bugs they eat fly randomly, too. So their 20-mph progress toward South America must be zigged and zagged in order to keep their tanks full of insects and thus have enough energy to reach their eventual winter home in Argentina. The nighthawk's cavernous mouth is kept open along the way like a trawler to scoop moths and dragonflies and at least 50 other species of insect—one dissected nighthawk stomach held more than 500 mosquitoes, and another held 2,175 ants! The insects just go right down the hatch—no chewing, no swallowing, no tasting. The huge flocks are beautiful to watch as the nighthawks flutter by on long narrow wings through the deepening sky at sunset.

Nighthawks are not a hawk at all (though they superficially resemble a small falcon in flight) but are members of the nightjar family (Caprimulgidae), a group remarkable for their wide mouths, around which many species have long rictal bristles (though nighthawks lack these), and for their crepuscular (at dawn and dusk) or nocturnal feeding habits. Identification of nighthawks is rather easy—both genders are slim brown-gray birds with a broad white bar across the wings. The male has a white band across his tail and a white throat.

Nighthawks utter a *peent* or *beer* call, a buzzy sound most frequently heard at dusk and dawn. They nest in open country and in cities on flat rooftops, beaches, gravelly fields, little-used blacktop areas, in piles of sawdust and chips around sawmills, and in burned-over areas. The female won't win any Good Housekeeping seals of approval—she just lays two eggs on the ground, not messing around with any nest-building whatsoever.

The adult male's nuptial flight in late May is an exceptional event to witness. I watched it for the first time in a rocky canyon area, and the "booming" dives of the male had me running back to camp to find out what this bird was. The male dives toward the ground at high speed, making a booming sound at the bottom as he pull ups and air rushes through his primaries, vibrating them in a loud *woof* or muffled boom. This can be a dangerous courtship in cities due to power and telephone lines.

To see at dusk and into the night, the nighthawk's eyes have evolved to be heavier than its brain, and they're set far enough back on the head so that nighthawks can see above and behind themselves, a handy adaptation for spotting insects on the wing.

Hot Spots

The **Duluth Lakewood Pumping Station** on the northeast tip of the city is the place where a major passerine count takes place every fall, while up above on Hawk Ridge the hawk-watchers count the incredible numbers of hawks funneling down from Canada and northern Minnesota (see chapter 51). Take Hwy. 61 northeast through Duluth and continue on North Shore Scenic Drive along the lake, where the road divides at the edge of town. About 2 miles up the Scenic Drive is the Lakewood Treatment Plant—park in the lot on the left side of the road by the large brick building. If you walk around the back side of the building, usually you will see a counter nestled in a lawn chair checking birds off as they go by. This is the site of the systematic counts that last from early August through October and average about a quarter of a million individuals of many species every year. Notable one-day records from here include 43,960 nighthawks, 9,000 flickers, 3,402 blue jays, 62,700 robins, 7,110 pine siskins, 29,300 warblers (mostly palm and yellow-rumped), and 3,882 cedar waxwings. No other migration of land birds remotely compares with this anywhere in Minnesota, or anywhere else in the Upper Midwest that I'm aware of.

If counting at a pumping station isn't your idea of an aesthetic experience, or if you don't want to bother the counters, try anywhere along the lake nearby, possibly at the mouths of either the French or Lester Rivers. Take Stony Point Drive, another 7.5 miles north on Lakeshore Drive, for a roadside hike that will give you good vantage points from which to look for nighthawks and other songbirds as well as waterfowl out on the lake.

46

Red-Necked Grebes

Until 1989 it was not known what migration corridor red-necked grebes used to reach their wintering grounds on the Atlantic Coast. Then, in that autumn, over 1,000 were counted passing by Whitefish Point in the Upper Peninsula of Michigan between September and November, a number that turned out to be only a hint of the multitude that was soon to be discovered. In 1992, with counts beginning in early August, a record 14,812 birds were seen off the point. That total was staggering, given that red-necked grebes were rarely seen in flight anywhere in the Midwest, much less in the thousands. Since then Whitefish Point has been recognized as the place to be in the Upper Midwest to view these elegant birds. Single-day totals have exceeded 5,000 individuals in flocks containing from 1 to 56 birds. The bulk of the eastern population of red-necked grebes is thought to pass by Whitefish Point during daylight hours.

Seen up close, red-necked grebes are distinguished by the red neck and chest, which contrasts with a whitish gray throat and cheek patch outlined by a white crescent. The dark forehead and yellowish, long, daggerlike bill are further defining characteristics. Most red-necked grebes observed at Whitefish Point won't be seen close up, though. The majority are "fly-bys" seen well off the point over Lake Superior. Still, their dazzling numbers create quite a spectacle. To identify a grebe in flight, remember that all grebes have a characteristic humped posture, where the head, neck, and feet are held lower than the body. At a distance, a red-necked grebe can be specifically identified by its large bill, prominent cheek patch, and white patches on the leading and trailing edges of the wings. Clark's and western grebes have similar markings, but given their western breeding range, they are highly unlikely visitors to Whitefish Point.

The fall migration of red-necked grebes peaks in mid- to late August, though it's well under way by late July and continues with individuals seen into late November. Comparatively few are seen in the spring—they appear to migrate nocturnally then.

Days of mass movement occur when steady northwest winds prevail, particularly if they follow weather patterns out of the south. Southerly winds tend to bunch migrating birds up while they wait for more favorable winds. Depending on the weather conditions, you may see no red-necked grebes if there is a southerly warm front, but if a cooler front comes in from the northwest the next day, bingo.

Most Midwesterners have never even seen a red-necked grebe, much less thousands in migration. Red-necked grebes breed uncommonly and locally in Minnesota and are rare breeders in western and central Wisconsin. None are known to breed in Michigan.

Red-necked grebes nest on water on floating masses of vegetation anchored to upright plants. All grebes are fish-eaters, but they also consume a smorgasbord of other aquatic creatures, such as amphibians and insects, along with a few plants. Grebes even eat their own feathers by the hundreds—an astonishing 50 percent of a grebe's stomach content may be feathers! This odd behavior may cushion their stomach linings to help protect against the sharp fish bones that pass through their digestive systems, and may also help slow down the digestive process so the bones can be better assimilated.

Red-necked grebes are currently under study to answer questions such as where they go after passing Whitefish Point and how far. Do they stage somewhere en masse? If so, where? Do they fly at night, and if so, how many? Since most other grebes (and other birds) are already in their winter plumage, why are most red-necks still in their breeding plumage in late August, and when does their molt take place?

Whitefish Point Bird Observatory is arguably the best site in Michigan from which to watch fall migrations. Shorebirds arrive in late August, including lesser golden plover, black-bellied plover, semipalmated plover, sanderling, and Baird's sandpiper, along with rarities like piping plover and red-necked phalarope.

September brings a flush of songbirds and other birds. In fact, September is considered the best month of the year at the observatory. And the third weekend in September may be the best weekend of the entire year, with the highest volume of migrants and peak opportunities for rarities like long-tailed jaeger, Sabine's gull, Harris's sparrow, and Smith's longspur. The observatory is the hot spot for jaegers in the upper Great Lakes—all three species may be seen in September.

October brings thousands of waterbirds past the point daily in a nearly continual stream of loons, grebes, geese, and ducks of all kinds.

Possibly best of all, if the weather systems don't cooperate and the birds are sitting tight somewhere, the peninsula itself is beautiful, as is the surrounding region. A trip here at any time of the year is wonderfully rewarding.

Hot Spots   To get to **Whitefish Point Bird Observatory,** take Hwy. 123 north to Paradise, and then turn north on Whitefish Point Road (Hwy. 123 bends west here) to the very tip of the peninsula and the parking lot at the lighthouse and the bird observatory.

47

August Shorttakes

Butterfly Migration

Monarch butterflies migrate some 2,500 miles to Mexico in early autumn, often flying along the same migration corridors as hawks. To see them in large numbers in Wisconsin, try **Kohler Andrae Park** along Lake Michigan. In Michigan, **Peninsula Point** is at the very end of the long peninsula that juts into Green Bay. A 40-foot lighthouse tower sits at the tip of the peninsula and serves as a great viewing platform. From Rapid River, go east on U.S. 2 to County Road 513 and turn right (south). Follow this road for about 18 miles to its end at Peninsula Point.

At the **Lake Bluff Audubon Center** along the Lake Michigan shoreline, often large groups of monarchs stop here to rest in August. From Manistee, go north on U.S. 31 and turn north (left) onto Michigan 110. After 1 mile on 110, turn onto Lakeshore Road. Lake Bluff Center is located on the left (east) side of the road at 2890 Lakeshore Road. Call the Michigan Audubon Society at (616) 889-4761 for more information.

In mid-August at **Tawas Point State Park,** monarchs congregate on the peninsula point jutting into Lake Huron to rest. From Tawas City take Michigan 23 and turn right (south) onto Tawas Beach Road. Go 2.5 miles to the State Park entrance.

The **Metrobeach Metropark,** a 750-acre peninsula jutting into Lake St. Clair with 7 miles of shoreline, often has large numbers of monarchs and hummingbirds flying over or stopping to rest. From Detroit, take I-94 east to Exit 236. Turn right onto Metro Parkway (16 Mile Road) and go 3 miles to the park entrance.

Ripe Blackberries and Thimbleberries

One of the best places I've ever been for picking thimbleberries is **Isle Royale National Park** (of course, it's one of the best places I've ever been, period). Blackberries come ripe along old logging roads, open fields and edges, anywhere where there is full sun. Wear protective clothing no matter the heat—the thorns can rip you up. See chapter 37 for directions.

Bat Hibernation

At the **Bat Mine in the city of Iron Mountain,** Michigan, all you will see is the mouth of an abandoned mine with steel mesh across it to allow bats in and out. This is a critical breeding and hibernation site for nearly 1 million bats—one of the largest concentrations in the world! Big brown and little brown bats hibernate here in late August and early September and won't emerge until late April to early May. The best time for viewing is dusk, when the bats emerge from the 300-foot-deep mine (visit early in August, before they begin hibernating). From the intersection of U.S. 141 and U.S. 2, go west on U.S. 2 for 1.8 miles to Park Avenue and turn right (north). Drive 1 mile to the parking area—the entrance to the cave is a brief walk uphill from the parking lot. Call (906) 774-8530 for more information.

Autumn Shorebird Migration

Shorebirds are among the first birds to migrate south, some beginning as early as late July. Visit **Wilderness State Park's Waugoshance Point,** a peninsula that juts westward 3 miles into Lake Michigan, and **Pointe Mouillee State Game Area,** another peninsula jutting into Lake Erie with a series of dikes that makes for excellent hiking and biking. Some of the best shorebird viewing in the state occurs here, especially in late summer and early fall. Call Audubon Rare Bird Alert, (810) 477-1360, for information on current rare sightings that may be in the area. Call (313) 379-9692 for more information on Pointe Mouillee.

48

A Closer Look: Great Lakes Migration Corridors

Migratory hotspots like Duluth, Whitefish Point, Brockway Mountain Drive, the Straits of Mackinac, and Lake Erie Marsh are like the narrow spouts of a series of broad funnels. Bird migration generally moves in a broad sweep up through the Upper Midwest in the spring and back down in the autumn, except when the birds run into an obstacle they can't cross, and then they have to go around it. The largest obstacles birds face in the Upper Midwest are the Great Lakes—Superior, Huron, Michigan, and Erie. An Arctic-nesting bird comes screeching to a southerly halt in the fall when it encounters something as imposing as Lake Superior. Most birds don't like to cross large bodies of water, so they willingly follow the shoreline in whatever direction winds and instinct may lead them. They ultimately get forced through narrow geographical corridors, or funnels, to the great joy of bird-watchers. Once through the constrictions, they then spread out and get back on course to their destination.

These funnels can spit out phenomenal numbers of birds on certain "record" days. A record day usually occurs after a number of consecutive days of the "wrong" weather—southerly winds in the autumn, northerly winds in the spring, or lengthy rainfalls or fog, anything to stack the birds up like airplanes waiting to land at a socked-in airport. When the weather finally changes and the winds turn, the birds come through in droves and bird-watchers need swivels on their necks and an adding machine to keep count. Usually peak periods in the fall are the second day after a cold front moves through, providing steady winds and ample sunlight to produce *thermals,* updrafts of warm air caused by the sun's heat, upon which hawks can ride effortlessly.

If a great flight is interrupted by a rainy, still, or foggy day, the hawks often settle on trees and other perches to wait it out. One peak broad-winged hawk day at Duluth's Hawk Ridge had such a large number of hawks coming through that not all made it by nightfall, and many settled down for the evening in trees in Duluth, often quite close to backyard bird feeders. Laura Erickson, a Duluth native and author of *For the Birds,* tells about the next day, when the morning was slow to warm up and the only thermals the hawks could find were over the large and rapidly heating asphalt parking lots of grocery stores and malls. The store owners were calling Laura to ask why so many hawks were circling right over their businesses—I suppose it made them nervous.

The corridors don't always hold true for both migratory seasons. Duluth's Hawk Ridge may be as good as any hawk site in America in the fall but has virtually no action in the spring because the hawks aren't forced that way. Brockway Mountain Drive in Michigan's Keweenaw Peninsula and White-fish Point farther to the east are two peninsulas that offer hawks the shortest crossings into Canada in the spring, but Brockway offers only great scenery in the fall and has no more hawks than anywhere else. Whitefish Point changes to specialize more in migratory waterfowl, passerines, and shorebirds.

Peninsulas projecting into the Great Lakes often are the best converging funnels for land birds in daytime migration. Don't just go to the areas suggested in this book. Look at maps of the coastlines of all three states, find the peninsulas, and check them out—you could experience excellent migrations if you hit the right day. Peninsula Point near Escanaba in the UP is a good example of a long peninsula that serves as the closest launching pad for birds wishing to cross Green Bay to reach Wisconsin. A 40-foot-tall lighthouse tower at the end of the peninsula makes the viewing all the more enjoyable. Even monarch butterflies may concentrate on this point in their 2,500-mile flight to Mexico.

Most hawks don't begin migrating until later in the morning—they're waiting for thermals to strengthen and give them the lift they need to fly more effortlessly. Flights usually end by 4:00 P.M. for the opposite reason—thermals are declining as the day cools off. The high rock ridges of Hawk Ridge and Brockway Mountain Drive are ideal for forming warm updrafts that the hawks ride right up, sometimes coming over the ridges so low that they are at eye level, at other times riding the thermals so high that they're little more than dots way up in the blue.

Broad-winged hawks, peregrine falcons, and ospreys winter in South America, but most other hawks head for the central and southern United States, Mexico, and Central America. A few, like goshawks, rough-legged hawks, and bald eagles winter right here in the Upper Midwest.

Not all hawks come through in the same time periods. At Hawk Ridge in fall the first migrants pass through in mid-August, and the last appear in late November and early December. Two peak periods occur: the first in mid-September, when massive kettles of broad-winged hawks (as many as 47,000 in one day) and sharp-shinned hawks (as many as 1,600 in one day) come through, as well as good numbers of falcons; and the second in mid-October, when the red-tailed hawks, goshawks, rough-legged hawks, and eagles soar by. Even golden eagles are here; a record 23 were counted on October 24, 1994.

September

Notes

49

Wild Rice Ripening

Canoeing through a dense stand of wild rice feels much like walking through a tall-grass prairie. The grasses (wild rice is a grass too) reach so high that one becomes lost among the swishing stems. On one lake I've canoed in northern Wisconsin the rice covers virtually every inch of the 94 acres of water, appearing from the boat landing more like a field of oats than a lake. But launch your canoe into the "standing field" and 4 feet of water supports your weight. Paddling is difficult and slow through the dense stems, but that's the right speed for gathering rice.

Traditional ricing is done by two people: one standing in the back of the canoe in order to see over the stalks and pushing the canoe along with a long pole, while the other sits in the front (facing the stern) with two rounded sticks, each a yard long. One stick is to gather and bend the rice stalks over the middle of the canoe, the other is to knock the rice into a rain of kernels onto the bottom of the canoe. Done right, the poler and the gatherer work in harmony to efficiently harvest a stand, though still losing some of the rice into the water, on purpose. Wild rice grows annually, and without some "waste," it won't come up the next year.

A quiet music accompanies the ricing process—the sound of the pole dipping in the water, the bow of the boat scraping through the rice, and the rattle of the sticks as they gather and knock, gather and knock.

An experienced ricing pair can gather 100 pounds of rice a day and return to the same stand several times over the following few weeks, for wild rice ripens unevenly, the field being ready for harvest again and again. Only about 10 percent of the fruiting head matures at a time, and the ripened grains "shatter," or fall off, immediately.

The Native Chippewa moved to ricing camps in late August along the shorelines of lakes and rivers. They saw the work as a ritual of great religious and social significance, symbolizing the peak of the natural cycles of earth, air, water, and sun joining to provide sustenance. Once the rice was gathered, it was dried on sheets of birch bark and then parched over an outdoor fire to loosen the kernels from the husks. Next, someone would "dance" on the rice, supporting himself or herself with poles so as not to crush the rice. And then the rice was winnowed, tossed into a wind that would blow the lighter husks away while the heavier kernels fell onto the ground.

Wild rice is the only cereal grain native to North America, and along with maple syrup was the most important indigenous food used by the

Native Americans in the Upper Midwest. Rice is estimated to have provided 25 percent of the total calories in their diet. The Menominee tribe in central Wisconsin took the name *Menominee* because it means "wild rice people." Thirty thousand Natives in the wild rice district of northern Minnesota and Wisconsin were supported by the seemingly endless stands of rice. Sandy Lake in Aitkin County, Minnesota, was said to be a "great rice marsh some five miles long and three miles wide." The rice not only fed the people but also fed myriads of waterfowl that could also be harvested while foraging in the beds. That's still part of the pleasure in ricing—one never knows when a flock of blackbirds or wood ducks or mallards will burst from the rice in an explosion of wings.

Today, wild rice occupies far less territory. Drained farmland, channelized streams, dammed rivers, and ditched wetlands are part of the story of twentieth-century agricultural progress. Wild rice requires some water movement, and it prefers fluctuating water levels, which help reduce competition from other aquatic plants. Still, some substantial rice stands await the harvester who wishes to engage in a simple reenactment of history with a culinary reward. Rice processors mechanically finish the rice after its gathering, so you needn't parch, dance, and winnow, unless you want to.

A note about domesticated "wild" rice packaged as *real* wild rice: Paddy rice farming took off in the 1970s in Minnesota and California, and today California holds over half of the world market in "wild" rice. Domesticated wild rice yields 1,000 pounds to the acre and is harvested mechanically, whereas true wild rice usually provides only 40 to 50 pounds per acre for harvest and is harvested by hand from a canoe. If you see wild rice sold at $2 per pound, it surely is paddy rice, because the Real McCoy should sell for about $7 per pound due to the far greater time and difficulty of collecting it.

In Wisconsin one may harvest wild rice on designated lakes, but an $8 license is required, and a unique set of rules governs the process. No boat longer than 17 feet or wider than 38 inches may be used nor can it be propelled by a motor of any kind. Only a paddle or pole may used. And no other method of gathering may take place other than by "the use of smooth, rounded, wooden rods or sticks, not more than 38 inches in length, and which are held and operated by hand." Harvesting may not begin until the opening date is set by the Wisconsin DNR, usually around September 1.

Gathering rice is remarkably easy. When ripe, the rice literally cascades into your canoe, so even the novice ricer can experience success. Call the department of natural resources in one of the northern lakes regions to find out about the local regulations and the designated lakes—the ducks won't mind sharing a pound or two.

In Wisconsin, **Vilas and Oneida Counties** are renowned for their density of lakes. The Wisconsin DNR has designated a number of lakes for ricing, though the list may change a bit annually. Try **Allequash, Aurora, Nixon, Irving,** and **Devine Lakes** in Vilas County, or possibly **Atkins, Big, Little Rice,** and **Gary Lakes** in Oneida County. Allequash Lake has two lobes, the southern lobe providing dense stands of rice with only a narrow channel through them. Allequash is located just off County Road M south of Boulder Junction. Head south for approximately 5 miles on M from Boulder and turn left at the boat-landing sign for Allequash Lake. Black terns nest back in the aquatic vegetation, too. Ospreys, eagles, and loons nest on the lake as well.

In Minnesota, **Rice Lake NWR** encompasses 18,000 acres, 4,500 acres of which are in the shallow waters of Rice Lake. Wild rice and wild celery beds attract huge numbers of migrating ducks and geese—up to 70,000 ring-necked ducks use the lake during their fall migration. The Chippewa traditionally have riced here every September and may still be seen harvesting a portion of the wild rice crop. Mid-October is best for seeing huge concentrations of waterfowl. A 9.5-mile auto tour gives a perspective of the changing face of this area. Stop 6 is at an observation tower overlooking Rice Lake. The refuge is located in Aitkin County about 5 miles south of McGregor. From McGregor, take Minnesota 210 east and turn right (south) onto Minnesota 65. The entrance to the refuge will be on your right in about 5 miles.

Tamarac NWR is made up of about 40 percent watery habitat—21 lakes plus marsh and bogs. Here the Dakota and Chippewa waged war over the abundant wild rice crops. Wild rice stands are still harvested in the traditional way here, both by people and by rafts of 35,000 ring-necked ducks and up to 30,000 coots. From Detroit Lakes, take Minnesota 34 east for 8 miles to Becker County Road 29, and follow it 10 miles north to the refuge headquarters.

The 30,665-acre **Sherburne NWR** draws in waterfowl by the tens of thousands in October to feed on its wild rice. From the Twin Cities, take I-94 northwest about 40 miles to Rogers, then take Minnesota 101 north to Elk River, where it becomes Minnesota 169. Follow 169 to the refuge sign 4.5 miles north of Zimmerman.

50

Autumn Foliage

Poet Edna St. Vincent Millay wrote that the autumn trees "ache and sag and all but cry with color. They bend and blow and burn against an October sky." The number of human "leaf peepers" attests to our love affair with this tapestry of colors. The brilliant transformation of the northern deciduous forest from a lush summer green to a riot of autumn colors combined with the invigorating bite of northern winds makes autumn the favorite season of many people.

Leaf change is analogous to pulling aside a curtain and revealing the true picture of a forest. Chlorophyll masks a number of other pigments that can't be seen until the tree stops its chlorophyll production in the autumn. The combination of shortening days, colder temperatures, and usually a reduction in moisture triggers the formation of a hardening layer of cells at the junction of the leaf stalk and twig. Eventually this layer grows, choking off the leaf's circulatory system, and the leaf drops. But for about two weeks prior to leaf fall as chlorophyll production ceases and the green fades, the chemical system of each tree is revealed in its appropriate colors. Trees with carotenes, carotenoids, and xanthophylls turn yellow. Trees with tannins turn a yellow-brown. Trees with anthocyanin, which develops as it's exposed to sunlight, turn red and purple. Combinations of these chemicals can deliver a palette of colors. Some leaves can be both brilliant red and yellow, the red indicating where sunlight reached the leaf, allowing the anthocyanin to form, the yellow indicating where the leaf was shaded.

Once the leaves fall, look closely at the twig on the tree and you'll see many buds. Here spring resides, enclosed in a series of scales that help protect the new twig and its undeveloped leaves, which are patiently awaiting the awakening song of April and May.

You can use a general color guide for identifying tree species by color alone, though one of the first laws in the natural world is to expect variation.

Gold and yellow: hard maples, poplar, beech, aspens, birches, honey locust, hickory, cottonwood, some ashes.

Red, orange, and purple: soft maples, sumac, blackberry, maple-leaved viburnum, white oak, red oak.

Brown: Oaks and ironwood turn colors but eventually turn brown, and many hang on to their leaves throughout the winter.

Rust, green, and yellow: butternut, walnut, elm, sycamore, catalpa.

The Porcupine Mountains in the UP offer beautiful vistas for leaf peepers and hikers. Photo by Carol Christensen.

Note that peak color varies at different latitudes. In the North Woods look for peaks from mid- to late September; in central counties, from late September to mid-October; and in southern counties, from early to late October. The shorelines along the Great Lakes tend to peak several weeks later than areas just inland due to the moderating effect of the water, so adjust accordingly. And the factors of varying local moisture levels and temperatures make for differences in colors within a region, too. It's best to call ahead to a local department of natural resources or chamber of commerce to see when peak colors are expected to occur in an area.

Hot Spots

In Michigan, the **Keweenaw Peninsula** and **Brockway Mountain Drive** in particular offer a feast of colors. The last 11 miles of Hwy. 41 leading into **Copper Harbor** are lined with overarching hardwoods. Once in Copper Harbor, turn left (west) on County Road 26 to drive up Brockway Mountain Drive, which will dazzle you with panoramic lake and forest valley views. (See chapter 28 for directions.) Because of the influence of Lake Superior, the peak color often doesn't arrive until the first weekend in October.

While in the Keweenaw, drive **Houghton Canal Road** to **Covered Drive**, and through **Redridge** and **Beacon Hill**. Pick up the Canal Road heading west out of Houghton on the south side of the Portage Lake Ship Canal.

The **Tunnel of Trees Shore Drive** near Harbor Springs is 13 miles long, following the north shore of Little Traverse Bay. Take Lake Shore Drive west out of Harbor Springs.

The **Porcupine Mountains Wilderness State Park Escarpment Trail** runs along mid-America's highest mountain range, offering spectacular views of Lake of the Clouds and wooded hills flowing to and away from Lake Superior. An overlook parking lot at the end of Michigan 107 provides easy driving access to the rock outcrops. Take the trail east or west if you wish to hike along this rugged ridge.

Of the nearly 3,246 planned miles of the **North Country National Scenic Trail,** 872 will be located in Michigan, and about 500 miles of trail are completed as of this writing. The section in the **Ottawa National Forest** and Porcupine Mountains State Park in the far western Upper Peninsula provides one of the wildest pieces of the whole trail. The UP also has the longest continuous completed section of the trail in the entire system, a 200-mile stretch from Munising to St. Ignace, which includes hikes through the **Pictured Rocks National Lakeshore** and **Tahquamenon Falls State Park.** Contact the North Country Trail Association (P.O. Box 311, White Cloud, MI 49349) or local Michigan DNR offices for maps of areas you would like to hike.

About 60 miles of the trail cross the Ottawa National Forest. Try the **Black River segment,** which begins at the Copper Peak ski flying hills on Gogebic County Road 513 north of Bessemer. It parallels the gorgeous Black River from the peak to Black River Harbor on Lake Superior and is mostly downhill. The trail crosses a footbridge and turns back south again, paralleling the river to a point just upstream of Rainbow Falls, then turns eastward to Gogebic County Road 519. The total length is 10 miles, but do just the first half for a combination of beautiful fall colors and rushing rapids and waterfalls.

In Minnesota, Lake Superior's **North Shore Sawtooth Mountains Fall Color Tour** is a self-guided journey through the Sawtooth Mountains that runs parallel to Lake Superior's shoreline. The "mountains" ("hills" might be more appropriate) rise sharply into jagged ridges that look out over the big lake. The Lutsen Tofte Tourism Association, in cooperation with Superior National Forest, produces a *Fall Color Tour* pamphlet with designated routes and highlighted points of interest. Write to Box 2248, Tofte, MN 55615. The pamphlets are also available at the Tofte Ranger Station and most businesses in the area.

Two seasons of fall color occur due to the moderating effect on temperatures created by the vast waters of Lake Superior. From September 10 to October 10, inland colors are peaking, and driving back roads will often bring you to spectacular vistas overlooking Lake Superior. The interior offers a medley of reds and oranges from red maples and sugar maples, contrasting with the deep greens of northern conifers. From October 5 to 20 the colors pulse along the shore of Lake Superior as you follow scenic Hwy.

61. The shoreline tends to be a patchwork of yellows from aspen, birch, and poplar, which often contrast with an understory of flaming red sumac.

Carlton Peak at 927 feet is the highest point on Minnesota's North Shore, and the summit offers impressive views of the surrounding Sawtooth Mountains and Lake Superior. An easy 3-mile ascent on the Superior Hiking Trail will bring you there. Pick up the trail at **Temperance River State Park** and follow the powerful Temperance River with its canyon views to the peak. **Britton Peak** provides another beautiful vista and is easier to reach. Take the five-minute walking trail marked by a sign on the Sawbill Trail (County Road 2) 2 miles north of U.S. 61.

The **Border Route Trail** follows high cliffs with exceptional views of forests and lakes while traversing the most rugged section of the **Boundary Waters Canoe Area Wilderness**. The hiking trail parallels the water routes along the Canadian border. The eastern trailhead is at Little John Lake at the end of the Arrowhead Trail (County Road 16), about 20 miles north of Hovland. The western trailhead is off the Gunflint Trail (County Road 12) at the end of the road to Loon Lake and about 30 miles north of Grand Marais.

In Wisconsin, the 3 miles of **Skyline Drive** in **Peninsula State Park** is claimed by some to have the most interesting and beautiful miles of paved road in Wisconsin on which to ride a bicycle. The drive offers three vistas of Lake Michigan and its islands and is wooded and shaded for its entire length. Peninsula Park is located off Hwy. 42 just north of Fish Creek in Door County.

The unglaciated coulee country of **Buffalo** and **Trempealeau Counties** winds you up and down ridges and through wooded valleys in a zigzagging progression through seemingly ever more beautiful areas. Check a good atlas and the roads here look like squiggly spiderwebs— it's mighty difficult to find anything straight or level in these counties. The beauty of the area emanates from its topographical creativity, and although numerous farms and small towns dot the landscape, the hills grow trees that turn every color you might desire. Try **Skyline Drive** (Hwy. 93) in Trempealeau County between Centerville and Arcadia, or "**Alligator Slide**," a steep descent off Hwy. 95 into the Trempealeau River Valley and Fountain City. The many bluffs along the Great River Road (Hwy. 35) provide exceptionally panoramic vistas over the Mississippi River. Try **Granddad Bluff** in **Wyalusing State Park** in Grant County for a view of the confluence of the Wisconsin and Mississippi Rivers, or **Brady's Bluff** in **Perrot State Park** in Trempealeau County. Contact the Indian Head Country office for fall color-tour routes at (800) 472-6654.

If you like to hike, a 60-mile section of the North Country Trail traverses the northern half of the **Chequamegon National Forest**. The trail begins at County Road A near Lake Ruth just south of Iron River and ends on Forest Road 390 just 2 miles west of Mellen. The eastern half of the trail is most rugged, traveling as it does through the rock outcroppings and ridges of the Penokee Hills. Thirteen miles northwest of Mellen, St. Peter's Dome, a granite summit of about 1,600 feet elevation, is a favorite destination of many hikers on the trail. On clear days a visitor can see Lake Superior 20 miles to the north. It's a 1.5-mile hike in from the parking lot at Forest Road 199. From Clam Lake, take County Road GG north and turn left (west) on Forest Road 187. Follow 187, and turn left (west again) on Forest Road 199, which takes you to the parking area.

The Wisconsin Department of Transportation produces a booklet entitled *Wisconsin Rustic Roads,* which lists all the officially designated "rustic" roads in the state. Write to the Department of Transportation, P.O. Box 7913, Madison, WI 53707.

In Wisconsin a fall foliage hotline may be called after Labor Day for information on fall foliage dates throughout the entire country: (800) 354-4595.

51

Hawk Migration

September at Hawk Ridge in Duluth, Minnesota, can defy superlatives. It's one of the major global sites for observing fall hawk migrations, and 2,000 or more broad-winged hawks may pass over in an hour. The record single-day high of 47,922 broad-winged hawks occurred on September 18, 1993. The total number of broadwings for the entire year of 1993 was a record 148,615!

Hawk Ridge ranks as one of the top three sites in the United States from which to watch the fall hawk migration. Owned by the city of Duluth and managed by a committee of the Duluth Audubon Society, the ridge sits high above the city, overlooking Lake Superior. Migrating birds coming south from Canada and northern Minnesota funnel over the ridge because of their reluctance to cross large bodies of water like Lake Superior (see map on page 216). Hawk Ridge, because of its commanding view, offers the ideal site for watching the stream of birds exiting the north before the winter hits. And because of the ridge's height, hawks, particularly sharp-shinned hawks and falcons, ride the updrafts and often stream in low over the ridge right at or below eye level to add to the thrill of seeing such great numbers of birds.

Full-time hawk counting between the months of August and November began in 1972, and records for every species of hawk counted have been kept, as have records of hawks and owls banded at the banding station on the ridge. The numbers confirm how spectacular a good day at Hawk Ridge can be. On September 24, 1993, a record 1,683 sharp-shinned hawks crested the ridge. On September 7, 1993, a record 51 ospreys were counted. On September 22, 1992, 37 Cooper's hawks came through, and 545 American kestrels soared by on September 3, 1988. On October 24, 1994, 23 golden eagles flew through.

The best time of day for viewing the migrations is from 9:00 A.M. to around 4:00 P.M. The midday hours provide the strongest winds and thermals for the birds to ride.

Two peak periods normally exist: one in mid-September for broad-winged and sharp-shinned hawks, and one in mid- to late October, when the "big" hawks head south, including the northern goshawks, rough-legged and red-tailed hawks, and eagles.

The best days are when the winds are from the northwest or west. These winds blow the hawks to the southeast toward Minnesota's North Shore,

Hawk Ridge is one of the best sites for watching the fall hawk migration. Photo by Carol Christensen.

and ultimately Duluth. The westerly element of the wind appears most important, because days with a straight north wind tend to produce only fair numbers of birds. If the wind is from the south, southeast, east, or northeast, stay home, because the birds will stay put as well. If there's rain, fog, or a low overcast, the hawks move little, though these are good days to check along the lakeshore for the passerine migration that might be momentarily "stuck" on Minnesota Point (see chapter 26).

Autumn is the only time to see hawks in any numbers along the ridge. The funneling effect of the North Shore doesn't affect northbound migrants in the spring, and the summer and winter are quiet too, because few hawks breed or winter along Hawk Ridge.

Hawk Ridge is the best hawk-watching site, but there are others that are very good, too. The barrier of the Great Lakes creates a series of land corridors between and around the lakes that most birds gratefully choose to follow, rather than risk the crossings that, with a shift in wind, could easily doom them. The following are some of the best corridor sites.

Hot Spots

To get to Minnesota's **Hawk Ridge**, take Hwy. 61 /London Road in Duluth to 45th Avenue East and turn left. Follow 45th to its end, then turn left onto Glenwood. Go 0.5 mile to the Skyline Parkway at the top of the hill, turn right, then go 1 mile on Skyline to the Main Overlook.

In Wisconsin, **Outer Island** in the **Apostle Islands National Lakeshore** is exceptional for passerines. About 97 percent of the many thousands of birds that stop over and fly across here are robins, juncos, and warblers. Following the passerines are falcons, and here is an outstanding opportunity to watch various predator-prey interactions. Peregrine falcons chase merlins, the merlins chase kestrels, and all three falcons chase songbirds. In 1991, 105 merlins and 66 peregrines were recorded here. Getting to the south end of Outer Island, where the migration seems to concentrate, is quite difficult, however. Lake Superior's conditions in autumn are at best unpredictable, and at worst quite dangerous. It's 18 miles by boat, so this may be one site that the birds get to keep mostly to themselves.

Along the **Mississippi River,** a number of bluff sites offer outstanding vistas from which to watch hawks. In **Wyalusing State Park,** take South Wilderness Road to its end for a magnificent view over the Mississippi River (see chapter 26 for directions). At **Nelson Dewey State Park,** the vista from the ridge in the park is excellent for migrating raptors (see chapter 26 for directions). **Genoa Old Settler's Park** is located 4 miles south of Stoddard or 2 miles north of Genoa. Look for the sign to the park along Hwy. 35 or for Spring Coulee Road. The park is an old quarry. **Buena Vista Park,** a 400-foot-high bluff with a magnificent vista overlooking the village of Alma, offers an excellent vantage point for fall hawk flights. Peregrine falcons attempted to nest here in the 1980s. Take Hwy. 35 into Alma and turn east onto County Road E, which will lead you to the road entering the park.

Along Lake Michigan, **Harrington Beach State Park** provides good hawk-watching. The Wisconsin Society for Ornithology usually leads a fall hawk watch here every year. Take I-43 north from Port Washington and exit east onto County Road D, which takes you to the northern edge of the park. Hike the wooded trails and along the lakeshore.

In Michigan, **Silver Mountain** in the **Ottawa National Forest** in the UP offers excellent spring and fall viewing of migrating hawks as they catch the updrafts pushing up the mountainside. It's a bit of a climb—250 boulder-strewn steps to the top. From Baraga, go west on Michigan 38 nearly 10 miles to Prickett Dam Road (also Forest Service Road 2270) and turn right (south). Follow the signs to the Silver Mountain parking area.

Along Lake Michigan, the **Kitchel-Lindquist Dunes Preserve** represents a full sand dune ecosystem from bare beach areas to climax dune forest and not incidentally is great for viewing hawks (see chapter 42 for directions).

Grand Mere State Park has forested sand dunes and beaches along Lake Michigan along with three small lakes, and heavy hawk migrations on east winds (see chapter 42 for directions).

The **Sarett Nature Center,** a Michigan Audubon Society sanctuary, has over 5 miles of elevated earth or boardwalk trails and eight observation platforms. From I-196, turn west on Red Arrow Highway (Exit 1) and take the first right onto Benton Center Road. The nature center is 0.75 mile north.

Hawk Migrations in the Upper Great Lakes Region

P.J. Hoffmaster State Park has a high dune platform that provides an excellent migrating-hawk lookout over the 2 miles of beach on the shore of Lake Michigan (see chapter 42 for directions).

Muskegon State Park offers outstanding autumn raptors, particularly on northeast winds. This is also a beautiful and diverse natural area with climax hemlock and beech-maple forests as well as jack pine scrub, white cedar swamp, and all the stages of dune succession. Take U.S. 31 north out of Muskegon and the Business Route U.S. 31 exit west toward North Muskegon. Go 1.5 miles and turn right on Michigan 120. Continue to Ruddiman Street, turn left, and take Ruddiman for 5 miles to the state park.

Peninsula Point in Delta County is a stubby peninsula jutting south into Lake Michigan that often concentrates hawks over the point. About 2 miles east of Rapid River on U.S. 2, take County Road 513 south. Follow 513 for 18 miles to the Forest Service picnic ground at the end of the peninsula. An old lighthouse may be climbed here as well.

Along Lake Erie, Lake Erie Metropark is an ideal hawk-watching location where the Detroit River empties into Lake Erie. In 1992, 59,000 raptors were recorded—30,000 broadwings in a single day, sometimes in kettles of 3,000! The best conditions are moderate winds from the north with broken clouds—hawks often fly too high to be seen well on clear days. Most watchers congregate in the northeast corner of the Great Wave parking lot. September 12 through 20 is ideal, though 51 golden eagles were seen in late October and November in 1992. From Detroit, take I-75 south to the Gibraltar Road exit. Turn left (east) onto Gibraltar and drive about 1 mile to Jefferson Road. Take a right (south) and continue to the park entrance on your left.

52

Elk Bugling

A concert put on by bugling bull elk is truly memorable. In September, a bull gathers a harem of 5 to 20 cows (the average harem size is around 10) for breeding, and then defends his entourage by breaking brush with his antlers and bugling to intimidate his competitors. Now you'd expect an 800-pound animal, four times the size of a large white-tailed deer, to make a deep, resounding bellow of some sort when it bugles, particularly to defend that many females, but not so. The sound has been variously described as a "low wheezing, almost asthmatic whistle that ends in a series of evil-sounding grunts," and as "a shrill shriek descending the scale into a blasting bawl." In other words, you have to hear it for yourself.

Today, free-ranging elk herds exist in 22 states. Thirteen thousand elk have been translocated from Yellowstone National Park to repopulate these areas, and the present North American population numbers around 600,000 animals. In the Upper Midwest, elk were extirpated from Minnesota, Wisconsin, and Michigan in the mid-1800s, but were reintroduced in Michigan and Minnesota in the early 1900s. Wisconsin is currently studying the effects of a recently introduced herd to determine if it wants to bring elk back—their prodigious appetites could have significant undesirable botanical effects.

Hot Spots

In Michigan, the largest free-roaming elk herd east of the Mississippi River is found in the **Pigeon River Country State Forest**. Over a thousand elk, Michigan's only elk herd, wander this 95,000-acre state forest, all of which are descendants of seven Rocky Mountain elk that were released here in 1918.

The best viewing occurs during weekdays in September due to the crowds that tend to gather over the weekends. The elk can be seen anytime, but the bulls rut in early fall and are most active then. Early morning and twilight offer by far the best opportunities for viewing elk. Interestingly, the Pigeon River Country State Forest's management is overseen by an outside group, the Pigeon River Country Advisory Council. Their number-one objective is "to provide favorable habitat for elk."

Four elk-viewing areas have been designated and are managed with plantings of rye, clover, buckwheat, and alfalfa to provide the elk with food aplenty. Parking areas with the best visibility have also been created.

Elk again reside in the Upper Midwest. Photo by Jeff Richter.

The best viewing is done from a car with binoculars or a spotting scope to prevent disturbing the elk. Like all wild animals, elk follow their own schedule and don't appear on demand like Old Faithful, so be patient.

From Vanderbilt, just off U.S. 75, go east on Sturgeon Valley Road for 10 miles to one of the designated elk-viewing sites (though you may see elk in many other areas). The Forestry Field Office on Hardwood Lake Road (3 miles farther on Sturgeon Valley Road and turn north) has maps and more information. Elk-viewing is also good from late April through early May. Elk-tour maps with designated elk-viewing sites marked are available at the forest headquarters or by mail. These sites are clearly marked and easy to reach by car.

In Minnesota, the state's only elk herd is located in **Beltrami** and **Marshall Counties** near Grygla. Twenty-seven elk were reintroduced here in 1935, and the population grew to nearly 200 by 1940. Today's free-roaming population hovers at around 30 animals, which are usually found in three townships, the best being **Velt Township** just to the east of the Thief Lake WMA. The best probable location of the elk is along County Road 54 on the border between Marshall and Beltrami Counties. Take Hwy. 54 north from Grygla for about 4 miles to the intersection with County Road 53. Work your way a mile west on County Road 53 and a mile or two north on County Road 54 at dawn or dusk for good sighting opportunities. The best viewing times are before spring leaves and after leaf fall in late September.

In Wisconsin the last native elk was shot in 1866, but in 1995, 25 elk were released as part of a four-year study to determine if elk should be reintroduced into the state. The site is located near **Clam Lake** in the **Chequamegon National Forest.** The 18 females and 7 males were culled from the Pigeon River Country herd in Michigan. Where the elk will finally settle down remains a mystery as of this writing. Solar-powered transmitters were installed in the ears of several elk to keep track of their movements and to test the devices for further use. Microchips were also implanted in the elk for identification purposes in the event the ear tags fell off.

Project coordinators hope the elk will remain in the Clam Lake vicinity. This area was chosen because it fits the general habitat requirements of elk—forests interspersed with openings, brushland, and grassland. To get to Clam Lake, take Hwy. 77 east from Hayward. Consider calling ahead to the Chequamegon National Forest headquarters in Park Falls to find out where in the area the elk have finally decided to call home.

53

September Shorttakes

Mushroom Peak

Mushrooms push up through the humus in early autumn to spread their spores, if we (and a variety of other animals) don't pick them first. Go "shroomin" at the **Fall Mushroom Mania** at **Walloon Lake** in Charlevoix County, Michigan; call (616) 535-2227. Or try the **Fungus Fest** at **Runkle Lake Park** in Crystal Falls, home of the Humungus Fungus; call (906) 875-3272.

For more information about mushrooms, write to the North America Mycological Association, Kenneth Cochran, 3558 Oakwood, Ann Arbor, MI 48104-5213, or call (313) 971-2552.

Staging Great Blue Herons and Great Egrets

Upper Lake in Pierce County, Wisconsin, just across from Red Wing, Minnesota, is a staging area for great blue herons and great egrets in mid-September. It's also good for fall shorebirds on the mudflats of the lake. Take Hwy. 63 south from Hager City for 2 miles. The lake is to the east, just before the bridge to Minnesota. Park along the highway to view the lake.

Autumn Wildlife Events

"Confusing" fall warblers stream through on their way to southern climates, testing the best birder's identification skills. See chapter 26 for more information.

Chinook salmon start spawning in September and peak in October. Brown trout begin spawning in late September. See chapter 56 for more information.

Shorebird migration continues into September—check out **Bradford Bathing Beach** in Milwaukee. From I-43, take the Hwy. 57/190 (Capitol Drive) exit east until it meets North Lake Drive. Turn right (south) on North Lake Drive to Lincoln Memorial Drive. Turn left and follow the lakeshore for about 3 miles until you see Bradford Bathing Beach on your left.

54

A Closer Look: Prescriptive Fires

Smokey Bear might faint to hear it said, but fire can be good. Let's go one step further: Not only can fire be good, it's necessary. Take a look at a Smokey Bear wildflower poster. Over half the species pictured do better after a fire.

A good number of earth's plant and animal species evolved in concert with lightning-caused fires, and many depend on flames for their survival. Fire helps create and maintain diversity. It performs an ecological service for many wildlife species, for instance, sharp-tailed grouse, prairie chickens, Kirtland's warblers, coneflowers, shooting stars, and bluestem grasses, that might otherwise decline in numbers and possibly disappear.

Fire has always played an essential role in Upper Midwest ecosystems. A 1941 study of the vegetation of northern Wisconsin noted that 95 percent of the area's virgin forests had been burned within the previous five centuries and that the fires "were periodic and ecologically normal events in the life of the forest," not "conflagrations of catastrophic proportions."

Fires usually leave a mosaic of burn patches, killing some plants, scarring others, missing still others altogether. Most animals easily sidestep fires, and the soil insulates ground-dwellers. Temperatures at the ground's surface may be 2,000°F during a fire, but the soil 4 inches below may only be 100°F, and then only briefly as the fire sweeps by. Many plants and animals not only survive but thrive after a fire and thus are called "fire-dependent."

Prairies are fire-dependent ecosystems. In the 1800s, wildfires rightfully frightened prairie settlers, often roaring out of control and destroying homesteaders' homes and crops. But those fires also killed the new stems of brush and young trees like willow, dogwood, and aspen that were trying to invade the open grasslands not yet under the plow while also clearing the grass litter from past growing seasons. The ash nutrients and open sun made possible by fire fueled the growth of prairie plants that had evolved to put two-thirds of their biomass underground in order to thrive after the fires. Some 65 percent of tall-grass prairie plants have roots that extend beyond a depth of 5 feet—some even to 23 feet! Switchgrass roots penetrate to depths of 11 feet, blazingstar has a taproot that reaches 16 feet down, prairie rose a root system that branches down 20 feet. It was fire that kept the "great green sea" lush.

The suppression of fire protected the new agricultural fields and homesteads but changed the landscape, closing up grassy openings that once

Controlled burns help reestablish and maintain prairies and pine barrens, which were once common in the region. Photo by Carol Christensen.

supported prairie chickens, upland sandpipers, marbled godwits, waterfowl that nested in the grasses, and a variety of small ground nesters. The Native tribes had set fires for as long as their collective memory could recall to bring up new grass shoots that would attract grazers and encourage extravagant berry growth. That 12,000-year-old process was snuffed out in the understandable urge to protect property, but we have since learned in the science of ecology that what is good for the goose is usually not good for the gander—species of plants and animals evolved to fill all the roles the earth provided, and there was a role for some to survive and thrive through fire.

Fires not only benefited grassland prairies but several forest ecosystems like pine barrens and Great Lakes pine forests. Most trees have scars—marks of experience—of many kinds, places where branches have been broken off by wind or snow or gnawed by animals. Fire also confers its badges of experience, often in the form of "catfaces"—charred areas extending from the ground several feet up a tree's trunk. In Itasca State Park in Minnesota, from 1650 to 1922 at least 32 fires occurred, 21 of which were considered major. Flames scored the park an average of once every 8.8 years; major fires occurred every 10.3 years. Red pine, of our three native pines, best survives fire, and today Itasca State Park is the best site in Minnesota for finding old-growth red pines; the park contains 15 to 20 percent of all of Minnesota's old-growth white and red pines. But since fires were eliminated in 1920, with only a few exceptions, pine seedlings are found only in quantity in road cuts and gravel pits. In 1954, 6,855 acres of red and white pine were considered "overmature" at 200 years or older. Today the park has considerable mortality in older trees and little seedling replacement—the park is evolving toward hardwoods and balsam.

Not all fires are alike, nor do all regenerate pines—there's a science to prescribing and managing burns. For instance, it is critical how intense a fire is. To regenerate pines it must destroy the leaf litter, expose mineral soil, and remove the shrub layer or reduce the overstory to let the sun in. There must be a ready seed supply to take advantage of the open ground when a fire happens. Too hot a fire will destroy white and red pine seeds. If another burn occurs too soon after a "good" burn, the seedlings will die, and usually aspen, birch, or brush take over. But if fires occur too infrequently, then succession takes over on suitable soils and the forest changes to northern hardwoods.

Species not only in the Upper Midwest but across the United States benefit from fire. In Florida's Big Cypress National Preserve, prescriptive fires are used to keep open the wet prairie that covers parts of the 700,000-acre preserve. The new growth after the fires feeds deer and feral hogs, who feed Florida panthers. Only 30 to 50 panthers are still thought to exist, 15 of them in Big Cyprus. Prescribed burns will be the salvation of sequoia groves in California, which are not regenerating without fire.

The Yellowstone National Park fire in 1989, which was highly controversial due to the National Park Service policy of letting natural fires burn themselves out within limits, rejuvenated Yellowstone's ecosystem. Lodgepole pines require fire to melt resin that holds their cones shut for decades. After the fire, 50,000 to 1,000,000 lodgepole seeds were dropped per acre. One black bear and 300 elk died, but no grizzlies did. The hardest-hit animal? Red squirrels, which eat pinecones.

Shawnee National Forest in Illinois uses fire to burn away the shrubby understory, allowing sunlight to reach the ground and release grasses and forbs and flowers. After a burn, one tally recorded 63 new plant species, which drew in wildlife from birds to butterflies.

The Kirtland's warbler, federally designated as endangered, only nests in Michigan jack pine stands from 8 to 20 years old and maintained by fire (see chapter 34).

Fire can be beneficial because it rapidly breaks down nutrients locked up in vegetation, which in turn enrich the soil and give plants a burst of natural fertilizer. The blackened soil absorbs sunlight and the warmed earth encourages seed germination. In a brief period of time, fire can duplicate the work of years of bacterial decomposition.

If we want to maintain all of this extraordinary world we were given, fire has its place. The departments of natural resources in all three states in the Upper Midwest as well as The Nature Conservancy use fire to maintain or re-create habitat of various kinds. Consider joining a fire crew—call your local department of natural resources or join The Nature Conservancy and become part of the effort to use fire as a tool to bring back much of our heritage.

October

Notes

55

Cranes on Stage

Imagine the sound and the sight of several thousand greater sandhill cranes flying, jumping, calling, dropping, and dangling their legs as they land in a whirl of action in one concentrated area. That is what awaits you at a sandhill crane fall staging ground. These staging areas are traditional sites that the cranes return to every fall but don't use in the spring in their haste to reach their breeding grounds. Here, in autumn fields and marshes, the cranes may remain for up to a month, feeding at their pleasure in apparently little haste to finish the migration south.

Why cranes stage at all no one can really say. During spring, sandhills drive away any intruders who venture near their territories, but in August crane pairs begin to become social, feeding together in the same fields and finally gathering together later in the fall in large flocks. The staging areas are usually about one-third of the distance to wintering areas in the South. In the spring, the Platte River in Nebraska fills with hundreds of thousands of cranes, and in the fall the Jasper-Pulaski Wildlife Area in northern Indiana supports tens of thousands of sandhills. The availability of food, safety, and the familiarity of one area, plus the loss of other areas that may have been historical staging areas, all contribute to funneling such enormous numbers into one spot.

Not all cranes stage in a few traditional areas. Whooping cranes don't, which causes serious management problems, because many potential stopover areas must be protected, given that no one knows what sites the whoopers will use in any year. And lesser sandhill cranes stage in the spring but not in the fall, just the opposite of greater sandhill behavior.

In the Upper Midwest we are blessed not with a Jasper-Pulaski but a number of smaller sites, island stepping-stones that still draw in thousands of cranes. The cranes look mostly gray, but many sport reddish brown plumage due to their habit of digging with their bills for insects in soil stained with iron. The iron gets transferred to their feathers during preening, resulting in a rusty-colored body.

You may see some dancing, even though breeding is long over. Dancing may be as much a reaction to stress as a mating ritual. Six-week-old chicks dance, so dancing may be more a string of aggressive behaviors than a romantic interlude.

Cranes fly about 150 miles a day on the average, but they can fly 300 to 400 miles if necessary. Surprisingly, they're not powerful flyers like Canada geese, who will fly from Hudson Bay to Wisconsin in one day. In fact, cranes are rather lackadaisical fliers. They leave their roosts well after daybreak, usually waiting for the day to warm up, and then use thermals to circle in, rising like pterodactyls. You may see groups of 75 spiraling together.

Best viewing is early morning, before the cranes scatter to feed, and late afternoon or early evening, when they come together to roost. By late fall the exodus to southern states like Georgia and Florida begins, with the cranes usually sailing a mile or more above the ground, riding like gliders on the northerly winds.

Hot Spots

In Minnesota, the **Borup area** in **Norman County** is famed for its concentrations of up to 10,000 staging cranes. Take Norman County Road 39 west from the intersection with Minnesota 32 for 7.5 miles and scan the corn stubble and the grassy fields on the south side of the road for cranes. There are no signs here designating the area, and in fact the cranes may be feeding on other fields anywhere in the general vicinity. Just drive slowly, try to stay on the road while you're scanning the fields, and the cranes should be nearby. When in doubt, stop and ask at a farmhouse—they'll know.

Agassiz NWR is host to several thousand sandhills in the fall. See chapter 37 for directions.

The **Roseau River Wildlife Area** may attract 8,000 to 10,000 cranes. To reach the headquarters from Minnesota 11 in Badger, take County Road 3 north almost to the border with Manitoba.

Cranes stage regularly in the **Rothsay WMA**. Take County Road 26 west out of Rothsay for 4 miles and turn right (north) to gain access to the southern end of the WMA.

The 8,199-acre **Twin Lakes WMA** in Kittson County harbors flocks of up to 2,000 cranes in **Twistal Swamp**, where they roost at night. Take Minnesota 11 4 miles northeast from Karlstad. The road bisects the WMA. Twistal Swamp is primarily on the north side of Hwy. 11.

Dugdale and **Burnham Creek WMAs**, southeast of Crookston, have had 2,000 to 5,000 cranes staging in recent years, and even a whooping crane in the fall of 1990. See chapter 33 for directions.

In Wisconsin, the **Sandhill Wildlife Demonstration Area** hosts one of the great wildlife gatherings in the state. Flocks of up to 2,000 sandhills wing their way into the refuge in the early evenings of October. During the day they disperse and forage in nearby fields, so viewing of large numbers is best in the early evening, when the birds roost together for the night. Sandhill is located north of Necedah, off Hwy. 80. Near Babcock on Hwy. 80, take County Road X north, and the entrance sign to Sandhill will be on your left.

Take the 14-mile self-guided auto tour, which winds through the wildlife area. Stop at the Marsh Tower (one of three observation towers on the property). The parking lot is to the left of the dike, which must be walked a short distance to the observation deck. The last half hour before sunset is usually most active.

Crex Meadows often has more than 1,000 cranes staging by late October. The area manager plants many hundreds of acres of crops to draw in the cranes. The entire northern section of the refuge has been restored to brush prairie and along with the flowage sites provides superb habitat for the cranes. Drive the dike road in the north-central area of the refuge for the best opportunities to see flocks of cranes. See chapter 37 for directions.

Navarino Wildlife Area, White River Marsh WMA, and **Grand River Marsh WMA** are traditional fall staging areas, too. See chapter 19 for directions. **Comstock Marsh State Scientific Area,** just south of Germania WMA, usually supports 1,000 or more cranes, too. From Hwy. 22 north of Montello, take County Road J east for about 1 mile to Edgewood Road. Turn left (north) and drive 1 mile to the small gravel parking area on the left. Park and walk west along Edgewood Road to a wooded ridge that forms the eastern boundary of the marsh. Viewing from this ridge is usually best for sighting cranes.

In Michigan, the **Phyllis Haehnle Memorial Sanctuary** is the place where most of southeastern Michigan's flock of sandhill cranes comes to stage before their migration south. Up to 2,000 cranes have been counted in an evening. Crane-watching is best between 3:00 P.M. and sunset from mid-September to mid-November. The birds feed on waste grain during the day in outlying fields, so large flocks may be seen from local roads in the area, such as **Seymour Road.** The nearly 900-acre **Michigan Audubon Society sanctuary** is closed to the public except for a 20-acre viewing area east of the parking lot. The sanctuary is located approximately 7 miles east of Jackson. From I-94, take Exit 147 and go north on Race Road 2 miles to Seymour Road; turn left (west) onto Seymour Road and drive 1.5 miles to a parking area.

The **Bernard W. Baker Sanctuary,** an 897-acre preserve that is also owned by the Michigan Audubon Society, is an exceptional marsh noted for migrating and nesting sandhill cranes. The best site for viewing the cranes is from the adjacent 131-acre tract, owned by the Battle Creek Kiwanis Club, which opens its land to the public usually on summer weekends and in October and November. Several platforms offer excellent viewing over Big Marsh Lake. Guided crane-watch tours are available; contact the Baker sanctuary manager for more information (see Appendix). To reach the Baker Sanctuary from I-94, take Exit 108 to I-69 and head north toward Lansing. Take Exit 42 west onto North Drive (Gorsline Road) and immediately make a right turn (north) onto 16 Mile Road. Go 3.2 miles to the sanctuary, keeping left on Junction Road at the Garfield Road intersection. The Kiwanis property is reached from 15 Mile Road just west of 16 Mile Road.

56

Salmon Running

Great Lakes fishermen know full well when the salmon spawn in inland creeks and rivers in early autumn—the chinook isn't called the king of salmon for nothing. Its tremendous fighting ability and delicious taste draw fishermen from all over the country to try their luck at catching one. But if you're not an angler, you've probably not had the opportunity to see a salmon up close. Now's your chance. Departments of natural resources in the lakes states have both fish-ladder viewing areas and egg-taking facilities where a fish-watcher can experience the thrill of seeing big fish on the move, sometimes jumping several feet into the air to clear obstacles on their migratory way.

In the wild on their native Pacific Coast, salmon (both coho and chinook) spawn in fresh water on clean gravel along stream bottoms. The females use their tails to dig nests and deposit their eggs, which are immediately fertilized by a male. The adults die soon after spawning, and the young eventually migrate to the ocean, returning in several years, guided by their sense of smell to their original natal creeks or rivers.

Great Lakes salmon follow the same pattern, homing in on their natal creeks through their use of smell. Here, though, the streams get too warm for the young to survive, so the department of natural resources strips the eggs from the adults and rears the young fingerlings at state fish hatcheries. At 6 inches long, the fingerlings are released into tributary streams, and the cycle begins again. The adults die a short time after spawning regardless of whether they spawn naturally or have their eggs stripped by department of natural resources personnel. The fingerlings grow rapidly and remain in the lakes for two to five years before returning to the stream in which they were planted (cohos return usually after only two years, chinook three to five years).

Both coho and chinook salmon were introduced intermittently since 1877 into the Great Lakes without real success until massive stocking programs began in 1967. The salmon were not only brought to the Great Lakes to provide a world-class fishery but also to exert their exceptional predatory skills on alewives and smelt, both non-native in the area. We have two species of Pacific salmon—chinook, which may reach 40 pounds, and the much smaller coho, which averages 10 to 15 pounds. Both species look alike, though the coho has white gums and the chinook has black gums. The body, ordinarily steel blue on the back with silver sides and white belly, darkens during spawning, and the males develop a hooked jaw and a slight hump on the back.

Salmon feed mostly in deep water on alewives, a small non-native herring that once had huge die-offs and was swept up on many shorelines, to the disgust of beachgoers. The salmon move inshore in late summer, congregating at river mouths, and they begin to move upriver by September. Chinook are best seen in mid-September through October, and coho spawn a bit later and are most numerous from October through November. Salmon in Lake Superior are notably smaller than those in other Great Lakes due to the sparse population of alewives, but the great number of suitable spawning streams around Lake Superior makes up for the scarcity of forage fish. No natural reproduction currently takes place in any of the Great Lakes.

Remember when trying to peer into water to use polarized sunglasses to cut the glare from the water surface.

Hot Spots

In Wisconsin, the **Kewaunee River Egg-Taking Facility** (also called the **Besadny Fish Collecting Facility**) has an underwater-glass viewing area for observing fish as they head upriver to spawn. The fish must make two jumps to get up the fish ladder. Wisconsin DNR personnel strip eggs from the salmon here, a process that can be watched—call after September 30 to find out when you can view this operation. Coho spawning peaks in mid- to late October, and chinook start in mid-September and peak in early October. The best time to see many species of fish is in early October—brook, brown, and steelhead trout should also be coming through here. The fish are most active in early morning and early evening, in low-light conditions, though in October fish can be seen all day long. In prime time, you many see three fish every 10 minutes in the cloudy waters. The facility is open every day for viewing during daylight hours and is located in Dana Farms County Park, off of County Highway F. From Kewaunee, take Hwy. 29 west and turn right onto County Road C, which continues west. Turn left onto County Highway F, and go 0.5 mile to Ransom Moore Lane. Turn right into the facility. (Signs for the facility begin at the junction of Roads C and F).

Egg-taking procedures can also be seen at **Strawberry Creek Egg-Taking Facility** on Strawberry Lane off County Hwy. U, south of Sturgeon Bay.

The **Root River Fish Facility** in Racine's Lincoln Park has a walk-in glass viewing tank for watching spawning fish. Call ahead, because in dry years the Root River water flow can be very low and the fish nonexistent. Egg-stripping can also be watched here. Call ahead to determine when the Wisconsin DNR will be taking eggs. From I-94, take the County Road K exit, which turns into Hwy. 38. At the edge of town turn right on Spring Street and then immediately take the first right into Lincoln Park (a large sign on the left side of the street announces the Root River

Facility). Go 0.6 mile to the parking lot. The glass viewing window is located 50 yards from the parking lot. The facility is located 2 miles up from the mouth of the river. Note: The water is cloudy here.

Chinook salmon may also be seen spawning at **Big Rock County Park** on the Sioux River near Washburn, **Pikes Creek Dam** in Bayfield (park your car at the Bayfield Fish Hatchery on Hwy. 13 and follow the trail), the **Horlick Dam** near the Holiday Inn of Racine, and **Quarry Park** in Racine.

Or consider visiting a hatchery where salmon are raised. **Wild Rose, Westfield, Kettle Moraine,** and **Lake Mills Hatcheries** all rear salmon as well as other species. Contact the Wisconsin Department of Natural Resources for more information and directions to these sites.

In Michigan, the **Sixth Street dam** in Grand Rapids prevents migratory fish from traveling up and down the Grand River. The **Grand Rapids Fish Ladder,** a series of concrete steps, was constructed to allow them to bypass the dam, and a specially designed viewing structure allows visitors to watch the procession. Large steelhead may be seen in the spring, and coho and chinook salmon are best seen in early fall. From U.S. 131 in Grand Rapids, go east on the Leonard Street exit and then turn right (south) on Front Street. At the end of the street turn left into a parking lot next to the fish ladder.

At the **Berrien Springs Fish Ladder,** a series of stair steps allows trout, salmon, and other migratory fish to swim around the Indiana Michigan Power Company dam in the St. Joseph River. Fish may be seen here every month of the year, but the fall run brings chinook and coho salmon, brown trout, steelhead, and even walleye and smallmouth bass through the ladder. Take U.S. 31 south from Benton Harbor into Berrien Springs. Turn left at the stoplight at West Ferry Street and go 1 block to South Main Street. Turn right and continue 5 blocks to Oak Street. Go to the T intersection and turn right onto a dirt road, which brings you to a small parking area. Walk on the gravel road past a metal barricade to the base of the dam. Though the ladder is surrounded by fencing, the fish are easily observed.

Michigan operates six fish hatcheries for raising game fish to be released into its rivers and lakes. The **Wolf Lake State Fish Hatchery** also houses the Michigan Fisheries Interpretive Center. Stocked in a clear show pond are an assortment of fish found in Michigan, which can be viewed from a long floating observation platform. Large fish, including chinook salmon and steelhead trout, can be seen up close here. The 7,000-square-foot interpretive center offers a multitude of displays and materials for learning about Michigan's fishery. It is located 8 miles west of Kalamazoo. Take Michigan 43 west to the large hatchery signs. Turn left (south) on Hatchery Road and go to the second drive on the right to reach the interpretive center.

57

Goose Migration

There are many exceptional sites from which to see migrating geese and other waterfowl in the Upper Midwest. The sheer numbers can overwhelm the uninitiated and still be a matter of amazement to the experienced. In Wisconsin and Michigan, long Vs of Canada geese slice down from their nesting areas along Hudson Bay in flocks of hundreds, and in total numbers over 1 million. Where geese concentrate at stopover sites, dozens of flocks may be in the air at any one time, coming and going in a cacophony of wing beats and honks. In the early morning and early evening, when the entire roosting flock gets up to go to feeding areas, the thousands of airborne birds can create an avian blizzard whose sound and sight stir the soul beyond words.

Canada geese take top billing in this waterfowl extravaganza, due in part to their size. A full-grown Canada goose will weigh between 7 and 10 pounds and glide on a 6-foot wingspan. Canadas are masterful flyers, able to attain speeds up to 60 mph but more commonly cruising at 40. When they leave their northern Canadian nesting grounds they usually make the entire 800-mile journey to a site like Horicon Marsh in one 12-hour flight, taking advantage of tailwinds that raise their ground speed to 70 mph. The V formation permits smoother flying because the air off the shoulder of a goose flying ahead is less turbulent than the air directly behind it. Geese rotate the point position to keep the lead bird from tiring.

Geese remind us a bit of ourselves in that they may mate for life, though if one mate dies the partner will choose another (and there are those ganders that are clearly polygamous, too). They're long-lived, sometimes to 30 years but more often barely making it to 5 because of the hazards of living in the wild. And they're obviously very social, at this time of year anyway. Hundreds will graze together, eating soft shoots, leaves, and buds off of grasses, cultivated crops, wild rice, and various meadow plants, as well as consuming grain crops and insects—about a half-pound of food per day satisfies one goose. If large numbers cause crop damage for local farmers, the federal and state governments have programs to pay for the losses. Unlike humans, male and female Canada geese are very difficult to distinguish, but if you see one larger goose chasing other geese away from a feeding area, that's usually the gander (male).

Heading the list of spectacular waterfowl-viewing areas is Horicon Marsh, near Waupon, Wisconsin. Get out your thesaurus and attach every superlative you can find to this site and you might still come up short. In a book filled with superlatives, Horicon stands at the head of the class. It is nothing short of astonishing, if seeing more than 200,000 geese and thousands of other waterfowl all in the same day fits that definition. This is more than just a goose marsh—Horicon is a complete wetland ecosystem, home to a marvelous array of birds, mammals, frogs, turtles, and fish, as well as wetland flora of great diversity.

Horicon attracts so many waterfowl because it encompasses 32,000 acres, 25,158 of which are marsh, open water, or wet meadow. It is the largest cattail marsh in the United States. Where possible, the higher ground is planted in moist soil plants such as smartweed and wild millet, which are attractive foods to ducks and geese. Horicon is also surrounded by fertile farm fields resplendent in corn and other grains that are necessary for feeding this waterfowl army. The Rock River flows through the middle of the marsh, and a dam at the town of Horicon allows control of the marsh water level.

Horicon Marsh qualified for inclusion on the List of Internationally Important Wetlands because of its size as the largest cattail marsh anywhere in the world, its support of such a large assemblage of rare or endangered species, its value as a genetic and ecological storehouse of flora and fauna peculiar to wetlands, and its special value as the habitat of plants or animals that are at a critical stage of their biological cycles. For instance, of the 1.1 million Canada geese in the Mississippi Valley population, over 80 percent stop for varying periods of time in the vicinity of Horicon Marsh. The fall 1989 migration population peaked at 700,000. Canada geese use the marsh for a resting area as they migrate from their nesting grounds in the Hudson Bay area to their wintering areas in southern Illinois, Kentucky, and western Tennessee.

During the last ice age, the Green Bay Lobe of the Wisconsin glaciation carved a basin 14 miles long and 3 to 5 miles wide here. Initially a lake, the Rock River eroded away the impounding glacial moraines enough to drain the lake and make way for the marsh. Horicon has been designated as one of the units of the Ice Age National Scientific Reserve because it is an outstanding example of an extinct postglacial lake. For the nearly 12,000 years since its waters thawed from the last ice age, the marsh has been used by prehistoric Native peoples and more recent tribes. The first recorded English name for the marsh was "The Great Marsh of the Winnebagos," in reference to the Winnebago people, who settled on the prairie lands west of the marsh.

The geese begin arriving in mid-September, peak in mid-October, and often remain until freeze-up in December. They may frequent the southern one-third of the marsh, which is a State Wildlife Area managed by the Wisconsin DNR, or the northern two-thirds, which is a national wildlife refuge administered by the U.S. Fish and Wildlife Service. The marsh is managed as a waterfowl area, but 265 bird species have been sighted here, about half of which are nesting species. Horicon is the largest nesting area for the redhead duck east of the Mississippi River. Mallards, blue-winged teal, ruddy ducks, coots, and pied-billed grebes also nest here, and you can expect large flocks of green-winged teal, widgeons, shovelers, scaup, gadwalls, and pintails to stop off in the marsh in their fall migrations.

Hot Spots

Horicon Marsh hotspots for viewing include Hwy. 49, which is the only public road that crosses the marsh, and though it's heavily used by trucks and cars, the road is one of the most popular areas to watch birds from—the daily flights of Canada geese at dawn and dusk are spectacular. Deep-water pools along Hwy. 49 provide a good variety of dabbling and diving ducks for viewing. Water levels in the pools are managed at varying depths, thus providing habitat for a wide range of birds, including many marsh birds such as great egrets and great blue and black-crowned night herons. If water levels are low, shorebirds in great number and variety show up.

Six miles of trails are maintained on the federal portion of the marsh, though most access to the federal refuge is very limited. The main dike road through the refuge is only open from April 15 to September 15. The state portion of the marsh is open for day use and offers far more viewing and recreational opportunities than does the federal refuge.

Another good spot is the Wisconsin DNR headquarters, which sits at the top of a hill providing one of the finest views of Horicon Marsh, though a scope is a must to identify species well out on the open water.

High-quality naturalist programs are offered to the public in spring and fall. Call (414) 387-7860 for more information.

Rather amazingly, Horicon is located only 65 miles northwest of Milwaukee, yet it is a true wetland wilderness. To get to Horicon from Milwaukee, take Hwy. 41 north and turn left (west) onto Hwy. 49, which cuts through the northern edge of the marsh.

Other sites in Wisconsin include the **Audubon Society's Goose Pond Sanctuary**, located 20 miles north of Madison. Over 245 bird species have been seen on this 174-acre property, including 30 species of waterfowl and 34 species of shorebird. To get there from Madison, take Hwy. 51 north into Columbia County, turn left (west) on County Road K, and after 2 miles turn right (north) on Goose Pond Road, then left on Prairie Lane. Viewing at sunset is best, when the birds are returning from feeding in local fields and ponds.

Nearby **Schoeneberg Marsh** also attracts large numbers of waterfowl. From Madison, take Hwy. 51 north and pick up Hwy. 22 north

Horicon National Wildlife Refuge

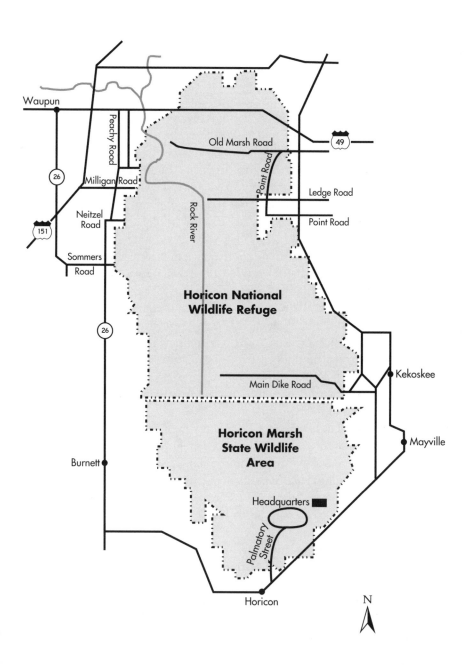

Waupun

Peachy Road

26

Milligan Road

151

Neitzel Road

Sommers Road

26

Burnett

Old Marsh Road

Point Road

49

Ledge Road

Point Road

Rock River

Horicon National Wildlife Refuge

Kekoskee

Main Dike Road

Mayville

Horicon Marsh State Wildlife Area

Headquarters

Palmatory Street

Horicon

N

where Hwy. 51 briefly swings west at North Leeds. After 1 mile turn right onto Priem Road and then left onto Harvey Road, which will take you along a piece of the south edge of the marsh.

Crex Meadows is an outstanding area for birding in general, and fall migrations of snow geese, diving ducks, Canada geese, and sandhill cranes can be exceptional. See chapter 37 for directions.

Necedah NWR supports peak populations of 30,000 geese and 55,000 ducks in the fall. Expect also snow geese, tundra swans, and 15 or more species of duck. Necedah has 44,000 acres of water, marsh, and upland for the birds, but much of it is inaccessible (adjacent to and west of the refuge is an additional 50,000 acres of federally owned land called the Meadow Valley Wildlife Area). Search the **Rynearson Pool** for geese in the fall—this is the most attractive spot. Tundra swans stop regularly in spring and fall on this pool. Take Hwy. 21 west from the town of Necedah for 3.5 miles to the large refuge sign pointing to the headquarters. The Rynearson Pool is behind the headquarters building. The **Sprague-Mather Pool** has an ideal dike for walking along its southern edge. Take Hwy. 80 north out of the town of Necedah for 8 miles to the town of Sprague and turn left (west). The dike runs along the right-hand side of the road. Pull off at a parking lot and hike the dike.

Trempealeau NWR, named by French settlers "mountain with wet feet" for the high bluff along the Mississippi River, has an observation deck from which one can scope a cormorant rookery and osprey and bald eagle nests. Tundra swans congregate here in the fall, and peak duck numbers reach 24,000. Travel west on Hwys. 35 and 54 from Centerville for 3.2 miles. Turn left (south) at the refuge sign. Drive for 1.2 miles, where a road to the right enters the refuge.

Siskiwit Harbor in Bayfield County is exceptional for diving birds, including red-throated loons and eared grebes as well as horned and red-necked grebes. Siskiwit Bay is located along Hwy. 13, where the Siskiwit River empties into Lake Superior at the village of Cornucopia. The drive into the main part of the harbor is just east of the Siskiwit River.

In Minnesota, the **Big Stone NWR** supports 20,000 various geese, 20 species of duck peaking at 40,000 birds, and flocks of tundra swans. See chapter 39 for directions.

The **Upper Mississippi National Wildlife and Fish Refuge** is exceptional for waterfowl—see chapter 64 for more information and directions. The refuge headquarters is located in Winona.

The **Minnesota Valley NWR**, located along 34 miles of the Minnesota River, supports 30,000 waterfowl in their fall migration, including snow geese, tundra swans, and rafts of coots—250 species of bird in all. The refuge is located in a series of noncontiguous units totaling 12,500 acres and combines with other areas managed by state and federal agencies to form a wildlife corridor extending 72 miles along the Minnesota River. From the Minneapolis–St. Paul Airport, take I-494 to the 34th Avenue exit, head south to 80th Street, then east. Follow the refuge signs from here.

Agassiz NWR holds snow geese in October and up to 250,000 ducks in mid-October. This is a true refuge, however. The birds come first, and access to viewing them is extremely limited. The refuge closes as of October 1—all dike roads are closed except the auto tour, but even so, the morning and evening flights can be worth it. You can try Farmes Pool on Marshall County Road 120 (a dirt road). Farmes Pool is the best waterfowl site in the area in October (it's also the only pool really accessible here) because it was recently created and grasses haven't filled it in yet. See chapter 37 for directions.

Silver Lake, in the middle of Rochester, harbors up to 30,000 geese in the fall and into the winter. A power plant keeps the small lake open. Scan from the lake's west side along West Silver Lake Drive between 7th Street NE and 14th Street NW. Rochester is located in southeastern Minnesota and may be reached by Hwy. 63, 14, or 52.

Lac Qui Parle WMA has 100,000 geese stopping over primarily in its three water impoundments. The Minnesota River valley serves as an important corridor for all avian migrants. See chapter 38 for directions.

Rice Lake NWR provides wild rice for 100,000 ring-necked and other ducks and geese to feed on, and 60 or more bald eagles prey on the ducks. The 18,104-acre refuge is mostly flat bog laced with glacial moraine. See chapter 49 for directions.

Sherburne NWR provides wild rice and other plants for tens of thousands of waterfowl to feed on in October. See chapter 49 for directions.

Tamarac NWR, with nearly half of its area in wetlands and open water, has large wild rice stands that draw in 35,000 ring-necked ducks and sometimes rafts of 30,000 coots. See chapter 49 for directions.

In Michigan, **Shiawassee NWR** commonly supports 30,000 ducks and 20,000 geese, including some snow geese and tundra swans. Shiawassee is considered one of the top 25 birding sites in America. An observation tower and 10-power scope provide excellent viewing opportunities into the surrounding wetlands. The refuge is located just outside of Saginaw, and rivers and streams converge here to drain 22 different counties, creating the largest watershed in Michigan. During October and November trails are closed on mornings of odd-numbered days for goose hunting, so come on the even-numbered days for the best bird-watching. All trails are closed in December. From Saginaw, take Michigan 13 south for 5 miles to Curtis Road. Turn right (west), and go a little less than a mile to the refuge headquarters or 4 miles to the waterfowl-trail parking lot.

St. Clair Flats and **Harsen's Island** lie in the delta of the St. Clair River and offer extensive marshes and canals for migrating and wintering waterfowl and raptors. Huge rafts of canvasbacks and redheads, some of the largest congregations in Michigan, can be seen in the channels, along the river, and in Anchor Bay. Take I-94 to the Algonac exit (Michigan 29, Exit 243) and follow Michigan 29 east for 17 miles to the Harsen Island Ferry at the Port-O-Call Restaurant.

Portage Entry in Houghton County is the south entry of the Portage Canal, which cuts the Keweenaw Peninsula in half. This area can turn up rarities like black scoters, surf scoters, oldsquaws, and king eiders, as well as the more normal diving ducks like scaup and mergansers. The breakwater provides protection from the rough waters of the bay. From U.S. 41 4.4 miles south of Chassel, turn east onto Portage Entry Road (marked with a large sign). Take this to the water's edge and scan for a while, then turn left onto North Entry Road, which parallels the canal. Stop at the public boat landing and the picnic area for an excellent view of the canal.

The **Presque Isle Peninsula** on Lake Huron has a tremendous duck and shorebird migration. The best days are cold with a blustery northwest wind. Take U.S. 23 to the north edge of Grand Lake. Turn east on County Road 638 and take it to the shore. Turn north and go 1 mile to a narrow spot on the peninsula before you get to the lighthouse.

Within its nearly 10,000 acres, the **Maple River State Game Area** contains 1,300 acres of wetlands, the largest wetland complex in central Michigan. Thousands of ducks, geese, swans, and shorebirds can be observed in the wetlands. The game area is located 8 miles north of St. Johns and is bisected by Hwy. 27. Note that this is a hunting area—call ahead to learn the opening dates so that you may arrive at another time if you intend to bird-watch.

More than 100,000 geese will pass through **Allegan State Game Area** in the fall, with as many as 40,000 possible in one day. The best viewing is in the **Fennville Farm Unit** on the southwestern boundary of the property. Snow, white-fronted, and barnacle geese have been seen here. The Fennville Goose Festival occurs in mid-October. Take Michigan 89 north into the city of Allegan and turn left (west) onto Monroe Road (joins 118th Avenue after 5 miles). Go 7 miles to the area headquarters. Posted refuge areas are off-limits to hikers, and during waterfowl season you must stay out of any area that is posted for hunting.

Birders at **Whitefish Point Bird Observatory** may see 70,000 waterfowl fly by in the fall, many of which are often rather rare species. See chapter 46 for directions.

Seney NWR is an enormous wetland complex—nearly two-thirds of the refuge's 95,455 acres are wet. As you might imagine, migrating waterfowl use an area this large extensively. From the town of Seney, go south on Michigan 77 for 4.5 miles to the road sign leading to the headquarters. The auto drive begins at the headquarters, though after September 30 the auto tour may only be walked or biked, and all dike roads are closed as of October 1. This is a great place to take a mountain bike or hike the over 80 miles of gravel roads—you'll have most of the refuge to yourself.

The **Muskegon County Wastewater Treatment Facility** may hold over 50,000 waterfowl during fall migration along with excellent shore-bird numbers. Although a wastewater treatment area hardly offers a wilderness retreat, this facility is huge, containing 10,000 acres of woodlands and fields and two 850-acre lagoons. Over 200 species of bird have been recorded here. Go east from Muskegon on Michigan 46 (Apple Avenue) for 7 miles and turn north on Maple Island Road. Drive 2 miles to the entrance gate and turn left into the facility. Go about 1 mile and turn right (south) onto the first paved road. Proceed to the administration building and check in for a guest pass. Then go around the building and turn left to the holding ponds and the lagoons. Check any drained ponds for shorebirds, too.

Review chapter 14 for notes on the following areas, which are also excellent in fall, but be aware that waterfowl-hunting severely limits access to some: **Tobico Marsh State Game Area, Pointe Mouillee State Game Area, Erie Marsh Preserve, Metro Beach Metropark,** and **Nayanquing Point State Wildlife Area.**

58

Moose Rut

One early July evening as my wife and I were watching the sunset on the shoreline of a lake on Isle Royale, we looked to our side, and there, standing on the sand about 50 feet away, was a bull moose. How it had come through the bush and onto the shore so close to us without our hearing will forever be a mystery to us. An animal that averages 800 to 900 pounds and stands 6 feet at the shoulder should not be permitted such stealth. After our initial astonishment we simply shared the sunset with him for several minutes until he moved quietly back into the bush and was gone.

Moose can do that. They can also make quite a racket during the autumn rutting season, when the bulls fight for dominance. They've been known to charge cars and trains in their hormonal craze. To call females they curl their lips and bellow and challenge any males to battle if they so choose. In August, bulls rub off the soft velvety covering of their antlers and polish them on tree trunks. They use their antlers, which can reach 7 feet across and weigh 75 pounds, in ritual combat with other bulls, rushing at each other and clanging antlers together until one masters the other. The battles commence in September and go into early October until the rut ends. During this time bulls can be aggressive toward humans. Eight months later, in May or June, the cows give birth to usually one calf, and sometimes twins in good habitat. The calves stay with Mom throughout their first year.

Two parasites that infest deer but don't kill them can kill moose, so moose don't tend to be found in areas with high deer numbers. A roundworm that is harmless to deer causes the greatest moose mortality. The deer passes on the roundworm's eggs through its droppings, and the larvae develop and reproduce in certain land and aquatic snails. The immature worm departs the snail and may be ingested by a hungry or thirsty moose. The worm then burrows into the brain and destroys the moose's neurological system. A liver fluke, also transmitted by snails, may cause severe liver damage in moose, too.

Moose need 50 to 60 pounds of browse a day. In fact, their stomachs can hold 110 pounds of food, so they need a reasonably large area to get them through a season. They prefer balsam fir as a winter browse, which is a starvation food for deer. *Moose* means "twig eater" in the Ojibwa language, and the best twigs are the young ones, so moose do well after fires because of the new young growth for browsing. In the summer they eat lots of aquatic plants like bur reed, pondweed, and water lilies.

Bull moose in rut have been known to charge trains and cars. Photo by Jeff Richter.

Moose sign is sometimes easier to spot than the moose—look for huge heart-shaped tracks and moose "marbles," marshmallow-sized droppings in a pile.

The principle predators of the moose are the gray wolf and, formerly, the mountain lion. A healthy kick from a moose can crush a wolf's skull, so wolf packs must take great precautions in attacking an adult moose. Wolves tend to take the weakest animals—the sick, old, and young—who place them in the least danger. On average, wolf-pack attacks on moose are successful less than 10 percent of the time, and wolves living off moose average one moose kill per wolf every 45 days.

Moose are powerful swimmers and regularly outswim canoeists. It's assumed they swam across Lake Superior to reach Isle Royale, a minimum distance of 15 miles. And they can run too if they must—up to 35 mph! So even though they may look awkward and gangly, they can get around quite effectively.

No guarantee can be made where a moose may be at any given time. You may see a moose crossing a highway before you ever see one in its prime habitat on a designated "moose-tour route." So go slow, and look for moose feeding along the edges of ponds, bogs, and lakes in the spring and summer, and browsing in willow shrub, balsam fir, and young aspen and birch in the late fall and winter. The best times to see them are at dawn and dusk, though they may be active at any time of the day.

Hot Spots

Minnesota is the state for moose; its moose population is in the range of 6,000 to 8,000. They thrive in two quite different habitats: the boreal forests and lakes of northeastern Minnesota and the aspen parklands of willow, aspen, and marsh of northwestern Minnesota. The two ranges total about 8,600 square miles, though between these two regions moose can occasionally be seen.

The **Superior National Forest** supports large moose numbers in the northeastern corner of the state. Over 3 million acres, including 1 million acres in the **Boundary Waters Canoe Area Wilderness,** are in public ownership. This vast area contains prime habitat for moose with its dense boreal forest interspersed with thousands of lakes and wetlands. Moose can be seen just about anywhere in Superior National Forest (they've even wandered down streets in Duluth), but try Forest Roads 325, 152, and 315. From County Road 12 (the Gunflint Trail) out of Grand Marais, turn left (west) onto Forest Road 325, which follows along the South Brule River. Forest Road 325 eventually ends at Forest Road 152, so turn right (northeast) and either take this slowly back to the Gunflint Trail, or turn left (north) onto Forest Road 315, which will eventually bring you back to the Gunflint, too. Near the northern end of Forest Road 315, check particularly around **Shoko** and **Swamp Lakes,** which are good moose watering holes.

Agassiz NWR and **Thief Lake WMA** are your best bets for seeing moose in northwestern Minnesota. About 250 moose populate Agassiz. There are no designated moose sites here because there are 10,000 acres of willow shrub in the refuge. The moose could be anywhere browsing in the willows. Slowly drive or walk along the willow thickets and hope you're in the favored willow grove of the day. See chapter 37 for directions.

Thief Lake WMA supports one to two moose per square mile in the better habitat areas. Contact the management office for current suggestions for moose-viewing. See chapter 37 for directions.

The Upper Peninsula of Michigan is home to free-ranging moose, too. **Van Riper State Park** produces a "Moose Locater Guide" that maps out several auto-tour routes that could turn up a moose. In 1985 and 1987 59 moose were released 6 miles north of Van Riper, so this remains the heart of the UP moose range. The moose were blindfolded, hoisted by slings, and airlifted by helicopter into Marquette County. By 1996, the herd size had reached more than 500.

Van Riper State Park is located 1 mile west of Champion on U.S. 41/ Michigan 28. Huron Bay Road and Tracy Creek Road are two of the auto-tour roads, both of which wind about 15 miles through good moose country. A video on the moose reintroduction can be seen at the information center in the park. A kiosk in the park carries the latest information on where moose were last seen.

Isle Royale National Park, at 45 miles long and a maximum 9 miles wide, is the largest island in Lake Superior and arguably the most beautiful. The only national park in Michigan, Isle Royale may also be the only national park in the United States that has no roads and requires all transportation to take place by foot or boat. Moose achieve the highest density here of any place in Michigan, and the continuing population interplay between the resident wolves and moose has resulted in some of the most intriguing wildlife studies ever undertaken. Although Isle Royale has rarities like moose, wolf, and nesting peregrine falcons, the island is also bereft of common species like white-tailed deer.

Getting to Isle Royale is more difficult in October, but a ferry does leave regularly until October 31 from Grand Portage, Minnesota. Contact the Grand Portage–Isle Royale Transportation Lines at (218) 728-1237 for more information. Although the crossing may be rough at this time of year, island visitors are few and far between, leaving this national park unpopulated for the more adventurous backpacker.

59

October Shorttakes

Loons Staging

Common loons lose their aggressive territoriality in late summer and often gather together in large flocks in fall prior to migration. **Mille Lacs Lake** in Minnesota is well known for the hundreds of loons that stage there in the fall. Scan from the northeastern end of the lake in Aitkin County, and be sure to have a spotting scope—this is a huge lake.

Turkey Vulture Staging

The bluffs surrounding **Devils Lake State Park** in Wisconsin are a great area to see up to 200 turkey vultures soaring on the thermals in early October. The best time is before sunset, or try early morning. The picnic area along the south shore is a good observation point, as is the nature center pine plantation on the north end. Take Hwy. 12 south from Baraboo and turn left (east) on Hwy. 159. Turn right (south) on South Shore Road, which will take you to a visitor information station and picnic area on the south shore.

Cranberry Harvest

October is the month for both wild and commercial cranberries to come ripe. A friend who manages one of the local cranberry marshes in nearby **Manitowish Waters** in Wisconsin notes that when he floods his marsh to harvest the berries, up pop scores of rodents who have nowhere to go but onto the dikes that run between the marshes, and nearly every fall a snowy owl shows up to partake in the easy meals. Put on your bog shoes and go picking.

60

A Closer Look: Autumn Leaves

I like to think of deciduous trees in the Upper Midwest as liberals, and conifers as conservatives (Democrats and Republicans, if you like). Each brings to the autumn a very different philosophy on how to live and how in particular to survive a northern winter. The liberal deciduous trees cast all their leaves onto the forest floor, spending nearly all the capital they gained over the summer in the optimistic belief that the nutrients they invest back into the ground will be repaid doubly the next spring. On the other hand, the conservative conifers like the status quo—they'll hold onto their leaves, thank you (needles are just modified leaves), and protect what they have, letting a little go now and again if they must.

The conifers believe in long-lived leaves, so they remain green. There are distinct advantages to being evergreen, particularly in the cold North Country. Because they hold onto their green leaves all year round, conifers can continue to photosynthesize on warmer winter days, and they can grow during warm spells in the later fall and early spring, during which their deciduous friends are leafless.

Conifers can also grow on poorer soils than hardwoods can, which is all they deserve anyway, because they refuse to invest their nutrients back into the soil through leaf-fall. This adaptation to less nourishment helps conifers survive in many of the poor soils left behind by the last glaciers—conifers can grow in nearly pure sand or on top of bedrock with only a few inches of soil covering it. Conifers can handle poor soils because they don't have to grow a whole new set of leaves every spring, so they require less energy.

Frugality is their motto. One author says conifers live on a "waste-not, want-not" system, while hardwoods look at life as "easy come, easy go." The conifers recycle nutrients very slowly, while the hardwoods work at a much faster pace. Not only don't the conifers drop many of their needles in a year, but their needles are very slow to decompose and hold comparatively few nutrients. Pine needles can take more than three years to fully decompose, while a sugar maple leaf may be soil within the year.

Many conifers are hardy trees, too. The deciduous trees drop their leaves because otherwise they would transpire more water through the leaf surfaces than what is available to their roots and would die of thirst. Remember that winter is a desert environment—very little water is available in the

Tamarack, the region's only deciduous conifer, turns into gold in the late fall. Photo by Carol Christensen.

frozen ground layer to roots that may only penetrate a foot or so into the soil. Still, many of the conifers thumb their noses at all the winter can throw at them because of a number of adaptations. They wrap their needles in a wax that protects them from losing moisture. They also place their breathing pores *(stomata)* underneath the needles, so little transpiration can occur—the white lines you see on the underside of a balsam fir or hemlock needle are the stomata. And the shape of the needles themselves is far better suited to holding onto water than are the big flat leaves that broadleaf trees flutter around in the summer. Conifers know how to hold on tight to what they have.

The leaves, or needles, that do fall on the ground decompose at a rate generally determined by their carbon to nitrogen ratio. The more carbon in the leaves, the harder it is for bacteria, fungi, and soil animals to do their work. Sugar maple has a 20:1 carbon to nitrogen ratio; alders are even better at 15:1. Basswoods are 37:1, a midrange ratio, and their leaves take about two years to decompose. A few hardwoods are in the high range, surprisingly, like aspens, which are 63:1. Tamarack may win the decomposition slow-track derby at 113:1, requiring more than three years for the needles to break down.

Finally, some trees, such as sugar maple, are "nutrient pumpers," meaning they pump most of their nutrients out into their leaves, which will eventually greatly enrich the soil. Other trees, such as oaks, squirrel those nutrients away in their roots and don't add much at all to the soil. As for the conifers, they may even deplete the soil by the acid composition and lack of recycled nutrients in their needles.

A few trees are independents. Tamarack is our only native deciduous conifer in the Upper Midwest—the needles turn a wondrous smoky gold in October and fall to the ground. Then there are the oaks and ironwood, two hardwoods that hold on to their dead leaves all winter, apparently unwilling to risk either a terrible winter thirst by letting the leaves live or the loss of any nutrients in those leaves by letting them drop.

November

Notes

61

Deer Rut

White-tailed deer are the Michael Jordans of the animal world. Their ability to effortlessly leap a 7-foot fence from a standstill, or bound away with more air under their hooves than earth, or their Houdini act of melting away into the bush, helps to give visual definition to the words grace, beauty, and power.

In the autumn buck rut, when the males become intensely single-minded in their mating desire, they become far more vulnerable to human observation and, as all hunters know, to being shot. Their hormone-induced frenzy leads them to extremes of behavior, reducing their normal wariness dramatically as instinct predetermines their movements. Here's the sequence of events in the autumn life of a buck.

In early September, bucks lose the velvet that grew to protect their newly forming antlers back in the spring. The antlers are now full-size, and the blood vessels to the velvet are shut off. Bucks may rub their antlers against trees or small saplings to help remove the velvet, but the velvet will fall off on its own in any case. The antlers now become ivory-colored at the tips. A secretion from a gland in the forehead is left on trees as a message to other bucks that this area is claimed. Such buck rubs are a good sign of a buck's presence.

By the end of the month, the bucks begin sparring to establish dominance, mostly pushing one another around in a not particularly violent confrontation, likened by one writer to offensive linemen scrimmaging on a football team.

By early October, bucks begin making scrapes, though they are usually not breeding this early. The bucks paw the ground bare in a number of areas, often urinating on the spot and leaving behind a secretion produced in glands between their toes. As the autumn progresses, these scrapes become much like an open letter indicating to does the buck's readiness for mating and to other males that this is their range.

By late October the does finally begin to come into heat *(estrus),* the oldest females first. The does begin to hang around the scrapes, and the males visit their circuits of scrapes in hopes of finding a willing doe. Subordinate bucks often try to hang around too, in hopes that the "big guy" won't show up in time to mate the available female, but they disappear when the dominant buck appears.

In early November, testosterone levels in the blood hit a peak, and the bucks show it physically. Their necks swell, their eyes become glassy, and one source says they smell awful. They now travel by day and by night in an effort to tend their scrapes. Bucks in this state of mind can be very aggressive—humans are best off staying a good distance away.

Late in November the rut declines rapidly, and the bucks, who have lost a quarter of their body weight by this point, now remember to start eating again.

In early December a few does who failed to be mated come into estrus again, but for all intents and purposes the rut is over, and the business of surviving winter now sets hard upon them. Some bucks are so emaciated from the rut that they are likely to die in a hard winter, succumbing much like weakened fawns. The does will give birth to their fawns in late May and early June, usually dropping only one, but twins are relatively common, particularly in good habitat.

White-tailed deer populations have reached numbers so large that many people perceive deer both as beautiful and as a major nuisance. In Wisconsin the 1995 herd was estimated at 1.4 million, and the annual hunt harvests over 300,000 animals. One-sixth of all Wisconsin traffic accidents in 1993 involved collisions between deer and vehicles—at least 22,819 accidents involving deer were reported. Deer in urban areas have become management nightmares because their population continues to escalate at the same time controls are not permitted within various city and suburban limits. Workable solutions remain elusive.

By the way, though blaze-orange clothing acts like a neon sign to humans, to deer it's just another leaf in the woods. Deer see reds and oranges as greens because they see color much the same way that a human with red-green color blindness would.

The best times for viewing deer are at the first and last light of day—deer are crepuscular and most active in twilight. Dawn seems best of all, because deer are the least skittish then. Spying of white-tailed deers is best done by learning where deer forage for food and where they go to rest and digest what they have eaten. In autumn, deer search for late-season grasses in forest openings and along field edges. In farm country deer forage the edges of corn- and soybean fields and will do so well into the winter if the snow accumulation is thin. After feeding, deer move to secluded areas in brush in open country and in thickets or forests. They'll usually remain in their sheltered areas from midmorning to midafternoon and seldom are seen. The home range of a white-tailed deer can exceed 500 acres, so the animals can cover some ground between feeding and resting areas. Look for droppings and trails that lead from the feeding areas to the resting areas. Once you recognize these areas, your success in observing deer should greatly increase.

White-tailed deer have a beauty that enthralls most wildlife watchers. Photo by Carol Christensen.

The deer season in the Upper Midwest attracts around 700,000 hunters in each state, a veritable army of pumpkin suits. The Native Americans, however, hunted in very different numbers and with varying techniques. John Muir wrote in his book *The Story of My Boyhood and Youth* that when he was a boy he frequently watched Native Americans hunt deer by running them down in the deep snow. He said the deer were followed to their deaths by the noiseless and tireless native people who ran like hounds on fresh tracks.

Ojibwa Indians are reported to have also used other methods for hunting deer such as:

1. The deer was snared and choked to death with a rope noose placed along known runways.

2. Sharp stakes were driven into the ground beside a log over which a deer was expected to jump, in hopes the deer would impale itself.

3. Deer were run by dogs into the water, where they were pursued by canoe and tomahawked, or they were simply exhausted in deep snow by the dogs.

4. Deer were killed with bow and arrow at salt licks or at customary feeding areas along lakes and streams. The bow and arrow only had a range of about 50 paces, so the Indians had to be good at still-hunting.

Deer were far less numerous in the United States prior to European settlement. Our creation of so much agricultural land and patchy forests has greatly increased the food in the cupboard for white-tailed deer.

One last note. The slang term "buck" for "dollar" originated with the custom of using a deer skin as currency, one skin having a value of roughly one dollar in trade.

Hot Spots

There are so many deer in the Upper Midwest that it is probably harder to find areas where deer are not found. Michigan has a few sites where deer have become so accustomed to human presence that you are virtually assured of seeing many whitetails. **Presque Isle Park** in Marquette in the Upper Peninsula recently released tame deer, and these animals will amble right out of the woods to be fed by hand.

Kensington Metropark in the Detroit area is noted for its approachable deer. Four nature trails leave from the nature center—try Deer Run Trail. Take I-96 west from Farmington Hills to Exit 151 or 153, where large signs will direct you to the park entrances. Kensington is on both sides of I-96 on Kent Lake just east of Brighton. Look also for deer in the open areas along the park roads.

Yankee Springs Recreation Area contains over 5,000 acres and is adjacent to the 17,000-acre **Barry State Game Area,** so there's 22,000 acres here to roam. From Hwy. 131 south of Grand Rapids in Allegan County, take Exit 61 and head east for 8 miles to the Yankee Springs headquarters.

62

Tundra Swans

Few superlatives can sketch for the uninitiated the beauty of the drifting, seemingly translucent formations of white tundra swans that sweep over the Upper Mississippi River National Wildlife Refuge in November. Thousands land to feed and loaf in the shallow backwaters of the river, appearing from a distance like popcorn scattered on the water. The swans often remain for many weeks, or until ice begins to form, and then it's move on or perish.

Their attraction in such great numbers to only a few sites in the refuge comes from their love of wild celery and arrowhead tubers, which grow abundantly in shallow, quiet pools found in backwaters off the river. An adult swan weighing 10 to 18 pounds and standing 4 feet tall has a large appetite and will feed on nearly 6 pounds of aquatic vegetation a day. Tundras plunge their heads underwater to feed, sometimes tipping up like a mallard does, their long necks and bills sweeping along the shallow bottoms to root out a meal. Even though their appetites are prodigious, their energetic digging usually improves the habitat by stimulating the growth of underwater plants so that next year the area will provide a bounty again.

Tundra swans (formerly called whistling swans) come by their name honestly, nesting high up on the Arctic coastline in tundra or sheltered marshes. The North American population totals around 200,000, two-thirds of which winter in California while the other nearly 70,000 head south into the Dakotas, following the tree line and eventually sailing down to the Mississippi. They begin arriving along the river the first week of November, but the peak usually occurs in mid-November, with large numbers remaining well into December if the weather holds.

The tundras eventually continue due east, flying across Lake Michigan and around Lake Erie and then southeast to winter in Chesapeake Bay. Tundras may fly up to 10 hours a day, and with good weather conditions can sail along in a V formation at 60 mph, thus traveling up to 600 miles a day. Their propensity for migrating at altitudes from 6,000 to 8,000 feet has resulted in at least two airplane crashes.

Tundra swans produce a high-pitched call, a *wow-how-ow,* that has been likened to a distant barking of dogs, soft musical laughter, mellow cooing, and something akin to a Canada goose honk, which amply demonstrates how limited human language is in describing the language of other animals. The origin of singing one's "swan song" is attributed to tundra swans, which at death are described by one scientist as singing a melodious, soft, muted series of notes: "When a swan is shot and falls crippled to the water, it utters this call as it tries in vain to rejoin its fellows in the sky."

All swans mate for life, though if a mate dies, the widow(er) will find a new spouse. While you are watching the tundra swans, note their strong family bonds and the squabbling that often occurs between family units. The young of the year, called cygnets, won't get their adult plumage until they're about 15 months of age and are easily distinguished by their grayish brownish coloring, their dark heads, and their pinkish bills.

To attract and hold thousands of swans for weeks in any given place requires an exceptionally rich habitat. The two finest sites in the Midwest are Reick's Lake Park, a backwater in Wisconsin where the Buffalo River enters the Mississippi River, and Weavers Bottoms, a backwater in Minnesota near the junction of Hwys. 61 and 74. These areas are the premier feeding grounds for tundra swans, drawing in up to 10,000 swans during peak times. The sight and sound of thousands of swans feeding, squabbling, taking off, and sailing in can be an overwhelming sensory experience.

Hot Spots

You can reach **Rieck's Lake Park** by taking Hwy. 35 (the Great River Road) north from Alma, Wisconsin, for 1 mile. Immediately after crossing the bridge over the Buffalo River, turn right into the park, where an observation platform with spotting scopes will aid you in seeing the swans "up close and personal."

Weavers Bottoms is located north of Winona near the junction of Hwys. 61 and 74. The backwaters begin just northwest of Weaver and extend southeast 4 miles to Minneiska. Vantage points may be found along Hwy. 61, though the traffic may drive you to distraction. The best spot is found by driving 1.7 miles south from Weaver on Hwy. 61 and then turning right just before the cemetery and heading to the top of the hill.

Both sites will provide ample numbers of migratory waterfowl, including Canada geese, wood ducks, green-winged teal, mallards, black ducks, pintails, canvasbacks, gadwall, widgeons, redheads, lesser scaup, buffleheads, and shovelers, not to mention great blue herons, common egrets, and bald eagles.

Spring tundra swan flights at these two sites are small in number, and the swans seldom hang around long enough for bird-watchers to be certain of their presence.

The chamber of commerce in Winona, Minnesota, in coordination with the **Mississippi River NWR**, holds annual swan watches every November. A Saturday-evening slide show precedes the Sunday-morning bus trip to the swan sites. The buses are usually led by refuge biologists who discuss the natural history of the swans and answer any questions. Call (505) 452-2278 for more information.

63

North Shore Migration—
The Last Flights

November bird-watching is not for the faint of heart. But neither is it a picnic for the last birds moving through. Lake Superior's North Shore from Duluth to Grand Marais provides the most concentrated avenue of descent in all of Minnesota for northern nesting birds to follow to their southern winter homes. In the first weeks of November this 110-mile stretch of shoreline can still offer up significant numbers of common passerines such as robins and cedar waxwings, who must be muttering to themselves, "I'm late, late, late" in the fashion of the White Rabbit in *Alice in Wonderland*. But the real allure at this time of the year are the more uncommon species of passerines, sea ducks, and hawks that are playing brinksmanship with the cliff called winter.

Hot Spots

For a whirlwind one-day birding adventure in early November, begin at **Hawk Ridge** in Duluth, where you should find a crazed hawk-counter or two still huddled in his or her lawn chair. The day could provide significant numbers of the last of the migrating hawks, such as red-tailed hawks, goshawks, rough-legged hawks, bald eagles, and golden eagles. With luck, you might hit a record day like November 10, 1963, when 204 rough-legged hawks soared over the ridge. Or maybe you'll hit "just" a good day like November 19, 1993, when 107 goshawks and 171 bald eagles traversed the ridge.

You can't win for losing in November, though. A good north to west wind pushes the birds through but brings along some bitter temperatures for standing around and counting birds. Wear more clothes than what you think the weather warrants, and then bring an extra layer or two.

When you've had your fill of hawks, or the cold wind on the ridge, take the Seven Bridges Road off Hawk Ridge down to the shoreline at the mouth of the Lester River and head north on County Hwy. 61 (North Shore Scenic Drive), the slower two-lane road that parallels Lake Superior much of the way up to Two Harbors. Stop first at the **Lakewood Pumping Station** to check for late-migrating passerines. On October 20, 1994 (I know it's not quite November, but it's close), in just three and a half hours, 19,740 robins cruised by out of a total of 26,352 birds that day. You may still find in early November a volunteer bird-counter on the top of the hill above the parking lot who can give you the lowdown on what's coming through. Rare songbirds that may be seen feeding in coniferous trees or fruit-laden trees like the mountain ash include boreal chickadee and Bohemian waxwing, or "lost" birds like mountain bluebird and Townsend's solitaire. The very last of the late-migrating warblers like the Cape May and the yellow-rumped may still be filtering through, as will all of the winter finches.

Continue north for 6.5 miles on the North Shore Scenic Drive, turning right on **Stoney Point Drive** to check for migrants on the water, over the water, and inland along the road. Snowy owls first appear at this time of the year, but expect flocks of red crossbills, pine siskins, goldfinches, and snow buntings flying overhead. The more spectacular finds will most likely be out bobbing on the water—seabirds like harlequin duck, oldsquaw, scoters (white-winged, surf, and black), and rarities like the Pacific loon. Check the skies over the water for other rarities like parasitic, pomarine, and long-tailed jaegers (though Park Point in Duluth provides the best opportunity for sighting these).

Stoney Point Drive loops back to North Shore Scenic Drive/County Road 61. Continue north to the **Knife River Marina** and scout the gravel beach, the grassy peninsula (for Lapland longspurs, horned larks, and snow buntings), and the docks for seabirds. The first state records for four different species were located right here in Knife River (king eider, red phalarope, black-legged kittiwake, and mew gull). Also check the mountain ash and spruce trees for Bohemian waxwings, bluebirds, and robins—and before you ask what is exciting about seeing robins, I'll tell you that robins can be quite a find when seen in the context of the North Shore transition between fall and winter.

Continue onward to **Two Harbors,** and stop at both bays, **Agate** and **Burlington,** to scan for seabirds. Scanning from the water treatment plant over Burlington Bay, I recorded my first Pacific loon. Remember that hawks should still be regularly coming down the coastline, so keep an eye out overhead and toward the ridges above town for them. Golden eagles too are a particularly fine present often given to the patient sky-watcher along the North Shore.

Heading north on Hwy. 61, stop at the turnout overlooking **Good Harbor Bay** south of Grand Marais. This bay has consistently been the best site for oldsquaws during the Christmas Bird Count.

When you reach **Grand Marais,** head for the harbor, where enormous flocks of gulls are common, with rarities such as glaucous and Thayer's gulls mixed in now and again.

And north of Grand Marais, stop at **Paradise Bay,** where a beautiful dark-sand beach stretches along the coastline, offering good opportunities for more sea-duck viewing.

If you've never searched big waters for sea ducks, I'd encourage you to pack a good spotting scope along with high-powered binoculars. Sea ducks don't mind the rough waters way out and thus can be frustratingly difficult to see if your equipment isn't up to the task. A typical birder's lament in such a moment sounds like, "Just what is that tiny black thing bobbing way out there?! Hey! Where'd it go? It dove! No, it's below the waves! No! There it is! Now, it's gone!" Etcetera.

A quality scope that's capable of defining those "little ducks out there" will make your bird-watching much more rewarding. A good tripod is equally important. If the winds buffet your scope because your tripod is unstable, the image you will see will shake with abandon, forcing you to give up the effort.

64

Waterfowl of the Upper Mississippi

The Upper Mississippi National Wildlife and Fish Refuge contains over 200,000 acres of wooded islands, waters, and marshes extending more than 260 miles southward along the river bottoms from Wabasha, Minnesota, almost to Rock Island, Illinois. The refuge boundaries are the longest of any refuge in the lower forty-eight states and touch four states—Minnesota, Wisconsin, Illinois, and Iowa. The river bottoms forming the refuge are from 2 to 5 miles wide and are favorite areas for thousands of brilliantly colored wood ducks as well as great numbers of marsh birds like herons and egrets. The refuge provides habitat for up to 60 percent of North America's tundra swans, which rest and feed on Weaver Bottoms north of Winona—some 10,000 may be seen here before embarking for winter on Chesapeake Bay. Up to 70 percent of all canvasback ducks in the world feed on wild celery near La Crosse. Other diving ducks like scaup, ring-necked, redhead, bufflehead, and ruddy may be seen by the thousands in rafts on the open pools above dams.

In total, 270 bird species have been seen along the river refuge. Eleven dams and locks within the refuge boundaries form a series of pools that vary from 10 to 30 miles long and create a maze of sloughs and channels that harbor waterfowl. Bald eagles concentrate in large numbers below the dams or near the mouths of tributary rivers.

The natural opulence here makes any visit worthwhile. But two species in particular, the canvasback duck and the common merganser, stick out for their sheer numbers and their reliance on the refuge as a stopover area.

The canvasback duck, a regal diving duck with a beautiful chestnut head and neck on the males, dark breast, and whitish sides and back, is considered the least abundant North American game duck. It suffered a dramatic population decline, from a high of 715,000 in 1958 to below 200,000 in 1972, due to a constellation of factors including habitat loss in the prairie pothole country where it breeds, increased predation of its eggs, a change in the main staging and resting areas along its migration route, and decline of its wintering habitat. But its numbers have been rebounding very well, and in 1994 the first legal hunt of canvasbacks in 23 years took place along the Mississippi River. Canvasbacks begin appearing at the refuge in good numbers around October 20 and usually remain until later November.

Up to 75 percent of the entire North American population of canvasbacks stage on the upper portion of the Mississippi, with great concentrations in pools 7, 8, and 9. In 1993, pool 7 (Lake Onalaska) held 70,000 canvasbacks, and pool 9 had 86,000 at its peak. Nearly 200,000 canvasbacks raft on the river pools, a phenomenal number for viewing.

Hot Spots

Lake Onalaska is just north of La Crosse, and there are a number of viewing areas where you might get a look at the canvasbacks. Lake Onalaska is 6 miles long, so the ducks could be most anywhere. Follow I-90 into La Crosse and take Exit 2 toward the airport onto French Island. Turn left as you get off the exit ramp, and then turn left again at the first intersection onto Fanta Reed Road, which will take you along the south edge of the airport. Go 4 blocks to Lakeshore Drive and turn right. Follow Lakeshore to Spillway Drive, turn left, and follow Spillway Drive to its end, where a dike intersects the road. You can walk a half-mile out onto the dike and view the south end of Lake Onalaska. Or follow Lakeshore Drive all the way to where it ends at **Nelson County Park.** You can launch a boat here for the best viewing of all, but one-half of the lake is restricted as a voluntary avoidance area in order to give the birds some breathing space (call the refuge office for current regulations).

Other viewing sites include a turnoff south of La Crosse on Hwy. 35 1 mile south of Goose Island County Park. The turnoff is just an area to pull off the road and look out over the lake. Or go on south to Stoddard, and at its south end, where Coon Creek enters the Mississippi, canvasbacks often congregate. This area is open to hunting, however.

Or take Hwy. 35 north out of La Crosse to **Trempealeau NWR,** where an observation platform allows you to look out over much of one of the large pools, which usually holds every species of duck, goose, and swan that frequent the area.

From La Crescent just over the river into Minnesota from La Crosse, south of the intersection of Minnesota 14/61 and Wisconsin 14/61/35, is **Blue Lake.** Pull off by the side of the road to view the area for canvasbacks.

One last spectacular overview of Lake Onalaska can be seen from the **Apple Blossom Drive** (Elm Street) in La Crescent, which takes you up a bluff and from there gives you an idea just how large the lake is and how many birds may be out there.

Common mergansers are sometimes mistaken for common loons at a distance. Their size and their dark heads and pure white underparts bear some minor likeness to loons, and because they both dive for fish, the mistake is understandable. The merganser's bright orange bill and red legs certainly distinguish it clearly upon a closer look, not to mention its lack of the loon "necklace." Common mergansers feed usually in shallow waters up to 15 feet deep and have toothlike serrations along their bills for grasping slippery fish.

On **Lake Pepin,** 30,000 to 60,000 common mergansers may be seen in their breeding plumage in late November all the way until ice-up. Common mergansers are the last of the migrants to come through, waiting until the last moment, it seems, so viewing is best around Thanksgiving, though in mild winters they may be seen out on the open water past Christmas. Lake Pepin must have a great fishery, because 60,000 common mergansers have a large collective appetite.

The village of **Stockholm** in Wisconsin is the hot spot on the lakeshore—scan from the village park for large rafts of lesser scaup, canvasback, redhead, and red-breasted merganser, too. Take Hwy. 35 north from Pepin for 6 miles to the well-marked road leading to the village park. Watch all along Hwy. 35 for vistas of Lake Pepin. In Pepin, turn south from Hwy. 35 on any street and proceed for 2 blocks to the lake to view the water.

On the Minnesota side of Lake Pepin, **Read's Landing** provides exceptional vistas of Lake Pepin from turnoffs north along Hwy. 61. A scope is a necessity for these long-distance viewing opportunities.

The **marina in Lake City, Minnesota,** has a good overlook, too. The refuge headquarters is located in Winona, Minnesota. Call for more information and directions to current hotspots (see Appendix).

65

November Shorttakes

Eagles Congregating

Lake Pepin, a very wide broadening of the Mississippi River, attracts huge flocks of waterfowl in November, but it is also a site for bald eagles that are often making one last push through on their way south just before freeze-up. Five hundred eagles were concentrated here in late November to early December of 1994, though that number is atypical. Scan the lower end of the lake and at nearby **Read's Landing.**

Rafts of Coots

Tens of thousands of American coots may all join together in rafts on individual lakes or flowages in Minnesota. In Minnesota, try the **Farmes Pool** in Agassiz NWR or **Lake Christina,** which lies mostly in Douglas County.

Snow Geese

Flocks of snow geese pour through the Upper Midwest in the spring and fall. Good viewing areas are along **Lake Traverse** and **Mud Lake** in Traverse County, Minnesota, on the South Dakota border, and along the **Minnesota River** in **Big Stone NWR** and **Lac Qui Parle WMA.**

66

A Closer Look: Snow Ecology

North Woods animals have four basic responses available to them as winter approaches. They can migrate to lawn chairs and piña coladas in the south, go into hibernation or torpor and not notice that winter is really going on, adapt and tough it out, or approach the winter as the season of choice, the season they were made for.

Winter weather is the limiting factor for most animal and plant survival in the North Woods. Five months of continual snow cover and temperatures consistently below freezing greatly reduce the number of species that can extend their ranges this far north. Imagine living outdoors in the average annual 200 inches of snow near the lakeshores of the Upper Peninsula of Michigan (the record is 393 inches in L'Anse!). Snow cover profoundly alters the environment, as does cold. The first snow changes the landscape so dramatically that it's like being on a different planet. Yet snow greatly differs in its effects on varying species based on its depth and character. What's considered positive by one species is often a negative for another. One inch of snow effectively covers the ground, preventing seed-eating birds from easily feeding on the ground layer, but it provides a great backdrop against which predator species like hawks can spot their prey—rodents are showcased on such a canvas.

But let 9 inches accumulate on the ground and the rodents are now happily ensconced in an insulated underworld where they begin a time of sheltered calm and bluish darkness. The snow, if light, is comparable to blown cellulose insulation because of all the air spaces it contains, and even if the temperature is 9°F outside, it's 34°F at the soil surface no matter how much the wind howls above.

For the red fox, 9 inches of snow becomes a problem. Fox can bound easily through 6 inches of snow, but at 9 inches they must walk trails to conserve energy that would be wasted trying to plow through so much snow. Ruffed grouse are pleased now. On extremely cold days they dive into powder snow to stay warm. Nine inches is enough to cover one up, though 18 inches would be better yet.

When a heavier snowfall drops that grouse-hiding 18 inches on the ground, white-tailed deer, who had been having little difficulty getting to woody browse, are forced now to "yard up" under conifers. Here one-third of the snowfall is caught in the evergreen branches, and the wind is cut down to virtually nothing. The deer are warmer here and expend less energy, but they're much more vulnerable to predation and to starvation.

Deep snow couldn't make the snowshoe hare happier. The heavy snows bend down branches or break them off, making the life of a small browser much easier. The hares leave behind their nutrient-rich pellets under the trees and shrubs in exchange.

Hares are the epitome of an animal efficiently designed for snowy winters. Fur covers their feet top and bottom, and if you could spread their toes, each foot would be as wide as the palm of an average human hand. Although the snowshoe hare weighs only 3 pounds, a 160-pound human would need a foot 12 inches wide and 30 inches long to provide the same support the hare gets from its feet. Nothing can move faster on top of snow than a snowshoe hare. Toss in for good measure its perfect white winter pelage for camouflage, and winter must certainly be the snowshoe's preferred season.

The deep snows force bobcats and wolves to travel on trails or wind-packed snow of northern lakes. If the snow builds up on tree branches, the tree-living animals like squirrels, chickadees, and crossbills can't find or reach the cones and buds that are their chief sources of food. So the birds must move to windy areas (or feeders) where the snow may be blown off the trees, and the squirrels must dig up their winter caches buried beneath the snow.

The character of snow, whether fluffy, wet, glazed, crusted, or dry and drifting, changes the behaviors of animals. A heavy crust cuts the ankles of deer and moose and acts just as effectively as an electric fence, immobilizing them to the trail system within their winter yards. The hard crust is detrimental to rodents too, because it holds in carbon dioxide from their respiration and from decomposition taking place at the ground level. They must build air shafts from their burrows to the surface, flagging their presence to predators. For lighter mammals that can skate along the snow surface, though, the crust opens up traveling opportunities that light or wet snows had closed.

A heavy wet snow breaks branches or bends them way down for browsers to reach. Sometimes in spring you can see buds browsed 15 feet up in a tree, and the image of Bigfoot may fill your mind when a snowshoe hare may have been the nibbler. Under a fluffy snow an open space forms as the snow melts and water flows to the colder crystals above, creating a delicate latticework of ice crystals above and room to move below, a virtual fairyland of pale blue light and moist warmth. But a wet snow weighs heavily upon this fairyland, compacting it and forcing more tunnel work.

Note while you're out in the forested North Woods how few herbaceous plants stand above the average 18-inch snow depth. It's no accident that most northern woodland plants grow no taller than 18 inches—staying under the snow prevents the drying winds of winter from further stressing them. In fact, many northern plants are evergreens, for instance, trailing arbutus, pipsissewa, and wintergreen, holding on to their leaves just as conifers do, but under the snow, where they have a measure of warmth and moisture.

Finally, note how many North Woods trees have bendable branches to shuck off the snow loads. A balsam fir branch bends and bends under the weight of snow like the bowstring of violin, and then the snow slides off and the branch snaps back to horizontal, and if it could sing a note like the plucked string of a violin, it would.

December

Notes

67

Christmas Bird Counts

Christmas Day was once a traditional hunting day when anything was fair game and contests were held to see who had shot the most game. In 1900, Massachusetts ornithologist Frank Chapman decided he would begin a new tradition of counting birds rather than killing them. He and 27 others in scattered locations across New England gave birth that Christmas Day to the Christmas Bird Count (CBC), a one-day survey that now takes place on over 1,600 sites in the United States, Canada, Central and South America, and islands in the Pacific and Caribbean. Over 43,000 people participate, identifying every year some 50 million birds in the Western Hemisphere.

Wisconsin was even represented that first year, and now 1,300 Wisconsinites take part in the count in nearly 80 locations. The National Audubon Society coordinates this massive event and publishes the results every year in its research journal, *American Birds,* providing a database for ornithologists throughout the world. The counts represent a single-day total that all involved realize doesn't assess the real total of birds in an area, but the numbers provide a benchmark for the day and a means to assess declines and increases in species over the years.

Each location of a CBC covers a 15-mile-wide circle, and that same circle is counted every year. The count does not really take place on Christmas Day but usually during the last two weeks of December and into the first week of January. It's nearly always on a weekend, and the actual date is set at the convenience of each CBC location. For 24 hours the individual team covers all the ground it can within that circle, counting and identifying every bird it encounters. Skis and snowshoes are often employed, though much of the counting is done from cars that simply stop at intervals along assigned roads; the counters listen and watch for a period of time before moving a little farther down the road.

All of the counting is done by volunteers, who run the gamut from very experienced birders to novices. All are welcome. Each team, usually composed of experienced and inexperienced members, is assigned a manageable area within the circle, and off they go to scour it as thoroughly as possible in a short December day. Nighttime or predawn counting takes place too, in order to pick up owls in the circle.

More often than not the count ends with a dinner at someone's house, and the day's totals, excitements, and frustrations are shared over a meal. That camaraderie may be the best part of the whole process.

Although counting birds is nearly always enjoyable, remember to prepare for an entire day out in the field in winter, which means plenty of clothes, a thermos filled with hot liquid, and snacks to keep you going. Like the postal service (well, better than the postal service), neither rain, sleet, nor snow stops the count. On the first count I participated in, we set out with the temperature at minus 22°F, and the day warmed up to minus 10°F. The windows in the car kept frosting up with a layer of ice that required continual scraping.

If you are a novice birder, jump right in and request to be sent out with experienced birders. You may not know all the identification characteristics, but you can help greatly simply by spotting birds for the more experienced to identify, and you will learn quickly, too. If you just can't see spending a day out and about in the cold (and who could blame you), you can sign up as a backyard bird-feeder-watcher, as long as your home is within the count circle. Some people attract hundreds of birds to their feeders in winter, and those numbers are very helpful to the count. In fact, I've walked miles back in the woods on counts and found fewer birds than were at my feeder. Therefore, much of the count is actually concentrated on residential areas where there are plenty of feeders and usually more open water to attract birds. Dams and power plants are good sites too, because they keep some water open.

Birders in the North Woods are lucky to find 20 species on any given winter day, whereas the southern-county birders often see 60 to 80 species. From the data gathered over the years we know that some birds are on the increase, like cardinals and red-bellied woodpeckers, who are clearly extending their ranges northward. Other birds are declining, like black ducks and tufted titmice.

Hot Spots

Maybe this should be called "Cold Spots," for that is what you are likely to encounter on a full day of winter birding. To find the CBC area closest to you, check the listings in the Appendix for your state coordinator, and give him or her a call. Then call the area coordinator, who almost assuredly will welcome you with open arms, because new energy is always needed.

Or contact your state ornithology societies, or the local birding club or nature center nearest you. You can also write to the Christmas Bird Count editor, *American Birds,* National Audubon Society, 700 Broadway, New York, NY 10003, for a list of counts and coordinators in your state. If no counts take place in your area and you wish to organize one, contact your state coordinator or the National Audubon Society for help.

68

Waterfall Cathedrals

Waterfalls hold a fascination for virtually everyone. Who can fail to be mesmerized by the liquid sounds of water splashing over rocks, the mists rising through rainbows at the bottom of a falls, or the perpetual motion of water swirling by but never running out? The Upper Midwest remains blessed with abundant clear rivers and waterfalls that often dazzle our senses.

But neglected by most of us are the same waterfalls in the winter, which may, in part or in total, transform into ice cathedrals. And in the midst of the silence that suffuses winter, the sound of falling water strikes the senses in some ways more powerfully than in the lushness of summer. The little pool of flowing water that is barely visible through a small hole in the ice speaks volumes about continuity, constancy, and inner strength.

Frozen waterfalls can be like perpetual ice storms, coating nearby rocks and plants with a sheen of crystal-clear ice. Along the underside of nearly every branch and twig hangs a comb of little icicles, once drips of mist but now frozen in gleaming pendants. Sometimes the ice glaze cracks in a shimmer of sound. And if you catch the sun as it rises or falls, streaming its horizontal light, the ice may work the miracle of 10,000 prisms, flashing color like someone tossing precious gems into the air.

A note of caution: Most waterfalls are rather treacherous to get to. Few have paths plowed out to them, and most lie across difficult ground or in ravines. Please navigate your way very carefully, and never test the ice anywhere around a falls. Take extra caution on platforms, steps, and overlooks, which may be very slippery and hazardous in the winter.

Hot Spots

In Michigan, nearly every waterfall in the state is found in the Upper Peninsula, and there are a great number of them. Some of the prettiest I've seen are the series of five named falls in the **Black River Harbor Recreation Area** in the **Ottawa National Forest**. From Bessemer, drive east on U.S. 2 1 mile to County Road 513 (Black River Road). Turn left (north) and drive for 12 miles until signs for each of the falls are seen. County Road 513 ends at Black River Harbor on Lake Superior, and the parking lots are closed all along the way, so you must park along the road and walk in to each of the falls. Remember that the snow in the UP is deep, so the going is tough unless you are on snowshoes. The beauty of the falls is further enhanced by the old-growth hemlocks and hardwoods that grace the surrounding area.

Presque Isle Falls (also called Manabezho Falls) in the **Porcupine Mountains Wilderness State Park** is one of four waterfalls occurring along the last mile of the Presque Isle River before it empties into Lake Superior. You may snowshoe on either side of the river, but both sides are quite rugged. South Boundary Road is closed into the park, so walk to the bridge just to the east that crosses the river and proceed down along the hiking trails toward the big lake. The river here is truly wild—please exercise extreme caution. Take County Road 519 north out of Wakefield to its end at Presque Isle and Lake Superior.

The upper falls at **Tahquamenon Falls State Park** are the second largest falls east of the Mississippi River, spreading 200 feet across and dropping 50 feet. The upper falls parking lot is kept plowed and the path is groomed, so the upper falls are easy to walk to even in the winter. Usually some water is still pouring over, but mounds of ice build up around the shorelines and edges. The trail in to the lower falls, a series of five smaller falls cascading around an island, is blocked off at the hill above the parking lot, but you still can park there and take the 0.75-mile walk in with snowshoes. Usually the trail is well packed from others hiking in. From Paradise, take Michigan 123 west about 6 miles to the entrance to the 38,000-acre park.

Munising Falls at **Pictured Rocks National Lakeshore** is only a 5-minute walk from the National Lakeshore Visitor Center. A paved path, kept clear in the winter, leads to a platform where you can view the sheer 40- to 50-foot drop of the falls into a canyon of multicolored rocks. A trail leads behind the ledge over which the falls drop. In winter the falls' ice remains suspended in air for its entire height, and there are those experts who practice climbing here with ice-climbing equipment. From Michigan 28 in Munising, turn left (east) on Hwy. 58 (Munising Avenue) and go about 1.25 miles to Washington Street. Turn left (north) onto Washington and go 0.5 mile to the parking area on your right across from the hospital.

For hardier souls, **Chapel Falls,** also in Pictured Rocks, is a frozen cascade, aptly named for the sense of serenity experienced in this pine canyon. A 6.5-mile unplowed road and trail lead to the falls, a long journey for most to snowshoe or ski, but well worth the solitude and beauty.

If that's a little far, try **Miners Falls,** a 3.5-mile ski or snowshoe trip off Hwy. 58. The ice stretches 30 to 40 feet down a secluded little canyon. A long series of steps must be descended to reach the falls, but as with most strenuous activity, the rewards make the effort seem small. The road in, Miners Castle Road, is 10 miles east of Munising on Hwy. 58.

Sable Falls, on the eastern border of Pictured Rocks, drops dramatically through a deep valley and is much easier to get to—only a quarter-mile walk on an unplowed path from the parking lot. Go west from Grand Marais on Hwy. 58 for 1 mile to the signed parking lot on your right.

If you're an ice climber, **Sand Point Road** offers ice climbing off cliffs near the National Lakeshore headquarters. Needless to say for the vast majority of us, this is a spectator sport only.

The middle branch of the **Ontonagon River** offers two easily accessible falls, though the short trails leading to their bases are rugged and steep. **Agate Falls** is a chain of miniature falls about 80 feet wide, with cascade after cascade to enjoy. From Trout Creek on Michigan 28, go west 4 miles to the Joseph Oravec Roadside Park on the left (south) side of the road. The park may or may not be plowed.

Bond Falls drops nearly 50 feet in a series of steps. From Hwy. 45 in Paulding, turn east onto the curvy Bond Falls Road and go about 3.2 miles to the parking areas on both sides of the road above the falls. The trail down is not plowed and is very steep.

There are several hundred more waterfalls in the UP. Get a good book (try *Michigan Waterfalls* by Laurie Penrose) and explore them throughout the year.

In Wisconsin, **Copper Falls State Park** offers several beautiful falls as well as 14 miles of groomed cross-country ski trails, so you can combine both activities. The main falls are easily accessible on a short path from the main parking lot. From Mellen on Hwy. 13 in Ashland County, take Hwy. 169 north for 2 miles to the park entrance road on your left.

Amnicon Falls State Park is a series of falls that pour for several hundred yards through a gorge. The park is located 2 miles northeast of the crossroads of Hwys. 53 and 2 in Douglas County, 15 miles southeast of Superior. Take County Road U north from Hwy. 2 to reach the park, which is open in the winter.

Big Manitou Falls is the largest in the state at a height of 162 feet and also one of the largest falls east of the Mississippi. Big Manitou Falls and its cousin, Little Manitou Falls, are located within **Pattison State Park**, 14 miles south of Superior on Hwy. 35.

In Minnesota, **Lake Superior's North Shore** is a highly concentrated area of spectacular falls. Head northeast from Duluth on Hwy. 61 and the state parks just form a line up to the Canadian border. They're all accessible with snowshoes, but in winters with little snow you can usually just walk back to the falls that so many people before you will have tramped the trails down. **Gooseberry Falls State Park** is the first state park north of Duluth and has five picturesque waterfalls and a series of cascades and rapids on the Gooseberry River, the largest estuary on the North Shore.

Tettegouche State Park is next in line, with three waterfalls on the Baptism River. The water was used at one time to baptize new converts to Christianity, hence the name. Here is Minnesota's second highest falls—80 feet. A 1.5-mile hike leads to the falls.

In the **Temperance River State Park,** the Temperance River tumbles through a stunning gorge and over waterfalls and potholes to its mouth.

Cascade River State Park offers five different waterfalls that can be seen from a footbridge dropping over a number of cascading steps into Lake Superior. The river drops 900 feet in its last 3 miles. In winter, this area is the largest deer yard in the state.

Continuing north, in the **Judge C.R. Magney State Park** the Brule River flows through the Brule River valley and is divided by a jutting rock at **Devil's Kettle Falls.** The eastern section plunges 50 feet into a gorge, and the western portion dives into a pothole and seems to disappear. Judge Magney helped establish the 11 parks and waysides along Lake Superior's North Shore.

Last, and certainly not least given that this is the largest falls in Minnesota, the Pigeon River dives 120 feet over **Pigeon Falls,** along the Minnesota-Canada border. Turn left off Hwy. 61 just before the customs station onto a paved side road that soon ends. From here, follow the narrow dirt road north for 0.5 mile or so to a short trail that leads to the falls. This is a generally unvisited area—you may have it all to yourself.

69

Winter Night Sky

Stars seem to shine more brightly at night in the winter, even though astronomers tell us there's no difference in clarity between a December night sky and one in June. Maybe the night sky seems brighter because there's just so much more time when it is dark—many of us are driving to work in the morning and home in the late afternoon, when it's already pitch black. It's possible we may just notice the stars more in winter because we spend more time out and about in the dark.

Two factors, though, really do make a difference in the winter sky. Cold winter nights drop so much in temperature that this causes a turbulence in the atmosphere. The rippling air passing in front of the starlight makes the stars appear to twinkle more, which draws our attention. And the number of bright stars visible in the winter is greater than during other seasons, so there's more to see.

The constellation Orion dominates the southern skies until late April, when it rises too far south for us to see it in the Upper Midwest, and it won't appear again until early November. Both Orion and the Big Dipper can be used as "pointer" constellations to help the amateur stargazer locate the major constellations in the night sky.

By using your hand to measure distances in degrees across the sky, the location of a particular star can be communicated easily. Hold your hand at arm's length away from you. Your little finger represents 1 degree, three fingers held together are 5 degrees, a closed fist is 10 degrees, the spread between your index and little finger is 15 degrees, and the maximum spread between your pinkie and your thumb is 25 degrees. Now you can explain distances between stars or constellations to others.

Find Orion in the southern sky by looking for the three stars in a line that make up his belt—nowhere else in the sky are three stars of this brightness so close together. Orion does actually look like the hunter he is supposed to be, unlike many other constellations, which require leaps of imagination to see. Above the belt are two stars marking the shoulders, and below the belt are two stars marking the legs. Rigel, in Orion's right foot, is the brightest star in the constellation and one of the brightest in the sky. It is nearly 55,000 times brighter than our sun, and the only reason this monster doesn't overwhelm the night sky is that it's 543 light-years away. No star puts out more energy than Rigel, but the light you are seeing began traveling toward us sometime around the year Columbus stumbled onto San Salvador, so it's come a long way.

Betelgeuse shines in Orion's left shoulder, the second brightest star in the constellation, and so old that it is ready to become a supernova anytime. With an estimated diameter of 800 times that of our sun's, Betelgeuse could wrap in its arms the orbits of Mercury, Venus, Earth, and Mars. It is a *supergiant,* one of a class of rare stars that are enormous but of low temperature. Betelgeuse even appears ruddy, underscoring its status as a red supergiant.

Locate Orion's belt and follow the belt to the left 20 degrees (about two fists). You should locate Sirius, the Dog Star, only 8.5 light-years away, and one of our closest celestial neighbors. Sirius is the brightest star in the sky and resides in the constellation Canis Major, the Big Dog. You may see a bluish tinge to Sirius, though it may seem to change color if the air is turbulent.

Trace Orion's belt in the opposite direction, to the right, for 20 degrees and you'll find Aldebaran, a bright star with an orange tinge—it's a red giant, too, but smaller than Betelgeuse. Aldebaran marks one eye of the zodiacal constellation Taurus the Bull. Keep going another 15 degrees to your right and you will be in the midst of the Pleiades, the brightest star cluster in the sky, known as the Seven Sisters.

From Orion's left shoulder (Betelgeuse) follow a line extending from the right shoulder through the left for 30 degrees (three fists) to Procyon. Or start at the far right star on Orion's belt, draw a line up through Betelgeuse, and continue on for 40 degrees, which will bring you to Castor and Pollux, which form the zodiacal constellation Gemini, The Twins.

Look just beneath Orion's belt with binoculars to see the Great Nebula of Orion, the brightest and nearest of thousands of such nebulae scattered throughout the galaxy. Nebulae are massive clouds of gas and dust where new stars are born, sort of like star nurseries.

You can use the Big Dipper, too, as your guide to finding many other constellations. The easiest way to find Polaris, the North Star, is to follow a line about 30 degrees from the bottom right star in the ladle up through the top right star in the ladle. Keep going another 25 degrees on that same line and you'll find the constellation Cassiopeia, which looks like a wobbly W.

These guidelines are all wonderfully mapped and described in Terence Dickinson's book *NightWatch,* a great resource for understanding what is in the night sky in any season. Equally useful is a computer program called Voyageur 2, which can print out a sky chart anytime for the location you choose. No more of those round rotating star charts, which tend to confuse some people.

Stargazing can be uncomfortable for your neck and legs. Take along a reclining patio chair to ease the burden on your neck, equip it with blankets, bring along a hot thermos with a drink that perks you up, and wear enough clothes that the cold can't seep in too quickly. Binoculars or your birding scope can be a great help in seeing the fainter stars or examining the moon. A red flashlight (put a red filter over your bulb housing) works great to allow you to read star charts without ruining your night vision.

Hot Spots

Stargazing is good anyplace you can get away from light pollution, a growing problem. Also be aware of the moon phase. A full moon overwhelms the stars with its light. A new moon, on the other hand, is ideal, for no moonlight will impair your view of the night sky. Higher elevations tend to be better because light pollution and air pollution usually settle in valleys.

70

Tracking

For every animal we may see in the woods, more than a hundred probably pass by us unobserved. Most wild animals are expert at being elusive, which is why I like botany so well—the flora always stay in one place. Plants are predictable, animals aren't. On the other hand, that elusiveness is what makes the sighting of wildlife so enjoyable. Humans are a fickle species—we put more value on those things we see less often. It's a version of the old "absence makes the heart grow fonder" routine. We appreciate the adventure, the seeking, and the discovery of wildlife. There's tension in the stalking and satisfaction in the find.

Most often, animals evade us quite successfully. Although most birds and a few mammals may be seen during the day, many mammals (and a few birds) are nocturnal and have learned very well how to avoid humans whenever possible. All we may see are the clues they leave behind, usually in the form of tracks or scat. Other clues are out there as well, like nesting or denning sites, food remains, the holes made to access food, deer rubs, scent piles, or matted-down vegetation indicating an overnight bed. Tracking isn't merely identification, it's the interpretation and understanding of an animal's actions. The clues all add up to a story to be read by the experienced observer.

Winter provides the best tracking opportunities, because if there's fresh snow, there will be tracks. Animals must eat, and to do so requires movement. Add to that the absence of leaves in winter and the white background of snow, and spotting an animal in many ways becomes easier.

To be a good tracker, one must think like an animal—think four-legged instead of two. It's not easy to get beyond our biases, because we tend to be anthropomorphic. We want to believe that animals act like humans; it's the Disney approach. But they don't act like us—their needs are different, and their behavior results from their needs. Wild animals respond primarily to their stomachs and their hormones. These animals have three drives—to eat, to avoid being eaten, and to reproduce. Prey species must remain close to cover for safety, and predators must travel significant distances to locate prey. But the mating urge may override caution in a prey species—most of us are familiar with the lengths the mating instinct will take a buck deer in rut.

Tracking requires understanding too of habitat, season, and location. Knowing what is possible and probable in a given time and place will narrow dramatically the list of suspects.

River otters leave an unmistakable tobaggon-like track as they run and slide through winter snow. Photo by Jeff Richter.

Unfortunately (or perhaps fortunately), tracking will never be an exact science but will always remain more of an art. You will not always be able to make a correct identification or read correctly the story of a trail. James Halfpenny, whose book *A Field Guide to Mammal Tracking in North America* is the best I've read, takes a laptop computer and calipers with him into the field. He measures eleven different parameters of every track, and each measurement is then fed directly from the calipers into the databanks of his laptop. Even with more than 20 years of data in his computer for comparison, an absolute identification is not always possible, because there is similarity in track size and gait between certain animals.

But the amateur tracker can identify a large number of tracks, or at least narrow them down to a small group of possibilities, and some stories can be clearly read. The pleasure of tracking often lies in the process of trying to unravel the mystery.

Winter tracking usually takes place on snowshoes, and my family and I now enjoy snowshoeing more than any other winter recreation. We pull out our topographic maps, search for a place that looks good, and head on out. Snowshoes leave a trail in soft snow that is virtually impossible to miss on the way back, thus eliminating the linear, start-to-finish, single-minded paths we so often confine ourselves to. In fact, tracking in the winter on snowshoes is the best means I know of to explore the North Woods. No mosquitoes, no blackflies—only the cold, the snow, and whatever has left its tracks.

So once you find a track, how do you know what you might have? To categorize the track into a family of animals isn't too hard.

Four toes on each of the front and hind feet equals the dog family (fox, coyote, wolf), cat family (bobcat, lynx, even cougar), or rabbit family (cottontail or snowshoe hare).

Four toes on the front foot and five toes on the hind foot equals the rodent family (mice, voles, shrews, chipmunks, squirrels, woodchuck).

Five toes each on the front and hind feet equals the raccoon and weasel families (weasel, badger, mink, skunk, fisher, otter, bear, beaver, muskrat, porcupine, opossum).

Two toes is the easiest of all. Those hooves belong to a deer or moose.

Numerous other factors can be looked at besides the number of toes, including whether claws are present, the length of the track, and the shape of the track. The basic law of variability applies, too. In other words, tracks may not do just what the books say they're supposed to—never say never, and never say always—expect variation.

Tracking offers wonderful challenges. But maybe more important is just being out exploring, poking around, and being part of the natural world. The snow provides the perfect textbook for learning more about animals. I encourage you to get out in the snows of December and try to read the messages there.

Hot Spots

Weekend tracking classes are given in many locations and provide the informational jump-start many people need to make sense of what they are seeing.

In Wisconsin, **Treehaven,** a 1,400-acre natural resource and education center near Tomahawk operated by the University of Wisconsin at Stevens Point, offers winter tracking and ecology classes. **Sandhill Wildlife Area** near Babcock offers Saturday tracking classes as part of its Outdoor Skills Center. A small fee is charged.

But as with any other skill, true learning can only take place out in the field and with practice over time. The "field" can be your backyard, a city park, or a national forest. Each site offers its plusses and minuses, but all are ripe for the curious of mind.

I like to snowshoe and track in wild areas, as far away from the sound of snowmobiles and the influence of people as possible. The **Boundary Waters Canoe Area Wilderness** in northeastern Minnesota and the **Porcupine Mountains Wilderness** in the Upper Peninsula of Michigan offer the largest wilderness expanses to explore. National and state wildlife refuges are prime areas for exploration too, as are national and state forests. Where you go depends on what you want to see and the amount of time you want to put into your experience. Consult the list of national and state forests, wildlife areas, and refuges in the Appendix. Call the manager of the specific sites and ask for any hotspots they know of because animals move around; the sites may vary from year to year.

December Shorttakes

Ice Skating

Although this event usually has little to do with wildlife, the first hard ice-up on northern lakes can be wondrous for skating. If the snow doesn't fly early, several weeks of sleek new ice can provide hours of glide time. A minimum of 2 to 3 inches of ice is considered safe, though the exercise of caution on any newly frozen body of water goes with living a long life.

Northern Lights

The aurora borealis is not a seasonal event, though I tend to see it more in December simply because it is dark so much of the time. Scientific explanations cannot begin to satisfy the overwhelming sense of mystery and grandeur the northern lights present. Keep in touch with your local weather forecaster, who will often know when the lights are occurring. Better yet, start up a northern lights phone tree, so if one person happens to see the phenomenon, a much larger group can be alerted. The nineteenth-century polar explorer Charles Hall wrote, "Who but God can conceive such infinite scenes of glory. Who but God could execute them, painting the heavens in such gorgeous display?"

A Closer Look: Chickadee Cheer

Many a bleak winter morning has been brightened by singing chickadees, who just don't seem to be fazed by the cold and snow. North Woods residents probably appreciate black-capped chickadees more than any other bird, because so few birds over-winter in the North Country. Any bird that can survive northern winters at just 5 inches long and only one-third of an ounce (three could be mailed with one postage stamp, notes author Laura Erickson) deserves all the appreciation it receives.

Life at the backyard feeder, though, is not so cheerful as it may appear. Although chickadees may seem to be unaffected by the rigors of snowstorms and windchills, nothing could be further from the truth. Their average life span is the simplest indicator of the hardships of living for a northern songbird. Individual chickadees have been known to live for 12 years, but probably half or more of the chickadees at any given backyard feeder are only 1 year old or less. Most of those won't make it to the spring, either—as many as 80 percent of chickadees will die before reaching one year. So it's not Disneyland out there, and though the chickadees appear to be taking polite turns at the feeder, they really are operating from a predetermined pecking order that is based on the survival of the fittest—Darwin's theory is hard at work at backyard feeders.

In any chickadee flock, there is one bird who wins all encounters at the feeder, whereas the majority of the flock win some and lose some. A few lose all the competitive interactions and are not long for this world. If two birds arrive at a feeder at once, the dominant one will lift its head to display its throat patch, or bib, which appears to be a signal to the other to back off—it may be that the bigger the bib is, the more dominant is the chickadee. Or at the initial encounter the subordinate bird may turn its back as if to say, "That's okay, I'll wait." The dominant bird may also emit a gargling sound that states its power in no uncertain terms.

Chickadees do interact in positive social terms, too. Their flocking is a good strategy for spotting food and danger. The first bird to spot a hawk will give a high *seet* sound as an alarm to the flock, a call so high-pitched that humans seldom hear it.

Chickadees also help one another out by sharing body heat. Chickadees feed until just before dark and then retire to a specific roosting area before total dark comes on. The flock may spend nights in a cavity in a dead limb or stump, or wedged under a loose piece of bark, or in an old woodpecker nest-hole, where the combined body heat helps keep the individuals warm.

When not feeding at a backyard feeder, chickadees use their short, strong beaks to uncover insect and spider eggs under tree bark and in deadwood, to gather seeds from plants, and even to strip suet from a deer carcass. Their *fee-bee* song is a location call saying, "I'm here," but it turns into a male territorial proclamation when breeding time occurs. The *chick-a-dee-dee* song repeated again and again is sung by both genders and appears to coordinate flock movement. The genders look alike, though the males have a slightly larger wingspan. Their behavior during breeding season, however, easily separates the genders.

But how does a little bird with an internal temperature of 109°F keep its body furnace stoked enough to stay warm on a subzero night? In brutal cold, chickadees will fluff out their feathers and turn down their metabolism to save energy. In summer a chickadee has about 2,000 feathers, but it adds several hundred more for winter to fluff out and trap air for insulation. Still, a strong wind can penetrate the feathers, so chickadees try to stay protected in conifers during the day. The worst-case scenario for a chickadee is an ice storm, even though oil glands keep their outer feathers reasonably waterproof. But freezing rain can slick feathers against a chickadee's body, killing it in minutes. Staying dry is the first commandment for chickadees.

Chickadees allow their body temperatures to drop 20°F at night in a form of self-induced hypothermia in recognition of the fact that the less warm the house needs to be, the less fuel need be burned.

And they eat and eat and eat. Chickadees need at least 20 times more food in winter than in summer, and so must eat 150 sunflower seeds a day to survive in mild winter weather, and 250 seeds a day when the temperature drops below zero. This amount of food represents about 60 percent of a chickadee's body weight. One researcher weighed birds early in the morning and found virtually no body fat, but the same birds weighed in late afternoon were bulging with fat.

Another chickadee adaptation to save heat is the horny scales that cover their feet and legs. These require little blood compared to our skin, and their legs are controlled by tendons, not muscles, and tendons use less blood too. So chickadees have evolved the means to lose less heat through their extremities.

One other way many birds stay warm in winter is to shiver. A chickadee's heart beats over 650 times per minute—their chest muscles quiver continually to produce heat. Chickadees never stop shivering once the temperature drops below 65°F.

The black-capped chickadee captures the hearts of North Woods residents. Photo by Carol Christensen.

Feeding chickadees in very cold winter weather can help them survive. A University of Wisconsin study compared the survival rates of 418 birds near feeders and 158 that foraged entirely in the wild. The feeder birds only obtained 20 to 25 percent of their daily energy from feeders, and the rest came from the woods and fields. During normal winter weather the chickadees were not dependent on feeders—when feeder food was withheld, the feeder birds survived at the same rate as those that never visited feeders. But when the temperatures skidded below 10°F, the story changed. Sunflower seeds at a feeder nearly doubled the survival rate of chickadees compared to those foraging in the wild. So if you feed birds and you're planning a winter vacation, try to go when the temperatures are high enough so the birds can forage with ease in the wild. If that's not possible, enlist a friend or neighbor to stock your feeders while you are away.

I know that we're not supposed to be anthropomorphic about animals, but with chickadees the temptation is hard to resist. It seems as if you can talk to them, and they'll sit close on a branch and look you right in the eye. With a little patience on your part they'll feed from your hand, and they're faithful and fearless—who else comes to your house every morning to visit even when it's minus 30°? I still go out for a few mornings every winter to entice them onto my hand. I like the feeling of their little claws on my fingers, as well as the fact that they trust me enough to share a meal. For me, December wouldn't be the same without the pleasure of chickadees.

Appendix

National Parks, Forests, and Lakeshores

Michigan

Hiawatha National Forest
Munising District Office
400 E. Munising
Munising, MI 49862
(906) 387-3700

Huron-Manistee National Forest
421 S. Mitchell St.
Cadillac, MI 49601
(616) 775-2421 or (800) 821-6263

Huron National Forest
Mio District Ranger Office
Mio, MI 48647
(517) 826-3252

Isle Royale National Park
87 N. Ripley St.
Houghton, MI 49931
(906) 482-0984 or (906) 482-3310

North County National Scenic Trail
North Country Trail Association
P.O. Box 311
White Cloud, MI 49349
(Or write/call state DNR offices for local North Country Trail information)

Ottawa National Forest
E. U.S. 2
Ironwood, MI 49938
(906) 932-1330 or (800) 562-1201

Pictured Rocks National Lakeshore
P.O. Box 40
Munising, MI 49862
(906) 387-2607

Sleeping Bear Dunes National Lakeshore
400¹/₂ Main St.
Frankfort, MI 49635
(616) 352-9611

Sylvania Wilderness and Recreation Area
Watersmeet Ranger Station
Watersmeet, MI 49969
(906) 358-4551

Minnesota

Chippewa National Forest Supervisor
Cass Lake, MN 56633
(218) 335-2226

Hiawatha National Forest Supervisor
2727 N. Lincoln Rd.
Escanaba, MN 49829
(906) 786-4062

Superior National Forest and Boundary Waters Canoe Area Wilderness
P.O. Box 338
Duluth, MN 55801
(218) 720-5440

Voyageurs National Park
P.O. Box 50
International Falls, MN 56649
(218) 283-9821

Wisconsin

Apostle Islands National Lakeshore
Rt. 1, Box 4
Bayfield, WI 54814
(715) 779-3397

Chequamegon National Forest Supervisor
1170 4th Ave. S.
Park Falls, WI 54552
(715) 762-2461

Ice Age National Scientific Reserve
Wisconsin DNR
Box 7921
Madison, WI 53707
(608) 266-2621

National Park Service
P.O. Box 5463
Madison, WI 53705-0463

Nicolet National Forest Supervisor
Federal Building
68 S. Stevens
Rhinelander, WI 54501
(715) 362-3415

St. Croix National Scenic Riverway
P.O. Box 708
St. Croix Falls, WI 54024
(715) 483-3284

National Wildlife Refuges

Michigan

Seney National Wildlife Refuge
HCR 2, Box 1
Seney, MI 49883
(906) 586-9851

Shiawassee National Wildlife Refuge
6975 Mower Rd., RR 1
Saginaw, MI 48601
(517) 777-5930

Minnesota

Agassiz National Wildlife Refuge
Middle River, MN 56737
(218) 449-4115

Big Stone National Wildlife Refuge
25 NW 2nd St.
Ortonville, MN 56278
(612) 839-3700

Minnesota Valley National Wildlife Refuge
4101 E. 80th St.
Bloomington, MN 55420
(612) 854-5900

National Wildlife Refuge Association
P.O. Box 124
Winona, MN 55987
(507) 454-5940

Rice Lake National Wildlife Refuge
Rt. 2, Box 67
McGregor, MN 55760
(218) 768-2402

Sherburne National Wildlife Refuge
Rt. 2
Zimmerman, MN 55398
(612) 389-3323

Tamarac National Wildlife Refuge
Rural Rt.
Rochert, MN 56578
(218) 847-2641

Upper Mississippi River National Wildlife Refuge
51 E. 4th St.
Winona, MN 55987
(507) 454-7351

Wisconsin

Horicon National Wildlife Refuge
Rt. 2
Mayville, WI 53050
(414) 387-2658

Necedah National Wildlife Refuge
Star Rt. W, Box 386
Necedah, WI 54646
(608) 565-2551

Trempealeau National Wildlife Refuge
Rt. 1, Box 1602
Trempealeau, WI 54661
(608) 539-2311

State Parks, Forests, and Recreation Areas

For all state trails and canoe routes, contact the appropriate district department of natural resources office, or the state department of natural resources headquarters.

Michigan

Bay City State Recreation Area
Saginaw Bay Visitor Center/Tobico Marsh
3582 State Park Dr.
Bay City, MI 48706
(517) 667-0717

Hartwick Pines State Park
Michigan Forests Visitor Center
Rt. 3, Box 3840
Grayling, MI 49738
(517) 348-7068

Huron-Clinton Metroparks (Indian Springs Metropark; Kensington Metropark; Lake Erie Metropark, Wetland Interpretive Center (800) 477-2757; Metrobeach Metropark)
13000 High Ridge Dr.
P.O. Box 2001
Brighton, MI 48116-8001
(800) 47-PARKS

Leelanau State Park
Rt. 1, Box 49
Northport, MI 49670
(616) 922-5270

Ludington State Park
Great Lakes Visitor Center
P.O. Box 709
Ludington, MI 49431
(616) 843-8671

Muskegon State Park
3560 Memorial Dr.
North Muskegon, MI 49445
(616) 744-3480

Nordhouse Dunes
Manistee Ranger District
Manistee, MI 49660
(616) 723-2211

P.H. Hoeft State Park
U.S. 23 N.
Rogers City, MI 49779
(517) 734-2543

P.J. Hoffmaster State Park
Gillette Sand Dune Visitor Center
6585 Lake Harbor Rd.
Muskegon, MI 49441
(616) 798-3711

Pigeon River Country State Forest
9966 Twin Lakes Rd.
Vanderbilt, MI 49795
(517) 983-4101

Porcupine Mountains Wilderness State Park
412 S. Boundary Rd.
Ontonagon, MI 49953
(906) 885-5275

Port Crescent State Park
1775 Port Austin Rd.
Port Austin, MI 48467
(517) 738-8663

Rifle River Recreation Area
Box 98
Lupton, MI 48635
(517) 473-2258

Saugatuck Dunes State Park
Ottawa Beach Rd.
Holland, MI 49424
(616) 399-9390

Tahquamenon Falls State Park
Star Rt. 48, Box 225
Paradise, MI 49768
(906) 492-3415

Tawas Point State Park
686 Tawas Beach Rd.
East Tawas, MI 48730
(517) 362-5041

Van Riper State Park
P.O. Box 66
Champion, MI 49814
(906) 339-4461

Warren Dunes/Grand Mere State Park
Red Arrow Hwy.
Sawyer, MI 49125
(616) 426-4013

Waterloo Recreation Area
Michigan Geology Visitor Center
16345 McClure Rd., Rt. 1
Chelsea, MI 48118
(313) 475-8307

Wilderness State Park
Box 380
Carp Lake, MI 49718
(616) 436-5381

Yankee Springs Recreation Area
2104 Gun Lake Rd.
Middleville, MI 49333
(616) 795-9081

Minnesota

Beltrami State Forest
Norris Camp
Bemidji Regional DNR Office
P.O. Box 100
Roosevelt, MN 56673
(218) 755-5955

Blue Mounds State Park
Rt. 1
Luverne, MN 56156
(507) 283-4892

Buffalo River State Park
Glydnon, MN 56547
(218) 498-2124

Cascade River State Park
HC 3, Box 450
Lutsen, MN 55612-9705
(218) 387-1543

Frontenac State Park
29223 County 28 Boulevard
Lake City, MN 55041
(612) 345-3401

Gooseberry Falls State Park
1300 E. Highway 61
Two Harbors, MN 55616
(218) 834-3855

Grand Portage State Park
HCR Box 7
Grand Portage, MN 55605
(218) 475-2360

Hennepin Parks
12615 County Rd. 9
P.O. Box 41320
Plymouth, MN 55441
(612) 559-9000

Itasca State Park
HCO 5, Box 4
Lake Itasca, MN 56460
(218) 266-2114

Jay Cooke State Park
500 E. Highway 210
Carlton, MN 55718
(218) 384-4610

Judge C.R. Magney State Park
Box 500
Grand Marais, MN 55604
(218) 387-2929

Kilen Woods State Park
Rt. 1, Box 122
Lakefield, MN 56150-6258
(612) 296-6157

Lac Qui Parle State Park
Montevideo, MN 56265
(612) 752-4736

Lake Shetek State Park
Rt. 1, Box 164
Currie, MN 56123-9715
(507) 763-3256

Myre–Big Island State Park
Rt. 3, Box 33
Albert Lea, MN 56007
(507) 373-4492

Nerstrand Big Woods State Park
9700 170th St. E.
Nerstrand, MN 55053
(507) 334-8848

Temperance River State Park
P.O. Box 33
Schroeder, MN 55613
(218) 663-7476

Tettegouche State Park
474 Highway 61 E.
Silver Bay, MN 55614
(218) 226-3539

Zippel Bay State Park
HC 2, Box 25
Williams, MN 56686
(218) 783-6252

Wisconsin

Amnicon Falls State Park
6294 S. State Rd. 35
Superior, WI 54880-8326
(715) 399-8073

Bong Recreation Area
26313 Burlington Rd.
Kansasville, WI 53139
(414) 878-5600

Brule River State Forest
Ranger Station, Box 125
Brule, WI 54820
(715) 372-4866

Copper Falls State Park
Rt. 1, Box 17AA
Mellen, WI 54546
(715) 274-5123

Devils Lake State Park
S5975 Park Rd.
Baraboo, WI 53913-9299
(608) 356-8301

Harrington Beach State Park
531 Highway D
Belgium, WI 53004
(414) 285-3015

High Cliff State Park
N7475 High Cliff Rd.
Menasha, WI 54952
(414) 989-1106

Kettle Moraine State Forest—Northern Unit
N1765 Highway G
Campbellsport, WI 53010
(414) 626-2116

Kohler-Andrae State Park
1520 Old Park Rd.
Sheboygan, WI 53081
(414) 452-3457

Nelson Dewey State Park
Box 658
Cassville, WI 53806
(608) 725-5374

Northern Highlands State Forest
8770 Highway J
Woodruff, WI 54568-9635
(715) 356-5211

Pattison State Park
6294 S. State Rd. 35
Superior, WI 54880-8326
(715) 399-8073

Perrot State Park
Rt. 1, P.O. Box 407
Trempealeau, WI 54661
(608) 534-6409

Point Beach State Forest
9400 County Rd. O
Two Rivers, WI 54241
(414) 794-7480

Wyalusing State Park
13342 County Rd. C
Gagley, WI 53801
(608) 996-2261

State Wildlife Management, Game, and Recreation Areas

Many state wildlife and game areas are in remote regions without an office or manager directly on the site. Most are managed as part of the duties of wildlife managers in district natural resources offices. Information requests are often handled through a central state office, which will refer you to the appropriate district office if it can't answer your questions.

Please note that major reorganization in both the Michigan and Wisconsin Departments of Natural Resources was taking place in 1995 at the time of this writing. Divisions and districts may no longer exist in the same manner as listed. Call the state headquarters to be certain of current designations. The addresses given here are accurate as of September 1995.

Michigan

For information and free maps of all state game areas and wildlife management areas in Michigan, write or call:

Michigan Department of Natural Resources Wildlife Division
Box 30444
Lansing, MI 48909-7944
(517) 373-1263

Allegan State Game Area
4590 118th Ave.
Allegan, MI 49010
(616) 673-2430

Crow Island State Game Area
Contact the Michigan Department of Natural Resources Wildlife Division

Erie Marsh Preserve
Contact the Michigan Nature Conservancy

Erie State Game Area
Contact the Michigan Department of Natural Resources Wildlife Division

Fish Point State Game Area
Contact the Michigan Department of Natural Resources Wildlife Division

Love Creek County Park
9288 Huckleberry Rd.
Berrien Center, MI 49102
(616) 471-2617

Maple River State Game Area
Rose Lake Wildlife Office
8562 E. Stoll Rd.
East Lansing, MI 48823
(517) 373-9358

Michigan Fisheries Interpretive Center
Wolf Lake State Fish Hatchery
34270 County Rd. 652
Mattawan, MI 49701
(616) 668-2876

Nayanquing Point State Wildlife Area
Contact the Michigan Department of Natural Resources Wildlife Division

Pointe Mouille State Game Area
37205 Mouillee Rd., Rt. 2
Rockwood, MI 48173
(313) 379-9692

St. Clair Flats Wildlife Area
Contact the Michigan Department of Natural Resources Wildlife Division

Tobico Marsh State Game Area
Contact Bay City State Park

Warren Woods Natural Area
Contact Warren Dunes State Park

Wigwam Bay Wildlife Area
Contact the Michigan Department of Natural Resources Wildlife Division

Minnesota

Burnham Creek Wildlife Management Area (Chicog Wildlife Management Area; Dugdale Wildlife Management Area)
Crookston Department of Natural Resources Office
203 W. Fletcher
Crookston, MN 56716
(218) 281-8452 or 281-6063

Colvill Park/Red Wing
Department of Natural Resources Nongame Specialist
500 Lafayette Rd.
St. Paul, MN 55155-4007
(612) 297-2277

Duluth Harbor Area
Department of Natural Resources Nongame Specialist
1201 E. Highway 2
Grand Rapids, MN 55744
(218) 327-4421

Roseau River Wildlife Management Area
Contact Bemidji Regional Department of Natural Resources Office
(218) 755-3955

Rothsay Wildlife Management Area
Fergus Falls Area Wildlife Office
1221 E. Fir Ave.
Fergus Falls, MN 56537

Thief Lake Wildlife Management Area
HCR Box 17
Middle River, MN 56737
(218) 222-3747

Twin Lakes Wildlife Management Area
P.O. Box 154
Karlstad, MN 56732
(218) 436-2427

Wisconsin

Ackley Wildlife Area
Antigo Department of Natural Resources
1635 Neva Rd., Box 310
Antigo, WI 54409
(715) 627-4317

Buena Vista Marsh
Ranger Station, Box 100
Friendship, WI 53934
(608) 339-3385

Crex Meadows Wildlife Area (Amsterdam Sloughs Wildlife Area; Fish Lake
Wildlife Area)
Box 367
Grantsburg, WI 54840
(715) 463-2896

Dunbar State Natural Area
Marinette Department of Natural Resources Office
Industrial Parkway, P.O. Box 16
Marinette, WI 54177
(715) 732-0101

Germania Wildlife Area (Grand River Wildlife Area; White River Marsh
Wildlife Management Area)
Berlin Department of Natural Resources
Box 343
Berlin, WI 54923
(414) 361-3149

Horicon Marsh Wildlife Area
W4279 Headquarters Rd.
Mayville, WI 53050
(414) 485-3000

Kewaunee River Egg-Taking Facility
(414) 388-1025

Killsnake Wildlife Management Area
Appleton Department of Natural Resources
1001 W. College Ave.
Appleton, WI 54914
(414) 832-1804

Mead Wildlife Area
SGV 129, County Highway S
Milladore, WI 54454
(715) 457-6771

Moquah Barrens
Contact Chequamegon National Forest

Namekagon Barrens
Spooner Department of Natural Resources
P.O. Box 160
Spooner, WI 54801
(715) 635-4089

Navarino Wildlife Area
Navarino Nature Center
P.O. Box 606
Shawano, WI 54166
(715) 524-2161

Pershing Wildlife Area
Ladysmith Department of Natural Resources
W8945 Highway 8
Ladysmith, WI 54848
(715) 532-3911

Powell Marsh Wildlife Area
Contact Northern Highlands State Forest

Riley Lake Wildlife Area
Park Falls Department of Natural Resources
P.O. Box 220
Park Falls, WI 54552
(715) 762-3204

Root River Fish Facility
(414) 263-8500

Sandhill Wildlife Area (Wood County Wildlife Area)
Box 156
Babcock, WI 54413
(715) 884-2437

Thunder Lake Wildlife Area
Rhinelander Ranger Station
Highway 17 S, Box 576
Rhinelander, WI 54501
(715) 365-2632

Turtle-Flambeau Flowage
Mercer Department of Natural Resources
Box 4
Mercer, WI 54547
(715) 476-2646

Department of Natural Resources Offices

Michigan
Department of Natural Resources
Box 30028
Lansing, MI 48909

Parks and Recreation (517) 373-9900 or 373-1270
Wildlife Division (517) 373-1263
Forestry Division (517) 373-1275
Grayling Department of Natural Resources Office (517) 348-6371

Minnesota
Department of Natural Resources
Information Center
500 Lafayette Rd., Box 7
St. Paul, MN 55155-4040
(612) 296-6157
(800) 766-6000 (in Minnesota only)

Aitkin Department of Natural Resources Office (218) 927-6915
Cass County Land Department (218) 947-3338
Cloquet Department of Natural Resources Office (218) 879-0883
Crookston Department of Natural Resources Office (218) 281-8452
    (Dugdale, Burnham Creek, Chicog Wildlife Management Areas)
Detroit Lakes Department of Natural Resources Office (218) 847-1578
Eveleth Department of Natural Resources Office (218) 749-7748
Fergus Falls Department of Natural Resources Office (218) 739-7575
Hinckley Department of Natural Resources Office (612) 384-6148
Park Rapids Department of Natural Resources Office (218) 732-8452

Wisconsin

Department of Natural Resources
Box 7921
Madison, WI 53707
(608) 266-2621

Parks and Recreation (608) 266-2181
Wildlife (608) 266-1877
Bureau of Endangered Resources (608) 266-7012
New London Area Department of Natural Resources (414) 424-3050

National Audubon Society Chapters and Sanctuaries

Michigan

Michigan Audubon Society (45 local chapters)
6011 W. St. Joseph Highway, Suite 403
P.O. Box 80527
Lansing, MI 48908-0526
(517) 886-9144

Bernard Baker Sanctuary
21145 15 Mile Rd.
Bellevue, MI 49201
(or write/call Michigan Audubon Society)

Fletcher Floodwaters
Contact Michigan Audubon Society

Lake Bluff Audubon Center
Contact Michigan Audubon Society

Phyllis Haehnle Memorial Sanctuary
Contact Michigan Audubon Society

Minnesota

Minnesota Audubon Society
30 E. 10th St.
St. Paul, MN 55101
(612) 291-2596

Wisconsin

Madison Audubon Society
222 S. Hamilton
Madison, WI 53703
(608) 255-2473

Goose Pond Sanctuary
Contact Madison Audubon Society

Schlitz Audubon Center
1111 E. Brown Deer Rd.
Milwaukee, WI 53217
(414) 351-4200

The Nature Conservancy

Michigan

The Nature Conservancy
531 N. Clipper St.
Lansing, MI 48912
(517) 332-1741

Minnesota

The Nature Conservancy
328 E. Hennepin Ave.
Minneapolis, MN 55414
(612) 331-0750

Wisconsin

The Nature Conservancy
333 W. Mifflin St., Suite 107
Madison, WI 53703
(608) 251-8140

Environmental/Nature Centers, Arboretums, Sanctuaries

Michigan

Blandford Nature Center
1715 Hillburn Ave. N.W.
Grand Rapids, MI 49504

Brockway Mountain Drive
Contact Michigan Nature Association
P.O. Box 102
Avoca, MI 48006-0102
(810) 324-2626

Chippewa Nature Center
400 S. Badour Rd.
Midland, MI 48640
(517) 631-0830

Dahlem Environmental Education Center
Jackson Community College
2111 Emmons Rd.
Jackson, MI 49201

De Graaf Nature Center
600 Graafschap Rd.
Holland, MI 49423
(616) 396-2739

Estivant Pines Sanctuary
Contact Michigan Nature Association
or call the Keweenaw Tourism Council (800) 338-7982

Gillette Visitor Center
Contact P. J. Hoffmaster State Park

Kalamazoo Nature Center
7000 Westnedge Ave.
Kalamazoo, MI 49007
(616) 381-1574

Kellogg Bird Sanctuary
12685 E. C Ave.
Augusta, MI 49012
(616) 671-2510

Lefglen Nature Sanctuary
Contact Michigan Nature Association

Sarett Nature Center
2300 Benton Center Rd.
Benton Harbor, MI 49022
(616) 927-4832

Seven Ponds Nature Center
3854 Crawford Rd.
Dryden, MI 48428
(313) 796-3419

University of Michigan at Dearborn
Department of Natural Sciences
Dearborn, MI 48128

West Bloomfield Woods Nature Preserve
3325 Middlebelt Rd.
W. Bloomfield, MI 48323
(810) 334-5660

Whitehouse Nature Center
Albion College
Albion, MI 49224

Minnesota

Deep Portage Conservation Reserve
Rural Route
Hackensack, MN 56452
(218) 682-2325

Raptor Center, University of Minnesota
1920 Fitch Ave.
St. Paul, MN 55108
(612) 624-4745

River Bend Nature Center
Box 265
Faribault, MN 55021
(507) 332-7151

Wisconsin

Bubolz Nature Preserve
4815 N. Lynndale Dr.
Appleton, WI 54915
(414) 731-6041

Havenwoods Environmental Awareness Center
6141 N. Hopkins St.
Milwaukee, WI 53209
(414) 527-0232

MacKenzie Environmental Education Center
W7303 County CS
Poynette, WI 53955
(608) 635-4498

Retzer Nature Center
W284 S1530 Rd. DT
Waukesha, WI 53188
(414) 896-8007

Ridges Sanctuary
P.O. Box 152
Baileys Harbor, WI 54202
(414) 839-2802

Riveredge Nature Center
P.O. Box 26
Newburg, WI 53060
(414) 375-2715

Sandhill Outdoor Skills Center
Contact Sandhill Wildlife Area

Thousand Islands Environmental Center
700 Dodge St.
Kaukauna, WI 54130
(414) 766-4733

Treehaven
2540 Pickeral Creek Rd.
Tomahawk, WI 54487
(715) 453-4106

University of Wisconsin Arboretum
McKay Center
1207 Seminole Hwy.
Madison, WI 53711
(608) 263-7344

Wehr Nature Center
9701 W. College Ave.
Franklin, WI 53132
(414) 425-8550

State Nature Magazines

All three states produce excellent magazines well worth the subscription price (Minnesota's magazine is free to Minnesota residents).

Michigan Natural Resources Magazine
Box 7355
Red Oak, IA 51591-0355
(800) MNR-0015

Minnesota Volunteer
Minnesota Department of Natural Resources
500 Lafayette Rd.
St. Paul, MN 55155-4046
(612) 296-0888

Wisconsin Natural Resources Magazine
P.O. Box 7921
Madison, WI 53707
(800) 678-9472

Wildlife/Environmental Organizations

Michigan

Michigan Nature Association
P.O. Box 102
Avoca, MI 48006-0102
(810) 324-2626

North America Mycological Association
Kenneth Cochran
3558 Oakwood
Ann Arbor, MI 48104-5213

Sigurd Olson Environmental Institute
Northland College
Ashland, WI 54806
(715) 682-1223
Watersmeet, Michigan, office (906) 358-4350

Whitefish Point Bird Observatory
HC 48, Box 115
Paradise, MI 49768
(906) 492-3596

Minnesota

Friends of Boundary Waters Wilderness
1313 S.E. 5th St., Suite 329-A
Minneapolis, MN 55414
(612) 379-3835

International Wolf Center
1396 Highway 169
Ely, MN 55731
(800) 475-6666

Minnesota Prairie Chicken Society
P.O. Box 823
Detroit Lakes, MN 56501
(218) 847-1579

Minnesota Sharp-Tailed Grouse Society
P.O. Box 3338
Duluth, MN 55803

Superior Hiking Trail Association
P.O. Box 4
Two Harbors, MN 55616
(218) 834-4436

Trumpeter Swan Society
3800 County Rd. 24
Maple Plain, MN 55359
(612) 476-4663

The Wildlife Society, Minnesota
Hennepin Park District
3800 County Rd. 24
Minneapolis, MN 55359

Wisconsin
Bluebird Restoration Association of Wisconsin
1751 28th Ave.
County Hwy. VV
Rice Lake, WI 54868

Central Wisconsin Environmental Station
7290 County MM
Amherst Junction, WI 54407
(715) 824-2428

International Crane Foundation
E-11376 Shady Lane Rd.
Baraboo, WI 53913
(608) 356-9462

Natural Resources Foundation of Wisconsin, Inc.
P.O. Box 129
Madison, WI 53701-0129
(608) 266-1430

Sigurd Olson Environmental Institute
Northland College
Ashland, WI 54806
(715) 682-1223
Watersmeet, Michigan, office (906) 358-4350

Society of Tympanuchus Pinnatus
930 Elm Grove Rd.
Elm Grove, WI 53122
(414) 782-6333

Timber Wolf Alliance
Contact Sigurd Olson Environmental Institute

Timber Wolf Information Network
E. 110 Emmons Creek Rd.
Waupaca, WI 54981
(715) 258-7247

Wisconsin Sharp-Tailed Grouse Society
P.O. Box 1115
Cumberland, WI 54829

Community Organizations/Chambers

Michigan
Crystal Falls, Michigan (Humungus Fungus Festival)
(906) 875-3272

Indian Head Country, Michigan (fall foliage)
(800) 472-6654

Walloon Lake, Charlevoix County, Michigan (mushroom festival)
(616) 535-2227

Minnesota
Wabasha, Minnesota, Area Chamber of Commerce (wintering eagles)
P.O. Box 105
Wabasha, MN 55981
(612) 565-4158

Winona, Minnesota, Chamber of Commerce (tundra swans)
(507) 452-2278

Wisconsin
Bayfield, Wisconsin, Chamber of Commerce (ice caves)
(715) 779-3335

Indian Head Country, Wisconsin (fall foliage)
(800) 472-6654

New London, Wisconsin, Chamber of Commerce (sturgeon spawning)
(414) 982-5822

Oscoda, Wisconsin, Chamber of Commerce
(800) 826-3331

Sauk Prairie, Wisconsin, Chamber of Commerce (wintering eagles)
(608) 643-4168
Eagle Watch Tours
(800) 68-EAGLE

Rare Bird Hotlines/State Ornithological Unions

Michigan
Michigan Statewide Bird Alert: (616) 471-4919
For Detroit area: (313) 477-1360
For Sault Ste. Marie: (705) 256-2790

Michigan Audubon Society
409 W. E Ave.
Kalamazoo, MI 49007
(616) 344-3857

Minnesota
Minnesota Rare Bird Alert: (612) 544-5016

Minnesota Ornithologists Union
Bell Museum of Natural History
University of Minnesota
10 Church St. SE
Minneapolis, MN 55455

Wisconsin
Wisconsin Birder Hotline: (414) 352-3857

Wisconsin Society of Ornithology
W330 N8275 W. Shore Dr.
Hartland, WI 53029-9732
(414) 966-1072

Fall Foliage

Nationwide Hotline (USDA): (800) 354-4595

Minnesota
(800) 657-3000 or (612) 296-5029

Wisconsin
(800) 432-8747, for fall color report referrals

Butterfly Organizations

Journey North
125 N. 1st St.
Minneapolis, MN 55401
(tracks monarch migration north in the spring on the Internet)

The Lepidopterists' Society
3838 Fernleigh Ave.
Troy, MI 48083-5715

Midwest Monarch Project
3116 Harbor Dr. SE
Rochester, MN 55904

North American Butterfly Association
4 Delaware Rd.
Morristown, NJ 07960
(201) 285-0907

Wisconsin Entomological Society
7119 Hubbard Ave.
Middleton, WI 53562

The Xerces Society
10 S.W. Ash St.
Portland, OR 97204

Young Entomologists' Society
Department of Entomology, Michigan State University
East Lansing, MI 48824-1115

Other Important Addresses

American Birds—Christmas Bird Count
National Audubon Society
700 Broadway
New York, NY 10003

For DeLorme atlases:
DeLorme Mapping Company
P.O. Box 298
Freeport, ME 04032
(207) 865-4171

Lake States Interpretive Association
Rt. 9, Box 600
International Falls, MN 56649

National Wildlife Federation
Region 7
735 E. Crystal Lake Rd.
Burnsville, MN 55337
(612) 774-6600

Michigan

Leelanau Conservancy
Box 1007
Leland, MI 49654
(616) 256-9665

Little Traverse Conservancy
3264 Powell Rd.
Harbor Springs, MI 49740
(616) 347-0991

Michigan Travel Bureau
P.O. Box 30225
Lansing, MI 48909
(800) 543-2937

Minnesota

For state trails and state canoe routes contact:
Minnesota Department of Natural Resources
Information Center
500 Lafayette Rd., Box 7
St. Paul, MN 55155-4040
(612) 296-6157
(800) 766-6000 (in Minnesota only)

Geological Society of Minnesota
2642 University Ave.
St. Paul, MN 55114-1057
(612) 627-4780

Minnesota Land Trust
70 N. 22nd Ave.
Minneapolis, MN 55411-2237
(612) 522-3743

Minnesota Mycological Society
220 Biological Science Center
1445 Gortner Ave.
St. Paul, MN 55108-1095
(612) 625-1234

Minnesota Native Plant Society
220 Biological Science Center
1445 Gortner Ave.
St. Paul, MN 55108-1095
(612) 625-3164

Minnesota Travel Information Center
375 Jackson St.
250 Skyway Level
St. Paul, MN 55101-1810
(612) 296-5029
(800) 657-3700 (for continental U.S.)
(800) 766-8687 (for Canada)

The Trust for Public Lands, Minnesota
420 N. Fifth St., Suite 865
Minneapolis, MN 55401
(612) 338-8494

Wisconsin

Great Lakes Indian Fish and Wildlife
P.O. Box 9
Odanah, WI 54861
(715) 682-4427

Ice Age Park and Trail Foundation
P.O. Box 423
Pewaukee, WI 53072
(800) 227-0046

Inland Sea Society
P.O. Box 1211
Bayfield, WI 54814
(800) 851-6004

Sierra Club Midwest Office
214 N. Henry St., Suite 203
Madison, WI 53703
(608) 257-4994

Wisconsin Department of Transportation
P.O. Box 7913
Madison, WI 53707

Wisconsin Division of Tourism
(608) 725-5855 or (800) 372-2737

Wisconsin Environmental Decade
122 State St., Suite 200
Madison, WI 53703
(608) 251-7020

Selected Bibliography

Ackerman, Jennifer. "Carrying the Torch." *The Nature Conservancy* (September/October 1993): 43–5.

Ashcraft, John D. "Kirtland's Warbler." *Bird Watcher's Digest* (July/August 1995): 17–6.

Auer, Nancy. "A Study of Lake Sturgeon." *Michigan Natural Resources* (March/April 1993): 63–2.

Bates, John. *Trailside Botany.* Duluth, Minn.: Pfeifer-Hamilton, 1995.

Black, C. Ted, and C. Roy Smith. *Bird Finding Guide to Michigan.* Lansing: Michigan Audubon Society, 1994.

Breining, Greg. *Wild Minnesota.* Minocqua, Wis.: NorthWord Press, Inc., 1993.

Brewer, Richard, Gail A. McPeek, and Raymond J. Adams. *The Atlas of Breeding Birds of Michigan.* East Lansing: Michigan State University Press, 1991.

Carney, Tom. *Natural Wonders of Michigan.* Castine, Maine: Country Roads Press, 1995.

Charles, Craig. *Exploring Superior Country.* Minocqua, Wis.: NorthWord Press, Inc., 1992.

Clark, Jim. "King Can." Birder's World (November/December 1988): 2–6.

Curtis, John T. *Vegetation of Wisconsin.* Madison: University of Wisconsin Press, 1959.

Daniel, Glenda, and Jerry Sullivan. *The North Woods.* San Francisco: Sierra Club Books, 1981.

Davis, Tom. "Great Stretches of Sand." *Wisconsin Trails* (July/August 1988): 89–4.

Dickinson, Terence. *Night Watch.* Toronto: Camden House, 1983.

DuFresne, Jim. *Michigan State Parks.* Seattle: The Mountaineers, 1989.

———. *Wild Michigan.* Minocqua, Wis.: NorthWord Press, Inc., 1992.

Dunne, Pete, David Sibley, and Clay Sutton. *Hawks in Flight.* Boston: Houghton Mifflin Co., 1988.

Eastman, John. "The Ghost Forest." *Natural History* (January 1986): 95–1.

Eckert, Kim R. *A Birder's Guide to Minnesota.* Plymouth, Minn.: Williams Publications, Inc., 1994.

Erickson, Laura. "Feathery Balls of Fire." *Wisconsin Trails* (January/February 1992): 33–1.

———. "Counting in a Winter Wonderland." *Wisconsin Trails* (November/December 1992): 33–6.

————. *For the Birds.* Duluth, Minn.: Pfeifer-Hamilton, 1994.

Evers, David C. *A Guide to Michigan's Endangered Wildlife.* Ann Arbor: University of Michigan Press, 1992.

Fassett, Norman C. *Spring Flora of Wisconsin.* Madison: University of Wisconsin Press, 1976.

Forbush, E.H. *A History of Game Birds, Wild-fowl and Shore Birds of Massachusetts and Adjacent States.* Boston: Massachusetts State Board of Agriculture, 1912.

Gruchow, Paul. "Coteau des Prairies." *The Minnesota Volunteer* (May/June 1995): 58–340.

————. "A Bit of Big Woods." *The Minnesota Volunteer* (September/October 1995): 58–342.

Haglund, Brent. *Wild Wisconsin.* Minocqua, Wis.: NorthWord Press, Inc., 1991.

Halfpenny, James. *A Field Guide to Mammal Tracking in North America.* Boulder, Colo.: Johnson Books, 1986.

Halfpenny, James C., and Roy D. Ozanne. *Winter: An Ecological Handbook.* Boulder, Colo.: Johnson Books, 1989.

Hamerstrom, Frances. *Strictly for the Chickens.* Ames: Iowa State University Press, 1980.

Henderson, Carol. "Great Views of Wildlife." *The Minnesota Volunteer* (May/June 1995): 58–340.

Huggler, Tom. "What Good Is a Prairie?" *Michigan Natural Resources* (March/April 1988): 57–2.

Jackson, Hartley H. T. *Mammals of Wisconsin.* Madison: University of Wisconsin Press, 1961.

Janssen, Robert B. *Birds in Minnesota.* Minneapolis: University of Minnesota Press, 1987.

Judd, Mary K. *Wisconsin Wildlife Viewing Guide.* Helena, Mont.: Falcon Press, 1995.

Kappel-Smith, Diana. *Wintering.* Boston: Little, Brown, 1979.

Kempinger, James J. "Against All Odds," *Wisconsin Natural Resources* (April 1989): 13–2.

Klein, Tom. *Loon Magic.* Minocqua, Wis.: NorthWord Press, Inc., 1985.

Klots, Alexander. *Eastern Butterflies.* Boston: Houghton Mifflin Co., 1951.

Kricher, John C., and Gordon Morrison. *Eastern Forests.* Boston: Houghton Mifflin Co., 1988.

Lanner, Ronald M. *Autumn Leaves.* Minocqua, Wis.: NorthWord Press, Inc., 1990.

Leopold, Aldo. *A Sand County Almanac.* New York: Oxford University Press, 1949.

Lisi, Patrick J. *Wisconsin's Waterfalls.* Oxford, Wis.: Wild Rivers Press, 1991.

Luoma, Jon R. "Restless Dunes," *Audubon* (November/December 1994): 96–6.

Madson, John. *Tall Grass Prairie*. Helena, Mont.: Falcon Press, 1993.

Marchand, Peter J. *Life in the Cold*. Hanover, N.H.: University Press of New England, 1987.

Mayfield, Harold. "Jack Pine Puzzle." *Birder's World* (July/August 1988): 2–4.

McPeek, Gail. "Invaders from the North." *Michigan Natural Resources* (November/December 1992): 61–65.

Meeker, Jim. "Taming Wild Rice." *Wisconsin Natural Resources* (September/October 1988): 12–15.

Meyer, Thomas. "Wild Beauties." *Wisconsin Natural Resources* (June 1990): 14–3.

Michigan Nature Association. *Michigan Nature Association Nature Sanctuary Guidebook*. Avoca: Michigan Nature Association, 1994.

Minnesota Department of Natural Resources. *A Guide to Minnesota's Scientific and Natural Areas*. St. Paul: Minnesota Department of Natural Resources, 1995.

Moyle, John B., and Evelyn W. Moyle. *Northland Wild Flowers*. Minneapolis: University of Minnesota Press, 1977.

Muir, John. *The Story of My Boyhood and Youth*. Madison: University of Wisconsin Press, 1985.

Nero, Robert W. "Denizen of the Northern Forests." *Birder's World* (September/October 1988): 2–3.

Penrose, Laurie. *Michigan Waterfalls*. Davison, Mich.: Friede Publications, 1988.

Pettingill, Olin S. *A Guide to Bird Finding East of the Mississippi*. Boston: Houghton Mifflin Co., 1977.

Robbins, Samuel D. *Wisconsin Birdlife*. Madison: University of Wisconsin Press, 1991.

Rogers, Patricia. "Secrets of the Prickly Pear Cactus." *Michigan Natural Resources* (Summer 1992): 61–63.

Rölvaag, O.E. *Giants in the Earth*. New York: Harper and Brothers, 1927.

Roth, Filibert. "On the Forestry Conditions of Northern Wisconsin." *Wisconsin Geologic and Natural History Survey Bulletin* (1898): Econ Series 1.

Runkel, Sylvan T., and Dean M. Roosa. *Wildflowers of the Tallgrass Prairie*. Ames: Iowa State University Press, 1989.

Schorger, A.W. *The Passenger Pigeon: Its Natural History and Extinction*. Madison: University of Wisconsin Press, 1955.

———. *Silent Wings: A Memorial to the Passenger Pigeon*. Madison: Wisconsin Society for Ornithology, 1947.

Seng, Phil. *Michigan Wildlife Viewing Guide*. East Lansing: Michigan State University Press, 1994.

Smith, Welby R. *Orchids of Minnesota.* Minneapolis: University of Minnesota Press, 1993.

Sutton, Patricia, and Clay Sutton. *How to Spot an Owl.* Shelburne, Vt.: Chapters Publishing Ltd., 1994.

Swengel, Ann. "A Wealth of Wisconsin Butterflies." *Wisconsin Natural Resources* (September/October 1988): 12–15.

Tessen, Daryl D. *Wisconsin's Favorite Bird Haunts,* rev. ed. De Pere: The Wisconsin Society for Ornithology, 1989.

Tocqueville, Alexis de. *Democracy in America.* London: Saundars and Otley, 1838.

Turner, John. "Safeguarding Shorebirds." *Birder's World* (June 1991): 5–3.

Umhoefer, Jim. *Guide to Minnesota's Parks, Canoe Routes, and Trails.* Mincoqua, Wis.: NorthWord Press, Inc., 1984.

———. *Guide to Minnesota Outdoors.* Minocqua, Wis.: NorthWord Press, Inc., 1992.

Vogt, Richard Carl. *Natural History of Amphibians and Reptiles of Wisconsin.* Milwaukee: The Milwaukee Public Museum, 1981.

Voss, Edward G. *Michigan Flora.* Part I. Bloomfield Hills, Mich.: Cranbrook Institute of Science, 1972.

Wauer, Roland H. *The Visitor's Guide to the Birds of the Central National Parks.* Sante Fe, N.M.: John Muir Publications, 1994.

Weaver, J.E. *Prairie Plants and Their Environment.* Lincoln: University of Nebraska Press, 1968.

Wisconsin Chapter of The Nature Conservancy. *The Places We Save.* Madison: The Wisconsin Chapter of The Nature Conservancy, 1988.

Index

About the Author

John Bates is an outdoorsman and naturalist who has worked for the Wisconsin Department of Natural Resources in the Northern Highlands State Forest and currently owns Trails North, a naturalist interpretive guide service. John is a part-time instructor at Nicolet College in Rhinelander, Wisconsin. He has written *Trailside Botany: 101 Favorite Trees, Shrubs, and Wildflowers of the Upper Midwest,* is a contributing author to *Harvest Moon: A Wisconsin Outdoor Anthology,* and writes a biweekly column called "A Northwoods Almanac" for the *Lakeland Times,* Minocqua, Wisconsin. John, his wife, Mary, and daughter, Callie, live in Manitowish, Wisconsin, population 29.